Learning Through Drama

# Learning Through Drama

Report of the Schools Council Drama
Teaching Project (10-16),
Goldsmiths' College, University of London

LYNN McGREGOR
MAGGIE TATE
KEN ROBINSON

Heinemann Educational Books
for the Schools Council

Heinemann Educational Books Ltd
22 Bedford Square, London WC1B 3HH
LONDON   EDINBURGH   MELBOURNE   AUCKLAND
SINGAPORE   KUALA LUMPUR   NEW DELHI
IBADAN   NAIROBI   JOHANNESBURG
PORTSMOUTH (NH)   KINGSTON


ISBN 0 435 18565 9 (paper)

Printed and bound in Great Britain by
Biddles Ltd, Guildford and King's Lynn

# Contents

# Preface

The Schools Council Drama Teaching Project (10-16) was set up to consider the aims and objectives of drama teaching; to find possible ways of assessing outcomes; and to suggest ways in which drama could be organized in the curriculum. This three-year project (1974-77) was based at Goldsmiths' College, University of London, and conducted by Lynn McGregor (director), Maggie Tate, and Ken Robinson. The project team combined a range of experience in sociology, linguistics and philosophy, and in practical drama teaching. Six local education authorities across England were chosen. A drama adviser acted as co-ordinator for the project's work in each authority. In each area three schools, covering the 10 to 16 age-range, were selected. Numerous and lengthy discussions took place between team members and teachers concerning their aims, methods and attitudes to actual work. Classes in each school were observed over a year so that development could be noted. During the year 159 lessons were observed.

In addition to research in schools, working parties were organized in each area to consider the place of drama in the curriculum. The six co-ordinators met regularly with the team to discuss their findings. Members of working parties represented a wide range of interests and included teachers, headteachers, advisers and members from colleges of education. The results of their discussions and recommendations were taken into account by the team when writing the book. A number of groups and individuals outside these areas made contributions to the project by submitting papers on a range of issues. Throughout the project national conferences and working parties were called to discuss such topics as 'The relationship of drama to English teaching', 'Teacher training' and 'Theatre in education'.

Two groups of people—the co-ordinators and the Schools Council Drama Teaching Project Consultative Committee—met the project team at least once a term to discuss and assess the project's development. During the second term of the first year, a weekend course was held for teachers to present and discuss with them the project's thinking so far. Another three-day course, which included members from all aspects of the project, was held the following Easter to discuss publication of materials. Two people have acted as evaluators throughout the project, assessing its feasibility in drama and methodological terms.

The first year was spent on research and the second on production of materials including a film. The film, *Take Three,* directed by John Slater, is an illustration of the work of three teachers and is intended to provoke discussion concerning the nature of drama and its assessment. (*Take Three* is distributed by the Educational Foundation for Visual Aids, and is available for purchase or hire from National Audio-Visual Aids Library, Paxton Place, Gipsy Road, London SE27 9SR.)

This book is therefore a result of continuous dialogue between the project team and those who participated in the project. Although it expresses ultimately the conclusions reached by three people concerning the nature of drama teaching, material for the book was gathered from people all over the country, either concerned with drama generally, or working in the classroom.

# Introduction

This book is about the nature of drama and how it can be used in the classroom. Although drama is an integral part of our cultural life, it is only quite recently that educationalists have begun to claim a separate place for drama teaching in the timetables of our schools.

Although the value of drama has yet to be widely accepted or fully understood, an increasing number of schools have begun to employ trained specialists in independent drama departments. Recently-built schools are now often equipped with custom-designed drama studios and, throughout the country, local education authorities employ drama advisers and advisory teachers to encourage and promote drama teaching at both primary and secondary levels.

In this book we are concerned with the aims and principles which underlie the work of drama teachers and with how these relate to the sorts of experience they structure in the classroom. What kinds of development can these experiences help to bring about in children, and how can teachers begin to evaluate them?

Our aims then in writing this book are:

1. To give teachers who use drama in the classroom some starting points for reflecting on the nature and value of *their own work in drama* and to suggest ways in which they might begin to tackle the problems of assessment and evaluation.

2. To give those teachers with an interest in drama, but little or no practical experience, some idea of what is involved in drama teaching and of the demands it might make of them and of their classes.

3. To give those with more general responsibility for curriculum organization—headmasters, advisers, and so on—some starting-points for considering the variety of roles drama may have in education, and to suggest some possible ways of organizing drama in the timetable.

## The aims of drama

One of the initial aims of this project was to 'attempt to clarify the range of aims and concepts in drama teaching'. It was clear from very early discussions with teachers and advisers that the greatest problems for any research project in drama would be those of definition.

Specialist drama teaching is a comparatively recent innovation in the curriculum and both its philosophy and its practice are the subject of considerable discussion. Traditionally the place of drama in schools has been seen in terms of the study of plays as literature. In some schools this has involved a wider look at the social and artistic history of the theatre. Generally speaking, drama in this sense was the responsibility of the English department. Many educationalists not directly involved in drama still see this as the job drama teachers ought to be doing.

The growing interest in drama as a specialism, however, is based on a much broader conception of its role in education. It is based on the use of drama as an active, social process which draws on the child's capacity for role-play—for projecting into imagined roles, characters and situations—as a way of exploring and expressing ideas through the body and the voice.

But what are the aims of such work? The teachers involved in the project listed such aims as 'developing the child's powers of self-expression', 'developing self-awareness, self-confidence, encouraging sensitivity and powers of imagination'. They showed a clear concern for the individual child's life of feelings and emotions and sensed that these are areas of the child's development that may be overlooked in a great deal of curriculum work. They also emphasized the importance of structuring work which encouraged the 'use of imagination'.

These are very general statements, of course, but they raise a number of immediate issues concerning the role and development of drama. Many of the aims of drama teachers are not unique to drama. Philosophically at least, drama is part of a much more general movement in education. Teachers in all areas of the curriculum—particularly in the arts and the humanities, but also in the sciences—discuss their aims in very similar ways. There is a growing awareness throughout the curriculum of the need to devise patterns of teaching and learning which recognize the child's inner world of emotions and imaginings. Recent developments in drama and in the arts as a whole in education have been both a contributor to and a result of this more general movement in education.

But saying this raises a second issue. If drama is part of a general movement, what distinctive and specific contributions can it make? This seems to be a question of defining clear aims. Are there within the general sorts of aims given above more specific aims which are exclusive to drama? Much of the debate in drama centres on this problem of defining clearer aims.

We want to suggest, however, that this may not be the first step in defining a role for drama teaching. The individual teacher must, of course, have clear aims in education as a whole. In this project we have begun by looking at the nature of the actual experiences which children may have in drama lessons and have asked the question, 'What are the possible *functions* of these experiences in relation to the child's overall development in education?' We feel that the distinctive roles of drama can best be unearthed by looking at drama in terms of the functions of the drama experience. This leaves an open question which only the individual teacher can answer. Are these functions, these developments, in line with what he is generally trying to achieve in education as a whole?

# Approaches to drama

The problems of defining drama are not only philosophical. Teachers vary enormously in the kind of activities they use in drama and in the way they organize lessons. During our observations we saw teachers adopting roles themselves, working alongside the children, while others tended to set activities and observe and control them from outside, so to speak. Some teachers emphasized a need for frequent discussion of the activities and their value; others preferred to keep such discussion to a minimum, letting the experience speak for itself. We saw children working together as a whole class, in small groups, in pairs and individually, sometimes closely directed by the teacher, sometimes with enormous freedom to select both the topic and the method of working. Some teachers see a clear connection between the improvisational techniques they use and the kinds of skills and techniques used in the theatre; others see little or no connection at all.

There is then an enormous range of teaching styles within drama. Much of the existing literature of drama in education describes or recommends particular ways of working and this has given rise to the idea that there are different and distinctive approaches to drama and even different types of drama. This presents a problem for the practising teacher. Faced with the idea of different types and approaches he has presumably to find out what they are and then decide which of them is best for him. Our own research suggests that the idea of different types of drama is misleading. There are, of course, many differences in teaching style, and many different uses to which drama can be put in schools. But that does not mean that there are fundamentally different sorts of drama all of which have to be explained separately.

We have tried to look for the common ground in drama teaching—for what may be the essential characteristics of all drama experiences. In looking at the work we have seen we have tried to pinpoint those features which are basic to it all and which identify it as drama rather than anything else. If a case can be made for drama, it ought to be sufficiently broadly-based to take in all examples of the work. There were those who felt that a project such as this should eventually be able to describe and recommend a number of distinct methods of drama teaching. Our conclusion is that this cannot be done, and that it would not be particularly helpful to attempt it. The essential task is to develop a framework of ideas, a rationale for drama, within which the teacher can begin to explore and develop his own way of working. Stylistic variations arising out of the uniqueness of each teaching situation ought then to be placed in their proper perspective. They emerge from individual differences within each group rather than out of basic differences in the nature of drama. The size of the group, the age of the children, their previous experience of drama and of the teacher, the teacher's own professional background are all crucial factors which affect the nature and the quality of the work, and the teacher must be sensitive to them in planning how to use drama in the lesson. The important question here relates to the teacher's specific intentions with this group, at this time and in this place. If there are different approaches, then it must be said that there are as many as there are teachers in schools. The problem then is not to attempt to classify these approaches, as each new teacher is likely to create a new category, but to try to give some theoretical basis for this work as a whole and, arising from this, some perspective from which the teacher can begin to judge the practical value of his own way of working, and of what he is trying to do with his classes. He must be free to develop his own style of drama teaching, based on a clear understanding of what drama has to offer.

## Drama or theatre?

As we have seen there are a number of problems in defining a clear role for drama in education. Some of these are to do with the existing vocabulary of drama in education. One problem is to do with the word drama itself. Does it mean the same thing as theatre and, if not, what is the difference? Some teachers maintain that there is a world of difference between the meanings of these two words, others see none at all. If there is a difference, what in any case is the point of making it and insisting upon it?

For most of those who are not directly involved in drama teaching, drama and theatre are the same thing—they are about plays, writers, actors, directors, rehearsal and performance. If this is the meaning of drama, then drama teaching should centre on the study and appreciation of them. If it is to be practical it should have something to do with performance and audiences. But this would be a very limited view of what most drama teachers are actually doing. If a teacher is more concerned with the process of exploration, of sharing and challenging ideas, than with products and presentation or professional skills, as many are, this other idea of drama may seem to be very restrictive. And yet the fundamental similarities between the way that statements are made and arrived at, in both the theatre and within a drama lesson, suggest the need for a closer look at the relationship between the two. Both essentially rest on the ability to adopt and develop roles and characters within 'as if' situations; they rely on the body and the voice as the main media of expression, and make the same symbolic use of space and time. Here again it may be more useful to look for similarities rather than differences in trying to pin down a relationship.

## The nature of this book

During the course of the project we observed a great deal of practical drama work throughout the country. We would have found it impossible to make any judgements about either the quality or the value of what we were seeing without continually trying to confront the more general questions about the underlying functions of drama. Before discussing how drama can be used in practice, therefore, we feel it is necessary to present a broader theoretical view of drama in an attempt to gain a clearer perspective on some of the central issues we have outlined here.

We begin by setting down the theoretical position we have come to hold. We then consider some of the implications of this view for the practice and evaluation of drama work, using illustrations from lessons we have observed. Finally, we discuss some possible ways of organizing drama in the curriculum as a whole, the resources needed for drama and the implications for the training and provision of teachers.

Throughout the project and in writing this book we have kept a number of central questions in our minds. These include:

*On drama in general*

Does drama have distinctive and unique functions? If so, what roles do they suggest for drama in education?

What kinds of learning processes are involved?

Is there a relationship between drama in the classroom and the theatre? If so, what is it?

*On the role of the teacher and his relationship with the learner*

What is the nature of the relationship between the drama teacher and the learner?

How can the teacher begin to realize his specific educational intentions through drama? What does he need to know in order to do this?

*On methods and strategies*
What kinds of decisions must he make within a lesson in terms of
methods, strategies and social structures?
What kind of roles should the teacher take up and what are the
likely effects of these?
*On assessment and evaluation*
How can the teacher begin to assess the effects of a lesson on the
children? What criteria can be used to judge its value?
*On organization of drama in schools*
Is drama a fundamental part of the child's education?
Should it be included within the timetable? Or can it be
accommodated as an option or extra-curricular activity?
Is drama a subject or a method of teaching, or neither of these?
Does drama require specially trained teachers?
Does it require special facilities, time and space?
Should drama be annexed to an existing department or should
separate drama departments be established?

Any attempt to explain anything so diverse as drama is bound to
run into complications. Some of what we have to say in this book
may seem over-simplified; in other parts it may seem over-detailed.
We have tried to avoid both extremes. But drama is not a simple
process, and the questions raised above have no easy answers. In
the end only the individual teacher can decide what qualifies as a
helpful attitude towards what he does. We have not tried here to
present a comprehensive account of the views of all of those who
helped in the project. This book is not a survey in that sense.
Instead we have presented a specific point of view which we feel
throws some light on the problems of teaching drama as we
conceive them. There is a temptation to defend a point of view by
systematically dealing with all possible objections and implications
at each stage of the argument. The danger is that the overall thread
of the argument is lost in a tangle of diversions and qualifications.
For the sake of directness and coherence we have painted a general
picture of drama, often in very broad strokes. We hope that
individual teachers will find enough starting-points here to
continue the inquiry in their own terms and according to their own
specific interests.

# Chapter 1
# Drama as Art

In any discussion, anywhere, where the place and value of drama in education is being talked about, the chances are that sooner or later somebody will ask, 'What is drama? What do you mean by the word?' After a moment, somebody may offer a definition. And then the debate will start. Although drama in schools has been steadily expanding for over twenty years, the problem of saying what drama is has stayed with us. This is not surprising. Both inside and outside education 'drama' has lent its name to a tremendous variety of activities and events. It covers a range of work in the performing arts. In the news media, virtually any situation of tension is a 'drama'. On both sides of the Atlantic the word has attached itself to developing techniques in group therapy—sociodrama, psychodrama—and now in schools a multitude of creative activities and innovation is being called drama. But what is it? The family of drama has become so large and widespread that it is becoming more and more difficult to spot any natural resemblance among all its relatives.

The need to define drama is particularly urgent in education. Drama in the classroom can generate enormous enjoyment and commitment in children of all ages. Within this enjoyment there seem to be real opportunities for positive and sustained educational achievement. But generating this commitment and building on the opportunities it presents can be a very random business for the teacher unless he has a clear sense of where this work can lead and an equally clear sense of the kinds of experience the children are undergoing. Clearly the way that teachers conceive of the nature and purposes of drama will affect their role in the classroom and, of equal importance, their sense of priorities when they come to judge the value of what they see the children doing.

So how is drama to be defined? As a subject? If so, what is its content and how can it be taught? As a medium of self-expression? If so, is it a valuable and accessible medium for all children or just for those of an extrovert nature? Is it a method of teaching? If so, a method of teaching what? Or if it is none of these, how else can we describe it and how can we best use it in our schools?

There are a number of ways of trying to define the contributions of drama to education. Firstly there is the question of aims.

Interviews with many drama teachers revealed a considerable overlap in what they are trying to achieve through drama. There was a common concern for the development of the child as an individual. There was a commitment to developing powers of imagination through creative activity. Teachers were directly interested in correcting an imbalance in educational priorities which emphasized the development of intellectual skills and the transmission of information apparently at the expense of the child's private life of feelings and personal responses. There was, overall, a concern for the child as a member of a group—that in education we should recognize and cater for the challenges of the child's social development. The problem in pursuing the idea of aims for drama is that, however much they can be defended or argued against, many of them, in themselves, are not distinctive or unique to drama. Such principles now underlie a great deal of thinking about the place and value of many subjects across the curriculum.

Then there is the question of content. It is in relation to this that the question of drama as a subject begins to come into sharper focus. Teachers are using drama to explore an enormous range of content. Through drama children may look, for example, at social themes (housing, pollution), historical topics (civil war, industrial revolution), current events (politics, apartheid laws), concepts (trust, love, deceit) and so on. The very versatility of drama in terms of content is a tremendous recommendation for its potential across the school day. But in saying this it becomes difficult, in terms of content alone, to define drama, as it is being used, strictly as a subject. There is, of course, much more to be said about the aims and content of drama teaching and we will return to these issues as we go on.

Initially, however, the key to the problem of defining drama, and its possible value in education, lies in what children and adults alike actually do in drama, and in the nature of the experience itself.

# Acting-out:
## the distinctive feature of drama

The essential and recurring feature of all school drama work is that it involves children, as participants, projecting into imagined or assumed roles or situations. We have called this process of projection 'acting-out'. It is the foundation of drama upon which the case for its place in education must first be built. What then are the essential characteristics of acting-out? What might its educational functions be and what light does this throw on the place of drama in schools?

A group of six fourteen-year-olds have been discussing the ideas of privilege and deprivation. They are particularly intrigued by the paradox that so many of the world's population are dying at the feet of an overfed minority. They want to explore this idea through drama. They begin by deciding on a situation which will symbolize this paradox. They agree on a situation and decide who is going to be who. After some preliminary planning they begin.

Four of the group, three boys and a girl, sit at a table. A second girl is a maid. They are a well-to-do family sitting in the dining-room of their sumptuously furnished house. The father reads the financial index in the evening paper. He complains to his wife that the company is going to lose several thousand pounds this year. She is trying to listen but is actually more interested in telling the maid off for being so slovenly. The children are toying with their food. They are only half way through the main course but already they're full. Suddenly there is a knock at the door. The maid answers. It is a collector for a national charity. She walks into the dining-room and asks the family if they'd like to make a donation. They are annoyed at being interrupted. The father eventually complains that there's no point in giving to charities because the money never reaches the people it's intended for. Anyway, it's not their fault if people on the other side of the world are starving. They started with nothing and had to make their own way in the world. Why should they carry everyone else on their back now they've made a modest success of their lives?

In the middle of the argument the collector says she isn't very happy with the way it's going. She'll go out and come in again and try to be more polite and persuasive. They all agree. They decide to have more 'food' on the table and to spend more time sorting out their attitudes before she comes in.

This group was using drama to explore an idea, the concept of privilege. They were tackling a particular problem of understanding. This is not the only way in which drama can be used, nor is it the only reason for doing it. The question here is, as they were acting-out, what were these children actually doing? Basically what did it involve for them?

Fundamentally, acting-out involves people making an imaginative leap from their actual situation or roles into a supposed one. In this example the group began by imagining a specific situation which could *represent* the conflict in attitudes which interested them. A rich, overfed family met a charity worker collecting for famine relief. As they began acting-out they had to project themselves into, and identify with, specific roles within the situation. So one became a maid, another the father figure, and so on.

There is a broad distinction to be made here, within the general idea of acting-out, between playing a role and playing a character. In taking up a role, as these children were doing, the individual is basically representing an attitude or set of attitudes. The role they are identifying with may be a pure stereotype—a charity worker, a company director. If the child begins to identify more completely with a personality behind the role, he begins to move into characterization. To represent a character is to assume and develop a more complex personality rather than to identify with a set of attitudes alone. It is an orchestration of many factors including attitudes, age, mannerisms, motivation, and so on.

This activity which we are calling 'acting-out' has been given many other names in the past. Most commonly it has been called 'improvisation'. We have a particular reason for suggesting a new name. 'Improvisation' can be used to describe any activity which involves an element of spontaneity or open-endedness. Music, conversation, movement can all be improvised. Improvisation does not describe what is being done, but a way of doing it. It is a mode of activity. Acting-out can be improvised, and it usually is. But it may be planned and carefully structured. In this sense 'improvisation' is too broad a term for the specific activities we have in mind.

Acting-out involves the participants in accepting a shift in the conventions of behaviour towards each other.
1.   There is an agreement to suspend the normal social roles with each other in identifying with the new imagined roles.
2.   There is an agreement to make a different use of the environment. In this case a desk becomes a dining-table laden with food, a chalk box becomes a cigar box, and so on. This different use of the environment includes a shift in the conventions of time. Events may be telescoped to give them greater or less significance. The usual conventions of space and time may be suspended during acting-out.

Children and adults alike naturally project into roles as part of their normal social behaviour. When playing, children spontaneously adopt roles and project into fantasy characters. This impulse and capacity for projecting into other roles persists into adult life, permeating our normal social relationships. Perhaps more than anything else, however, this facility for slipping in and out of roles in everyday life has led to the idea that drama is easy, both for the participants to do and for a teacher to organize. This is certainly a misleading impression. Acting-out, of the kind we are interested in here, differs in two significant ways from spontaneous role-playing.

First there is the matter of context. The role-playing which takes place outside the drama session is likely to result from more or less spontaneous impulses. As individuals tell stories or relate anecdotes, they may project into the roles of the people, real or imagined, whom they are describing. The kinds of roles they take up in this context may serve to reinforce the attitudes of the group and the status of individuals within it. To be asked to project into

roles within the more structured, more deliberate context of the
drama session often proves to be more difficult as individuals are
encouraged to adopt roles which deliberately challenge and extend
their social roles. It must be emphasized that drama in action
depends for its vitality on spontaneity and immediacy of response
within acting-out. It is this very immediacy of the process which
can lead children to insights and discoveries they might not
otherwise experience.

The second important feature of acting-out in this sense is that it
has an underlying sense of purpose. We will want to argue later that
acting-out can be used to bring about a range of developments. It
may be, as in the example given, that the explicit purpose of the
acting-out is to arrive at a clearer understanding of certain ideas or
concepts. In other cases the purpose may be related to developing
clearer ways of expressing oneself through drama. The emphasis
may be on the process of creation and communication of ideas. In
using the process of acting-out, however, both the teacher and the
group will be aware of some underlying purpose. The way that
intentions are understood by the group can critically affect the
nature and quality of their involvement. In considering drama in
practice and the teacher's role in structuring a session, this question
of intention and purpose will become increasingly significant,
particularly in relation to evaluation.

But saying what is involved in acting-out in this way does not in
itself answer the basic question of what this group was actually
doing. An essential element has so far not been touched upon. This
relates directly to the functions of acting-out, and therefore to the
whole question of the function of drama in education. Whatever
acting-out involves for those who do it, why should children or
adults be asked to act-out in the first place? What are its possible
functions? What promise, what value does it hold for education?

## Meaning and symbolizing

To return briefly to our example: what was the relationship of the
situation and the roles, through which the acting-out unfolded, to
the underlying ideas and feelings which were motivating the
group's work—the general concepts of privilege and deprivation?
These ideas could have sparked off numerous alternatives.

The situation was selected, as any of a range of others might have
been, because it functioned as a *symbol* of the conflict in which the
group were interested. It *represented* the paradox of privilege and
deprivation. Through representing these essentially abstract ideas
in symbolic form, the group were making them more concrete as a
way of making clearer sense of them, and also developing and
expressing an attitude towards them. It is in the light of the process

of symbolization—particularly as it applies to the arts—that the functions of drama can best be seen.

In general conversation, the word 'symbol' has a fairly limited use. Typically it conjures up ideas of trademarks, of flags, badges and insignia. Like drama itself, 'symbol' is an elusive concept. All of these things may function as symbols in so far as they are used to represent or evoke ideas. But we want to adopt a broader definition of symbol. A symbol is any item—a sound, a mark, an object or event—'whereby we are enabled to make an abstraction'.* This is best illustrated in the first instance by considering the way in which we use verbal language. Our experience of the world comes to us initially as a tide of impressions and stimulations through the senses. As we live through the constant barrage of sensory stimulation on which we base our actions in the world, we have first to make sense of what we experience, to give it meaning. In doing this we look for patterns and relationships in events. It is within this process of finding meaning in experience, in making sense of it, that the idea of symbolization has particular significance.

Spoken language is an orchestration of vocal noises. The power of these sounds lies in our ability to use them as symbols, to invest them with meaning. As the child grows through infancy he learns to associate events and to recognize similarities and differences in past and present experience. As he does so he prepares for future experiences. This is probably the most sustained and significant achievement of his mental life. Through the use of words we can call into the consciousness of others objects which are not immediately present in the environment. 'They . . . serve to let us develop a characteristic attitude towards objects "in absentia" which is called thinking of, or referring to, what is not here'.† Spoken language is then a system through which we are able to communicate and express our accumulated experience of the world to others.

A traditional view of language is that we use words primarily to communicate with each other. Although this is clearly an essential function of language, recent studies in the acquisition of language suggest it has a further and equally significant role; that we do not use language just to express ideas and communicate about experience, but that the development of language is intimately bound up in the growth of consciousness. We do not use words just to express our view of the world, but the language we use actually helps to shape what our view of the world is.

* S.K. Langer, *Feeling and Form* (Routledge & Kegan Paul, 1953).

† S.K. Langer, *Philosophy in a New Key* (Harvard University Press, Cambridge, Mass., 1957).

Thought is not merely expressed in words, it comes into existence through them . . . words play a central part not only in the development of thought but in the historical growth of consciousness as a whole.*

Our ability to use language is based on our power to represent experience in symbolic form. And the way we represent the world to ourselves, the way we symbolize it, affects how we come to understand it.† New concepts may radically affect the meaning we give to experience and alter our personal sense of reality. What is the relevance of this theory of symbolization to an understanding of drama? Although we have been talking here mainly about spoken language and verbal symbols, words are not the only symbols we use in making sense of the world. We use different kinds of symbols according to the nature of the experiences we are trying to understand. Through mathematical symbolisation, for example, we confront essentially abstract problems in the physical world.

But each individual lives in two worlds:

There is a world that exists beyond the individual, a world that exists whether or not he exists. The child needs to know about this world and manage himself in it . . . it is a world of facts, of public space and 'objects' . . . There is another world, however, a world which exists only because the individual exists. It is the world of his own sensations and feelings . . . the world of private space and the solitary subject.‡

If we look at the content and form of the arts we are confronted immediately with expressions from this inner world. Statements which have evolved deep within the inner world of subjective response and its interaction with the public world. A primary

---

* L.S. Vygotsky, *Thought and Language* (MIT Press, 1962). See also, for example: A.R. Luria and F.I. Yudovich, *Speech and the Development of Mental Processes in the Child,* trans. O. Kovasc and J. Simon (Penguin Books, 1971); E. Cassirer, *An Essay on Man* (Yale University Press, 1944); and E. Sapir, *Selected writings of Edward Sapir,* in *Culture, Language and Personality,* ed. David G. Mandelbaum (University of California Press, Berkeley and Los Angeles, 1949).

† The American psychologist, George Kelly, in *A Theory of Personality* (Norton, New York, 1963), talks of language as a template. It is a grid or framework which we place over the mass of experience, much as we would place a grid on a map, as a way of perceiving patterns and relationships. This capacity to see the world through symbols is a basic process of mind and understanding. The mind is often likened to a transmitter, sending and receiving messages between the individual and the outside world. This theory of symbolization and its role in the development of consciousness likens it, however, 'to a great transformer. The current of experience which passes through it undergoes a change of character . . . by virtue of a primary use which is made of it immediately: it is sucked into the stream of symbols which constitutes a human mind' (S.K. Langer, *Philosophy in a New Key,* op. cit.).

‡ R. Witkin, *The Intelligence of Feeling* (Heinemann Educational Books, 1974).

function of the arts is to make sense of the life of feeling through expressing and representing problems of subjective understanding in symbolic form. In music, painting, and drama and the other arts, we develop languages, symbolic forms through which we may understand this universe of personal response.

The arts, both inside and outside education, have tended to be seen as recreational, as something to do when we have time off from the business of the world. They are relaxing, even stimulating but they are not quite so important as getting on with the 'real business' of life. But if relaxation were their only purpose then going to sleep would be a much cheaper and less strenuous alternative. The persistent influence of the arts suggests that they fulfil a much more basic need. They are the product of a compulsion to make sense of, express and communicate from, the inner world of subjective understanding.

# The expressive process of drama

Artistic expression takes many forms and uses many media. To some extent the content of particular art forms is determined by the media themselves. The painter or the sculptor working in plastic media is directly concerned with expressing visual and spatial relationships as part of his work. In drama, the media are essentially the body and the voice. But drama also uses space, objects, light and sound and, importantly, time. Drama revolves around the process of behaviour, through interpersonal response. In acting-out, the individual himself is the prime medium of expression. *Acting-out then is the exploration and representation of meaning using the medium of the whole person.* It is precisely because of this that the content of drama is so broad. It can be tuned into a variety of topics. In a strict sense it is not so much the content of drama which is distinctive, but the way in which it is considered. It is seen through the lens of human behaviour, from the point of view of those involved. In our initial example drama was not being used to establish the facts of famine or even the facts of working for a charity, although it may well have started from them. It was being used to explore the attitudes which either led to or resulted from these circumstances. The group of children were looking at the situation through the behaviour of those who might be involved. *There are a number of characteristics of acting-out which lead us to define drama as a* process.

## A process in time

Drama takes place over time. It happens as a series of events. If a person is working on a painting he is involved in a process of discovery and creation. But in the middle of this expressive act is a physical object—a canvas. A finished object, a physical product remains when his efforts are complete. This is not true for those who make an expressive statement through drama. Their statement only exists in the act of making it. It is a sequence of sounds and silence, movement and stillness, which unfolds and dissolves through time. It exists only in action and does not linger in space when the action is done. In this sense drama is closer to music and, of course, dance. The participants may repeat their statement, if it can be repeated. They may write it down afterwards, recording the words which were spoken and the movements which were made. They may even write it beforehand. These are essentially records of drama. They are not themselves expressions in drama. Drama only exists as a process in time.

## Action and interaction: the negotiation of meaning

A drama statement exists in action and develops through interaction. As individuals assume a role or a posture, they enter a dialogue. As each one moves or speaks he affects and modifies the actions and behaviour of the others. They change and challenge the contributions of each other; they modify and explore the symbols they are using, so they may be drawn nearer to understanding the problem of meaning with which they are concerned. *This flow of interaction and reciprocal response is at the heart of drama.*

If two children face each other across an open floor and one asks, 'What are you standing on?', the response of the other will immediately begin to determine and shape all that is to happen. If he says, for example, 'I'm standing on a raft', the symbolic situation has begun to be defined and with it the possible area of exploration. As the interaction continues it may become clearer. The way in which each of them responds will determine the actions and potential involvement of the other. It is a shared process. As soon as a child begins acting-out with others he evokes and must provide an immediacy of response. As the symbolic situation is developed through this process of interaction, so the underlying meaning is explored. Drama revolves around this pooling and sharing of experience in the development of a joint expressive act. Through this process individual perceptions are aired and challenged and extended. *We are calling this process the 'negotiation of meaning'. It takes place on two levels—the 'real' and the 'symbolic'.*

A group of ten-year-old children have been discussing housing problems in their area. They are particularly interested in the antagonism between landlords and tenants. Using the chairs and rostra in the room they establish a living-room in a terraced house. Conditions in the house are very bad. They complain about the leaking roof and the cockroaches on the walls. One of the group comes in full of excitement. He has just been given a dog. The family are also excited about their new pet but they are worried about the attitude of the landlord. He has forbidden pets to be kept in the houses.

The landlord arrives suddenly. He is very proud of a new fur coat he has just bought. He sits with the family and they tell him about the repairs that need to be done to the house. He complains about rising costs and says that he would love to get the work done but they obviously don't understand his money problems. Suddenly the dog bounds into the room. He loses his temper and tells them that either the dog goes or they go. He doesn't want dirty animals lowering the tone of the neighbourhood. At this point the teacher stops them and they begin to discuss their reactions to the situation so far.

Before the acting-out began, the group had not decided what was going to happen. Nor had they settled on particular attitudes to be expressed. They had a rough idea of a situation and had taken on only general roles—landlord, parents, children. As they each contributed through their roles a picture of entrenched and conflicting attitudes emerged which on each side they had to defend. In doing so they each had to absorb and challenge the opposing views, working within and through the symbolic situation. They were negotiating at the symbolic level.

Although in acting-out the participants are negotiating at this level, the real social network in the group underlies and informs the nature and the quality of their involvement. It will also help to determine the actual issues and problems of understanding which become the focus of the acting-out. The symbolic situation may become the vehicle through which the underlying relationships in the group are expressed, and in their turn modified and developed.

In considering the value and significance of drama work, the teacher needs to be aware of the real personal and social challenges which are engaging the group during acting-out. Beneath the surface level of the represented situation is a deep structure of personal motivations and impulses. It is at this level as well that significant learning may be taking place.

# Drama and theatre

Let us return here to one of the original questions—the relationship of drama and theatre. How does this expressive, exploratory process relate to the world of scripts, actors, directors and audiences? Are they the same thing or are they totally unconnected? What light does the theory outlined here cast on this? It was suggested at the outset that it may be more useful to look for similarities rather than differences in trying to pin this relationship down. What are the similarities? They both rest on the ability to project into roles and characters; they both use space, time and objects as symbolic media. They both centre on the person as the main medium of expression. The distinctive dimension to the content of both is again interpersonal response—human behaviour and social action. Yet there are equally obvious differences. By far the most important of these is the idea of *performance*. The word 'theatre' means a number of things. It suggests a profession and the work of the artists and technicians who are part of it. But the concept of 'theatre' is to do with performance. Theatre exists in performance—in communicating with an audience. Drama in education, on the other hand, need not and, in most cases, does not, have performance as a goal. But the power and the appeal of theatre arises from and is based on the same impulse towards symbolic expression through role-playing and characterization which is the foundation of the expressive process of drama.

It is worth pursuing the idea of performance a little further. Performances mean audiences. Participants in a drama session are primarily aware of themselves, reacting with and for each other in an open-ended, often uncertain way. Their only audience is themselves—their sense of audience is introspective. If they are asked to take part in performance there is a shift of emphasis. They need to think of ways of communicating outward from and through the group to an external audience. This makes quite different demands on the involvement and participation of the group. The crucial question for drama in practice is whether or not for this group, at this time and in this context, such a shift in emphasis can fulfil any additional or worth-while function.

The question of theatre and drama raises a fundamental question related to the idea of form. Although performance may result from drama work it would be quite misleading to suggest or imply that it was its goal. Nevertheless drama does have a sense of destination but that destination is not in the first place a performance, and it is often not performance at all. The destination is the resolution of the problem of meaning or understanding which is motivating the work. To work in the arts is to tackle problems of understanding through representing them in symbolic forms. This revolves around a dialogue between the content of the expression and the form in which it is made. The symbolic form encapsulates the meaning. The symbols chosen critically affect the nature of the understanding which develops during the work.

Two groups of fourteen-to-fifteen year-olds are exploring the idea of 'a stranger who calls on people in a familiar situation and has a powerful effect on them'. They discuss this in their groups and decide how they can explore this idea. Their selection and treatment of symbols critically affects the nature and level of their exploration and understanding of the theme.

The first group—two girls and one boy—decide on the following situation. A married couple are driving along a country road. They see a girl hitch-hiker and stop to give her a lift. She gets in the car and suddenly pulls a gun on them. After trying this out in action, they decide that it needs to be elaborated and deepened. Everything has happened too fast. Subsequently they talk about the relationship between the married couple. The wife is seen as an overbearing woman. She is driving the car. The husband is bored and tense. The hitch-hiker needs a reason for being on the road alone and it is decided she is a baby-snatcher on the run from the police.

As they work through it again the tension between the couple is expressed and elaborated. The husband sees the hiker and suggests giving her a lift. The wife suspects his motives but eventually agrees. The girl gets in and almost immediately pulls a gun. At this the wife reverts to being a helpless female expecting her husband to defend her. The hiker stops the car and gets out.

The second group—three girls—also discussed a number of ideas. They eventually agreed that they would be on board a plane which was about to crash. The stranger would be the Devil. He would offer to save them from death in the crash if they sold him their souls.

When they began acting-out they encountered difficulties: they felt that their limited technical knowledge of aeroplanes and flying stopped them being involved; whatever they said sounded contrived and melodramatic; they became embarrassed at each other's attempts to take this seriously and decided to try another way in.

They decided that if they were to tell anyone about their experience they would be put in a mental hospital. Then as they began to act out the scene in the mental hospital the third girl was introduced to them as a doctor. They spent some time trying to represent their madness. The doctor then revealed herself as the Devil who had come to collect their souls. They then discussed how to represent the taking of souls.*

Starting from the same original idea these groups went in quite different directions. A major factor in this was the initial selection of the central symbolic situation through which to express the idea. In the first case this led the group to an exploration of the relationship of the married couple and their expectations of each other in different circumstances. The hitch-hiker acted as a catalyst for this. The girls in the second group were led to explore the broad theme of the conflict of good and evil. Their subsequent discussion involved a consideration of morality and of attitudes to insanity. The choice of symbolic structures is crucial in determining the nature of the explorations in acting-out. As the group struggle to elaborate the form of expression so they may plumb greater depths in the meaning of the theme or idea being represented. Similarly new insights and perceptions into the problem or meaning will

* A more complete description and analysis of this group's work appears on pages 62-4.

affect and shape the nature of the emerging form of expression.

There is a dual search in the arts—a search for adequate symbolic forms of expression which will both unearth and represent the problems of meaning. This is the primary sense of destination in drama work. The question of whether or not the group are then encouraged to move into performance—however formal or informal—can only be answered in its local context. It must be made in the knowledge that this is not an inevitable objective of the drama process.

There is a further point to be considered in thinking about the relationship of drama and theatre. We have been talking about drama work done by the individual or group for themselves. It may be appropriate, according to circumstances, for groups to share their work with others—to move into performance.

What then is the value for the child of experiencing other people's work, as a member of an audience? This is part of a much wider question. If, as we have suggested, drama and theatre are interrelated, in so far as they are based on the same impulses to explore and represent experience through the same media, how in practice does the work of the theatre relate to the educational process of drama? How if at all, can the child's own work in drama benefit from a knowledge of theatre forms and experience of seeing plays in performance?

The child does not develop his view of the world in a vacuum. He does so as a member of a group and, importantly, as a member of a culture. James Britton has this to say of the development of language, and it applies equally well to development through the arts:

We each build our own representation of the world but we greatly affect each other's representation so that much of what we build is in common.*

In expressing and communicating perceptions and attitudes through the arts the individual is contributing to a common pool of shared experience. As the individual finds meaning in personal experience through direct, active involvement in the arts so the culture, the society of which he is part, challenges and shapes, questions and expresses its corporate personality in its public arts. The music, literature, theatre, visual and plastic arts which characterize a culture provide a structure of perceptions, challenges and questions which feed and nourish the individual's own search for meaning in experience.

There is a difference between learning about the arts and learning through the arts. We are primarily concerned here with active

* J. Britton, *Language and Learning* (Allen Lane, Penguin Press, 1971).

participation in drama, with learning through drama. But the child's explorations need to be set in their wider cultural context. The teacher needs to ask how the child's own involvement in the arts can be enriched and enlivened through experience of the work of others—not through a dry study of artistic achievements but through an understanding and appreciation of the problems of meaning they are struggling to express and of the process of creation by which they are brought about.

# Drama, the arts and affective education

There is a danger in saying that drama is to do with the life of feeling. It may come to be seen as a form of therapy, as a way of releasing emotional tension or sorting out personal problems. The function of the arts in general and of drama in particular is not to provide an outlet for pent-up emotion. Alternatively, drama can be seen as non-intellectual, as a process best used in the education of the less intelligent child. The corollary of this is that it has little or no part to play in the education of the more intelligent child.

It is perhaps these views more than any others which have tended to keep drama on the periphery of the school curriculum. Certainly in a system which is geared so much towards examination success, the place of any work which apparently has no 'cognitive spin-off' is bound to be endangered. Similarly, any activity which is thought to centre on the release of emotional energy is bound to produce a nervous reaction in those with no direct experience of it.

This view of drama and the arts as peripheral to 'the real business of schools' is based on an interesting misconception. It is that feeling can be somehow disentangled from thinking and knowing; that these can be separated out from each other and taught in a kind of vacuum. This is certainly not the implication of the view of the arts in education which has been outlined here. Feelings and emotions cannot be filtered out of everyday life—for the purpose of developing them or for any other reason. The way we feel in a situation depends on what we know and how we interpret it. And the way we interpret it depends on the framework of ideas and concepts we bring to it. Clearly two people may react in entirely different ways to apparently similar circumstances. In his book *Education and Children's Emotions*, Geoffrey Yarlott* gives the example of a boy who is walking along the bank of a canal. He slips and falls in the water. He cannot swim. What is his emotional reaction likely to be? In all probability he will feel panic and fear. But if the same person had had the ability to swim his perception of

* Weidenfeld & Nicolson, 1972.

his circumstances would be different and so would his consequent emotional reaction. In this case he may feel anger and annoyance, but not fear or panic. The skills and knowledge with which he meets the situation help to determine his response to it.

The point here is that the individual's cognitive and affective development are completely interlinked, that it is extremely difficult to separate how we feel from what we come to know. What then is the role of teachers in the arts and in drama? It is two-fold:

1. To encourage the child to deepen and challenge his perceptions of himself and his world so that he gradually begins to make sense of the complexities and subtleties of his experience; acknowledges, accommodates and reassesses his world-view in the light of new experience.
2. To do this through enabling the child to use and express himself through the symbolic process of the arts.

Through drama the child explores problems and issues at the safety of one remove. He distances himself from them by behaving 'as if'. It is a vicarious involvement by which he can feel sufficiently removed from the issues to reflect on them and get them in perspective, and sufficiently involved, in the 'as if' sense, to deepen his understanding of them. The drama teacher takes part in the child's affective development not by providing cathartic experiences but by encouraging him to explore and question his ideas, attitudes and feelings, and in doing so to develop ways of making sense of, expressing, and communicating them. It is indeed this close interrelationship of knowing and feeling and the way in which they are combined, not separated, which opens up so many opportunities for drama in the education of all children.

## The components of the drama process

Drawing all of these considerations together, it is useful to think of the drama process in terms of four main components:

1. *Social interaction*. Drama is essentially social. As children participate they are encouraged to interact on both real and symbolic levels.
2. *Content*. Drama revolves around problems, questions and issues of understanding. The content of drama is united in that it is seen at the level of human behaviour and interpersonal response.
3. *Forms of expression*. As participants explore problems of meaning and understanding through drama they are experimenting with different ways of representing them through the roles and situations they devise.
4. *Use of the media—the 'language' of drama*. The way in which content is explored and the forms of representation which are

discovered and used are affected by the participants developing skills in the media of drama.

The ways in which these components are brought together or emphasized within a drama lesson affects, and helps to define, the kinds of learning which take place. Any lesson may focus on one or more of these. It is the way in which they are combined which helps to explain many of the differences between individual lessons.

# Conclusion

We began by asking 'what is drama'? What are its functions? We have argued that it is an expressive process which is best understood through the idea of symbolization and its role in the discovery and communication of meaning. There are not different types of drama, but the drama process is multi-faceted. It works through a variety of media and at a number of levels. As a result there are a number of ways in which drama can be used in education—and these require different aspects of the process to be emphasized. Through drama the child can gain greater experience in the use of the media themselves—voice, language, the body, as prime means of expression; and the associated media of light, sound and space.

The content of drama is wide-ranging. Through drama the individual can be brought closer to an understanding of a broad variety of topics, issues, themes and concepts, exploring them from the perspective of interpersonal behaviour. Drama revolves around social interaction. Through drama the child can explore his actual social relationships at the real level, and an unlimited number of hypothetical roles and attitudes at the symbolic level. Through testing out ideas and attitudes vicariously, he may experience a growth in self-confidence both in his ability to formulate and challenge ideas and in communicating and exposing his views to others. Through experiencing other people's drama he may find out more of their perceptions and interpretations of the world.

It is precisely because of this diversity of the process in action that it is impossible to prescribe aims for drama as a whole. The teacher needs to consider what he wants to achieve with the groups he works with in the context of the school of which he is a part, and to structure the drama work accordingly. The way a teacher works in drama depends on what he wants to achieve, and on his knowledge of what drama has to offer. His way of teaching drama will evolve in relation to the children he works with and the kind of learning he wants to encourage.

# Chapter 2
# Learning through Drama

In the last chapter we defined what we meant by 'drama' and discussed what its value in education might be. We suggested that the process of acting-out involves the exploration and representation of meaning through the medium of the whole person and that this is done through social interaction. In view of this, what kinds of learning should result from involvement in drama? They include: greater understanding of people and their situations; mastering the use of the process of representing, ordering and expressing feelings and ideas; controlling and using dramatic media; and working with others on both symbolic and real levels. To some extent all these kinds of learning occur when acting-out takes place. Some, however, may be stressed more than others. Depending on what teachers specifically want to achieve at a given time, different aspects of the process will be emphasized to achieve those aims.

In considering drama in practice, the following questions need to be asked: What distinctive kinds of learning can be achieved when teaching drama? What differences in practice may occur when teachers focus on certain aspects of learning? Conversely, what effect can different emphases placed on the process have on learning?

Through observation of a number of lessons, we have distinguished four main areas of emphasis within drama teaching:
1. Learning to use the process.
2. Understanding themes, topics and issues through acting-out.
3. Participating in presentation.
4. Interpretation and appreciation of dramatic statements by other people (i.e. experiencing other people's drama).
These will be discussed in some detail in the following pages.

This chapter is intended to give a basis for the ways in which aims and intentions in drama can be considered in practice. Descriptions will be given of how some teachers have encouraged certain kinds of learning through drama. It should be emphasized, however, that every drama session is the result of the unique interaction between the individual teacher and his pupils. There are no set ways of teaching drama even though some methods may better achieve certain ends than others.

# Learning to use the process

Drama work can be used to emphasize the development of acting-out as a creative process in its own right. This means that children, either on their own or with the teacher, are expected to find, select and create their own material. They are responsible for finding adequate forms of representation. Importance is attached to children finding their own ways of expressing and communicating meaning rather than working within an already defined situation or one which is mainly channelled by the teacher. This means that the work can be more open-ended than work that focuses on understanding particular themes, topics and issues. The child is expected to learn to use the process of drama to express his feelings and ideas. Because of this attention may be paid to the control and use of various media—movement, speech, space, physical objects and sound—in representing meaning.

Some teachers feel that work should be unstructured, enabling children to experiment and develop work in any ways they want. Other teachers feel that the process should be linked to the exploration of a theme, topic or issue, but that once a broad structure is given, children should be allowed to develop their own lines of inquiry. This does not mean that teachers may not intervene from time to time to improve or deepen work. What they actually do often depends on what they want to achieve and what children are capable of doing at a given time. For instance, children who find it difficult to work by themselves will need more help than those who do not. What are the advantages and disadvantages of working in different ways?

## *Exploration of meaning*

Where work is undirected, children are usually not given a particular focus for their work. They may be given a simple stimulus and be expected to arrive at their own definition of what they wish to explore, as well as the manner in which they want to work. This allows children to develop along their own lines. Children who have not had a great deal of experience of acting-out are sometimes allowed time for 'playing' in this sense, so that they can experiment freely without feeling pressurized. Some teachers feel that development occurs naturally as a result of the children having the opportunity to explore topics and issues of interest to them and chosen by them.

When a teacher asked a group of eleven-year-olds what they wanted to do they said they wanted to go on a boat journey. The teacher sat at the side of the class. With great excitement children ran around the room collecting chairs, tables and any other furniture they could find. Within five minutes they constructed a boat with imaginary oars. There was a little trouble in starting because they couldn't row together. One child shouted, 'One, two, one, two', and they started rowing in time. Another child saw the island they were going to. 'Look there it is, it's time to land.' Landing on the island was difficult because the picnic baskets were heavy and had to be carried by more than one person. Two girls and a boy started grilling meat on an improvised barbecue and other children waited until they were given some. Meanwhile a group of children had explored the island. 'Look, look, blackberries!' There was a scramble as everyone rushed to pick blackberries, some pricking their fingers with the inevitable child suffering from stomach-ache from eating too many. The teacher told them that they had five minutes left so they collected their things, got into the boat and rowed back.

One of the advantages of working in this way is that pupils are given responsibility for selecting their own subject matter and lines of inquiry. This allows them to choose to explore what is important to them. The problem is that many children will spend a great deal of time in deciding what they are going to explore. This often means that, in the limited time of a lesson, children reach the stage of selecting symbols to work with rather than exploring in any depth. At no stage except at the end did the teacher intervene. The children enjoyed themselves. Together they created a delightful environment in which a great deal of 'as if' activity occurred. One of the disadvantages of working in this way is that there is no guarantee that children will be challenged or confronted with problems that will stretch them. The quality of exploration is likely to be superficial unless the teacher injects an event into the acting-out that challenges them.

In more structured work, teachers may give children a stimulus or ask them to explore particular ideas by themselves and to find forms to express their feelings about them. In other cases he may help children by working with them but letting them make most of the decisions. Two examples of work follow, one where both teacher and children worked together and one where the pupils worked on their own.

The teacher asked a class of ten-year-olds what they would like to do some drama about. One boy quickly said that he wanted to do some drama about 'smashing up the school'. This had immediate appeal to others. The teacher asked them how they were going to organize this. They said the meeting should take place in an old air-raid shelter and when he asked who he could be in the play, after refusing to be the leader of the gang, a girl suggested he should be a tramp who sometimes lived in the shelter.

He went and huddled in a corner between two rostra and said that that was where he always slept. The children came in and began arguing about how they were going to get into the school. The tramp complained at being disturbed and asked them what they were doing in his home. They explained and he (furious) said that if they were so disorganized then they would be traced back to the shelter and the police would discover him and move him on. He said he was going out for food and when he came back they should either be properly organized or have left. He then withdrew from the drama. Two leaders emerged and the class began to plan the raid with more care.

Seven minutes later he returned. One girl asked where he had got food from. He said from dustbins at the back of a factory canteen. This made a great impact and the tramp was greeted with stunned silence. A boy said that they could have got him food. Several others said, 'Let's get him some proper food'. Within seconds the class left and went 'home' for food. They returned to find the tramp gone and decided to tidy the place up, laying food on the table.

The tramp came back and, after thanking them, told them that he could not accept their gestures as he was too used to living in filth and squalor. He left. At first the children were very angry at being rejected. They sat about despondently and uttered angry comments. Then one boy suggested that the shelter and some others be made habitable as a sort of transit hostel for tramps 'because if there were lots of them together they would probably enjoy it and be able to cope'.

Ways of raising money were discussed in some detail, together with design ideas for the shelters.

In this example the teacher confronted the pupils with something they had not considered before. This gave them a starting-point to develop the drama for themselves. Although he helped to heighten the drama and posed difficulties, they made most of the decisions about how the situation would be developed.

The following is an example of how meaning was negotiated by a group of children on their own.

A teacher asked small groups of fourteen-year-olds to work on any element of human weakness they cared to choose. She wanted them to select characters and situations through which they could explore the topic. One group, two boys and two girls, decided that they were interested in deception. After a heated argument where one girl said that people who deceived others, really deceived themselves and one boy thought that most people deceived others because it benefited them, they started to act-out. The situation developed in which two married couples met for dinner. After a while one of the husbands started having an affair with the other man's wife. The two other people pretended not to notice. At this point they stopped acting-out as one boy was unhappy about the way the girl had represented flirting with the other man. 'She wouldn't flutter her eyes like that. Too obvious.' 'It would be better if she pretended to be, oh, much better than everyone else. That would make it much worse.' 'It don't matter how she acts—she's got to keep it from her old man.'

The scene was repeated with some differences and elaboration, where the deceiving couple were questioned by their spouses. Dialogue was intense and went on for thirty minutes until the lesson ended. The husband convinced his wife that it was a mild flirtation and did not affect his feelings for her. The wife eventually admitted she had deceived her husband and broke down saying that she was so guilty that she hated the affair. Her husband walked out slamming the door. He was just coming back in when the bell went for the end of the lesson.

Both couples were exhausted and did not say much except for one who said, 'I don't think you can separate people's weakness from the better sides of them. Everyone's got both sides to them.'

During acting-out each child developed a definite character for the person he was playing. The children assumed certain attitudes to each other which were reflected in the ways they talked, related physically to each other, and the kinds of mannerisms they employed when doing simple things like drinking tea or lighting cigarettes. As the acting-out developed there was a marked increase in detail as well as children finding various ways of reinforcing the kinds of people they were representing. For example, one wife showed her anxiety by being obsessive about tidying the house. The value of the activity was that it allowed the children to pursue their interests as far as they wanted. It is possible that after a time they would have reached some conclusions which they might have wanted to express in a more coherent form embodying the complexity of what they wanted to say. At this stage they would have deliberately begun shaping.

## Shaping

*Shaping involves the organization and crystallization of ideas into a statement where there is an emphasis on form.* Shaping occurs when children have gone through initial phases including the selection and modification of symbols. The notion of form is an essential feature of shaping.

A primary teacher was working on the story of Theseus and the Minotaur with her ten-to-eleven-year-old class. She asked them to represent the journey of Theseus through the maze until he reached the Minotaur, fought and eventually killed him. They were to do this through the media of movement and sound. One group of eight children created a never-ending maze by forming chains and passages on different levels and of different lengths. As soon as one chain was formed the beginning of the link broke off, joined on to the end of the existing one and began again. While this was happening they hummed in a menacing way while Theseus crawled through the maze. The volume rose as he got nearer to the beast then stopped to indicate that the beast and Theseus were confronting each other. At that stage the children represented the struggle by forming a writhing shape through which Theseus emerged triumphant as the shape collapsed. From the children's conversation it was clear that they felt that they were representing some notion of good triumphing over evil.

This last example is an illustration of how children can synthesize their understanding of quite complex and abstract ideas through drama.

Appreciation of form does not, however, guarantee the quality of the meaning represented. There is a danger in encouraging children to produce an end-product. It may inhibit the natural development of the work and often forces children to cut short exploration and prematurely find forms of expression which can result in work of a superficial nature. Not all children are equally capable of organizing complex ideas. Some might not get beyond trial and error 'playing'. Some may reach exploratory stages without being able to shape their ideas. Other groups for various reasons—for example, capacity to come up with ideas, interpersonal relationships—arrive at partial statements in which they have an idea of shape but do not complete their work. Some children go through a great deal of trouble to reach a conclusion whereas others start with an idea of a finished plot and spend time on elaborating it. The teacher needs to be aware that not all children have an equally developed sense of form and therefore might need to devote some time to this particular aspect of learning. He may set up specific exercises to encourage the shaping of ideas with an ultimate view to improving the general quality of their exploration of meaning.

In using the process children must learn to use their own resources in finding and selecting symbols which will adequately represent their interpretations of what is being explored. They should develop a greater capacity to assume and build hypothetical roles and characters by responding to others and the situation inventively. Children should also become increasingly aware of the levels of superficiality and depth at which they are working so that they can become critical about the quality of their work both in terms of the content explored and whether they are satisfied with the accuracy of their forms of representation. Where learning to use the process is emphasized, the teacher is less likely to structure and more likely to encourage children to work on their own. His responsibility is to help them in their ability to use the process and improve the quality of their work. Where shaping is encouraged, children should be more able to order and clarify increasingly complex ideas into some form of dramatic structure. Problems of shaping may arise because some children find difficulties in organizing ideas. They may also arise because at a particular time children have not clarified their ideas enough to devise a statement about them. The teacher needs to take factors like these into account and also be aware of the dangers of forcing children to 'shape' before they are ready.

In general, drama is one way in which groups can learn to find forms of expression in which they can explore and express their understanding of people and situations. It is also a useful way of encouraging them to put their ideas together—a dramatic statement is an immediate, concrete and vivid experience which allows children to test in a short time whether they have been effective or not. This is even more apparent when they show their work to others.

## Learning through social interaction

So far we have discussed learning to use the process in terms of exploring and representing meaning. A basic component of most acting-out is that it is done through social interaction. It is therefore important to ask what kinds of learning can be achieved through this.

In the first chapter it was suggested that, because of the nature of acting-out, involvement takes place on two levels—the symbolic and the real. It is in these two areas and the links between them that learning takes place.

By working hypothetically, children are given the opportunity of experimenting with a variety of reactions and responses. They are also given the opportunity to increase their understanding of people and their circumstances through their changing perceptions of how they personally react on both real and symbolic levels within the acting-out. In other words, participation in drama can affect children's perceptions of social reality. Their reactions can help them become more aware of a wider range of people and how they behave, than they might otherwise encounter in their everyday life. By negotiating how to work and making decisions about the ongoing work itself, children are learning to communicate with each other on a real level as well.

In constructing characters and roles children draw on past experiences and understanding in order to project into new symbols and roles. Depending on the imagined roles they adopt and how people react to them, they respond and develop in the drama. Their symbols are derived from their perceptions and feelings about reality. These are affected by social expectations in the children's immediate environment—their home, their friends, their social and other influences such as television and magazines. These perceptions are often reflected in the forms of representation that children use, which can often be forms of stereotyping. It is one thing deliberately to use caricature as a means of finding a correct form of expression. It is another thing to believe that a stereotype corresponds to reality. By putting children in other people's positions they can learn to become more aware of the complexities of human situations and possibly even start questioning certain preconceptions and prejudices. It is one thing to believe that all black people do not deserve to have the same work as whites. It is another thing to be put in the position of someone who is trying to find work and is discriminated against because of colour.

It should, however, be said that there is a danger of reinforcing social attitudes and preconceptions by constantly giving children the same roles to play. This is most manifest in differences between male/female roles where girls are frequently given subservient roles and the boys are given dominant ones. If drama is to be used to develop flexibility of approach and to challenge the child by asking him to respond to situations unusual for him, it will not be helpful if the child merely imitates existing social patterns and attitudes limited to his own social environment and reinforced by practice.

Another way in which children learn is in the area of group problem-solving and group decision-making. In acting-out children are often given an idea and asked to go away and make something of it, perhaps to arrive at a dramatic statement which encapsulates their feelings and ideas about a particular topic or issue. This involves complex processes such as selecting and rejecting the right symbols; modifying and elaborating their ideas and organizing those ideas into appropriate coherent forms of expression. Equally important, it involves being able to learn to contribute, to accept and share other people's ideas, to build on them and come to corporate decisions about which ideas are thought to be appropriate to what the children want to explore and also whether adequate forms of expression can be found in which to say them. Drama can give children the opportunity to communicate between themselves and to arrive at corporate and positive decisions about what to do and how to do it. In view of the increasing tendency for both social and industrial decisions to be made collectively, it is important in the child's everyday education that he be given the opportunity to learn how to negotiate for himself, to discuss things with people and arrive at decisions and have opinions about the issues involved.

What has just been said could apply to any creative group problem-solving activity. What then is especially useful about drama in this area of learning? First, through acting-out, children can become more aware of other people's positions. Secondly, drama offers the opportunity of exploring a number of possible social situations in action and therefore discovering the practical implications. Thirdly, acting-out enables pupils to discuss what they want to do, how to do it, to act on their decisions, and to see whether these decisions are effective.

Acting-out combines both physical and verbal forms of communication. In everyday life our main means of communication are through interpersonal contact in different contexts. Our effectiveness is determined by our perceptions and how sensitively we respond to others. Through acting-out, children can become aware of the effectiveness of body language as a means of communication. By improving physical skills, often through movement training, and applying these skills to express himself, the pupil is given the opportunity to lose physical inhibitions and build up personal self-confidence through the control and command of his body. An important aspect of communication is how the spoken language is used to express feelings and ideas. Drama can play an important role in language development.

## Language learning through acting-out

Through drama the child is given the opportunity of using language to cope with and respond to a number of situations. He can become aware of the different linguistic demands placed upon him when put in various social roles—for example, in communicating with people in different social positions such as an employer, a doctor, or a social security officer; or responding in various social situations—from engaging in small talk at a party to discussing a friend's personal problems. Acting-out can help children experiment with the appropriateness of a number of social registers. It can help them build up a more flexible approach.

An advantage of acting-out is that it occurs over a clearly defined period of time. It elicits immediate response from others and also demands that the speaker responds quickly. As one child said when she was asked what she thought of the value of the activity, 'It teaches you to think on your feet'. It is possible for the child immediately to modify, correct or develop his use of language as he goes along.

One of the most important aspects of drama is not just the use of words in language but, very important, the effectiveness of voice as a means of expression. Research has shown the importance and complexity of the use of the voice, particularly intonation.* The way teenagers speak is often criticized by teachers and head teachers. As teenagers become more self-conscious, there is a greater tendency towards hesitation and using such phrases as 'you know'. In other words, when adolescents need to be able to express themselves more, it seems that there is a danger that some become more inflexible in their use of language and less able to express themselves. It could be argued that drama, by allowing them to act in hypothetical situations, enables this to be counteracted to a certain extent. The teenager can protect himself through acting-out in somebody else's role; he does not have to be as constantly self-conscious of his own voice and his own reactions.

* David Crystal, *The English Tone of Voice* (Edward Arnold, 1975).

However, not all cases of acting-out necessarily encourage improved language development. One of the many criticisms levelled against drama in education is that it allows children to use forms of language which would not otherwise be acceptable in schools and very often reinforces the mundane everyday poverty of speech used by some teenagers. This is often the result of the teacher's failure to present the children with a wide enough range. He needs to be aware of the kinds of language difficulties and habits that individuals in the class may have, so that if he is going to designate particular roles for children he can give them roles which will challenge and extend their actual use of language. The notion of competence and performance and the notion that the native speaker is capable of using an infinite amount of sentences* is only valid if opportunities are given to stretch children's ability to use language. It is up to the teacher to provide these opportunities. It is the duty of every teacher using drama to be aware of the quality of the kind of communication and language used and to provide opportunities for improvement.

# Understanding themes, topics and issues through acting-out

**Son:** Mum, stop sewing. Listen to me.
**Mother:** Yes, the candle is too dim. What is it?
**Son:** I want my supper.
**Mother:** You've had potato broth.
**Son:** You call that food! Two potatoes boiled in water! I'm leaving. I'm going to find work. There's nothing here. It's boring.

This dialogue occurred in a lesson with a class of ten-year-olds in exploring some aspects of the Industrial Revolution. Acting-out was used to explore the human implications of people leaving the country to go to the city to find work. The teacher fed in details about social life in the nineteenth century by reading to the children, showing them pictures and watching television programmes. She also talked them through a movement sequence of working in the country. Family groups were drawn up and two children in each group were given the task of persuading their families to let them leave for the city. There was a discussion at the end of the session when children were asked what reasons were given for going, whether they were valid reasons in terms of the details given and what it felt like to leave or be left in those particular circumstances.

Children can translate their understanding into concrete actions. They can become familiar with details fed in by the teacher and digest them through experience. The use of acting-out to explore

---

* N. Chomsky, *Language and Mind* (Harcourt Brace Jovanovich, 1972).

particular subject matter can be used across the curriculum. If drama is used in this way, it is part of the teacher's responsibility to give pupils enough information to work with, and see that they understand the relevance of details. Consistent use of details is important if children are to further their understanding of the particular characteristics of a situation. In this context it is no use to the teacher who wants to explore Roman social history if children decide to play at cowboys and Indians.

Drama can be used to extend children's immediate experience, or explore issues more directly relevant to them. The following examples show ways in which two teachers focused on particular issues by asking children to play selected roles.

### Examining different methods of persuasion

One of the most common topics explored by older children is work interviews. One pupil role-plays the interviewer and the other the interviewee. A teacher in a grammar school set up interviews with fourteen-year-old boys to look at the nature and techniques of persuasion. Boys were given roles in which they had to persuade prospective employers to give them work. After each pair had shown their interview, discussion centred round who had been most effective and why. The lesson continued with the teacher giving individual pupils the problem of selling things such as wallpaper that changes colour according to the mood of people in the room, or soluble chairs. 'I want to challenge your ingenuity by giving you difficult things to sell'. He wanted them to examine the difference between honest and dishonest methods of persuasion. At the end of the lesson it was interesting to note some of the boys' comments: 'Couldn't they have pretended it was better than it was and forgotten about the Trade Descriptions Act?'; 'You can make unlikely facts sound realistic'; 'An honest man might stick to a price but a dishonest man could start with a high price and then knock it down'; 'Service could make customers feel special. It could be personal so that people would buy things because they liked you'.

### Exploring the nature of love between mother and son

A fifth-year group were asked to focus on love between mother and son and to define a problem that would test that love and if possible resolve the problem.

Some of the pupils did not find this easy, possibly because the emotional intensity was too great. Their comments after the session revealed, however, considerable thoughtfulness about the problem. One group explored a mother's response to a son caught stealing. 'It's more shame, isn't it? What the neighbours think.' 'My mother would blame herself for bringing me up wrong.' 'Mothers will always make excuses for the child.'

A number of pupils remarked on the problems of coming up with solutions: 'We didn't really find a solution although we had ideas like I would get a day job and go out to work, but that didn't really sum it up.'

As a group they came to the general conclusion that in normal relationships the love between mother and son remained constant.

An advantage of these methods is that children can base their opinions on experience. Through discussion after the event they are given the opportunity to see their work in more general terms. It also allows them to reflect on how they, as individuals, react and interact in certain roles.

The next example shows how a teacher used a script to deepen understanding, not only of the historical plot, but also of the characters in the play.

A CSE group worked on the 'Cato Street' conspiracy for two terms. The group of fifth-year pupils came from a working-class catchment area. Some of them had reading problems. They chose 'Cato Street' by Robert Shaw, because they wanted to do an historical play written in modern language and had chosen this one after reading a number of plays. The plot concerned the Cato Street conspiracy in 1821 where people had plotted to blow up the cabinet. The attempt failed and most of the plotters were hanged. Some of the themes the teacher wanted the children to explore through work on the script were: the desperation that poverty produces; what redundancies mean; the problems of organizing change when there are no structures for organization. They were exploring this through reading and acting-out the text, improvisations and discussion about the background of the play and the script.

A great deal of in-depth characterization was done both through acting-out and in discussion. For instance, at a certain stage, one of the leaders lost confidence. A long improvisation occurred between her and her son in which she outlined her fears and fatigue and he talked about his father who had been hung for rebellion. The relationship between mother and son was reinforced by their sharing their fears and frustrations with each other. This was later maintained when they returned to the script and injected more meaning into it.

Towards the end of the year the teacher felt that their work was 'less superficial and more thoughtful'. There had been improvements in their ability to sustain characters and relationships between them. The teacher constantly challenged them about their level of involvement; '*Listen* to each other, then if you don't know the exact words, you get the meaning. Do you really *mean* what you say . . . When do you last remember being cold and hungry?'

By the time that pupils were ready to perform the play, they had given a great deal of thought to the issues raised in it. There were often discussions about the effects of poverty on people. 'If you don't have bread, you find something else, like potatoes.' 'What happens if you don't have no money for anything?' 'Then you steal it.' 'Nah, you wouldn't have no energy.' Discussions concerning characters also revealed that they had thought about the structure of the play. One girl who played the part of a leader said that her part was difficult. She was expected to go 'on and on about [her] husband's death'. 'I was always doubtful about whether the plot would succeed. Well, that isn't enough to go on, if you really have to feel you're a leader and make other people convinced.' One boy thought that one of the reasons why the conspiracy failed was shown in the play by the personal weaknesses of the characters. He felt this was the reason why one person had exposed the plot for a bribe.

Two pupils with severe reading difficulties said that they would never have explored the play in such depth if they had not been actively involved. They felt that working in this way had motivated them to try to improve their reading.

By studying characters in depth through their own explorations and the text, it was possible for pupils to build more detailed pictures of characters with their complexities and subtleties. Pupils go from more general conceptions of roles to a more detailed consideration of characters when they concentrate on understanding characters through acting-out. In that sense they are moving from the general to the particular. It is also possible in acting-out to move from particular experiences to a more general understanding of the nature of what is being explored. This means that the experience of acting-out can be used to understand the nature of themes and abstract concepts. The following two examples show how abstract concepts can be explored through drama. They also illustrate how drama can help children understand concepts in general terms and at the same time make them relevant in personal terms.

*Understanding the 'need for silence'*

A noisy class of twelve-year-olds were asked to examine the difficulties of keeping silent when necessary. They chose the idea of escaping from a prisoner-of-war camp. The whole class participated (with the teacher intervening at times when she felt that silence was being lost)—for example, constructing physical barriers across the room which gave out alarms when there was noise—with terrible repercussions. Throughout the lesson details were fed in—for example, silence was needed because the prison guards were catching up with them. Each child chose a particular part to play—some were children, ex-soldiers, etc. The session was conducted with concentration, in almost total silence, so that there was an atmosphere of tension throughout.

At the end of the lesson, the children said that what they had gained from the lesson was that if people had enough motivation to keep quiet, they would be silent. The teacher asked them whether they felt that previous drama work did not 'have enough meat in it'. They answered that they found the work exciting not only because of the storyline, but also because for the first time they had worked intensely together as a group on something that mattered to them and found the experience satisfying, and therefore they were emotionally committed to the work. One boy, who had responsibility for keeping children quiet during the drama, remarked on how difficult and stressful it had been because he had been aware that the noise of the children would have given the group away.

*'The nature of violence' and problems of decision-making*

A teacher had a dual purpose in working with a fourth-year class. He wanted them to start considering the nature of violence by working on a sequence of lessons on organized violence—for example, war. He also wanted them to explore the nature of decision-making by giving them real decisions to make during the lesson. The lesson began with the teacher asking pupils to be designers of postage stamps. He talked them through designing their stamps. Then in role, he started feeding in a military influence in which he ordered the designers to design and illustrate military slogans. As the session progressed, he put increasing pressure on them to finish quickly and to produce the most effective propaganda for war. Activity was stopped and an authentic propaganda record was played which expanded on how evil the enemy was and how they should be exterminated. Until that point the lesson had been carefully structured to give pupils a detailed context in which to work. The teacher then instructed the class to divide into two groups. Each was to organize and stage a political rally. At the same rally one group was to argue for war. The other was to plead for peace.

Groups were given fifteen minutes to work something out. One group devised a series of chants and marches which ended in the climax of the speech. The other group, because of interpersonal difficulties, could not organize themselves. The lesson ended with a tribunal conducted by the political leader (a boy in role) to analyse why the second group had failed. In this way, their actions were discussed in both real and symbolic terms, that is they had to work out what had actually happened to them during the session and the effect of their actions in symbolic role. Because of the atmosphere that had been built up they had also become aware that had this been real, the group that failed to organize themselves would have been punished for not carrying out orders properly.

Drama can be used to explore quite general concepts or themes. It can also be used to explore specific social or political issues. In such cases there is usually a greater emphasis on role-play within the drama session than on characterization. This can be done in the form of a structured game. The simulation would involve constraints and rules which are analogous to real pressures. This use of drama has led to the production of a number of 'ready-made' simulation exercises which can be used in the teaching of many subjects.* 'Tenement', a game produced by Shelter, the organization for the homeless, is intended to simulate the problems of finding a home through the existing social and economic system. A number of agencies are set up within the game—the participants having to offer advice and help within clearly defined limits. The would-be home buyers have to use the agencies to find and finance a home—again working within clearly spelt-out rules.

* For more detailed discussion and more examples, see R. Walford and J. Taylor, *Simulations in the Classroom* (Penguin Books, 1973).

## Practical implications

It is suggested that, if drama is used to explore particular problems of understanding, the main kinds of learning encouraged are:

1. Ability to apply information given by the teacher and sustain this with reference to the particular aspects of meaning being explored.
2. Greater facility in expressing understanding through acting-out in such a way that abstract notions can be represented and explored through action.
3. Improved ability to make experience gained through acting-out conscious and to understand the implications of the experience in both general and personal terms.

There are two major practical implications in using drama to encourage these kinds of development.
1. Teachers are more likely to take responsibility for content and the manner of exploration so that the main focus is kept on exploring a particular theme, topic or issue. This means that teachers have to be able to construct or control work in such a way that understanding can be deepened. It also means that often children will act-out within more closely defined contexts and therefore have more limited choices concerning the development of the work.
2. Importance is placed on the kind of understanding that has been gained. One of the features of this work is that teachers ask pupils to reflect upon their experiences in various ways, by translating and exploring what they have understood as a result of acting-out through other media, such as writing, art or music. Discussion is one of the commonest forms of reflection.

In a lesson considering the advantages and disadvantages of war, a teacher of ten- to eleven-year-olds asked children to express differences of conflict and peace through movement. Later she asked them to express these two concepts through drawing. The children produced abstract patterns expressing differences through shapes and patterns. She then gave groups a number of photographs including some of statesmen and civilians in war conditions. They were asked to develop roles and attitudes based on the photographs and in role either to argue for or against war. In cases where photographs depicted war-time conditions, pupils were encouraged to give their own personal stories of what had happened to them. In the discussion that followed 'in role' it became clear that pupils had considered a number of aspects: one statesman argued that by rights a piece of fertile land occupied by another country historically belonged to them. Now that there was not enough food to go round, he felt that they would have to retrieve it by war. A civilian replied that that would mean suffering for the other

country. Another felt she would rather starve than risk the death of her
family. One boy felt that if they did not attack first the other country
would.

At the end of the lesson there was no agreement among pupils
about whether they would support war or not. They were certainly
aware of some of the suffering involved in war and what their own
conditions might have been compared with existing peace-time
conditions. What they had done was to put themselves in other
people's places, and put forward a number of viewpoints they had
not thought of before. Discussion can be used as a bridging
experience. Teachers may stop lessons at various points to discuss
the implications of work, perhaps to extract generalizations from
particular experiences or to deepen the understanding of particular
characters or roles. Discussion also can take place at the end of
activities or lessons so that both pupils and teachers can share
ideas, discuss how successful the lessons have been and what may
be suitable for future work.

# Participation in presentation

## *Showing*

Sometimes children may want to show what they have done to
others (usually members of their class). Showing involves a shift of
emphasis from finding the appropriate forms to communicating
what has been created to others. The emphasis on sharing or
communicating often means that children organize their ideas so
that they can be appreciated by others. Showing often involves
three new learning processes: recall (the ability to remember and
repeat sequences of actions); improving communication skills; and
the shaping of ideas.

Numerous examples have been observed which illustrate some of
the values of successful 'showing'. Many children take great
pleasure in sharing their work with others, in communicating their
ideas and feelings, and gain from the reciprocal enjoyment of their
audience. Often the response of an audience to a particular child
will help him to build up confidence and motivate exploratory
work. For the rest of the class, watching and listening to other
people's work can help increase powers of concentration and
discrimination.

Unsuccessful showing can be counter-productive, making pupils
too self-conscious and nervous to enjoy working. The teacher
therefore has to be careful to see that children who are vulnerable
are not put in difficult positions. The production of work which is
slick or glib may easily be confused with work of quality. In other
words there is a danger that children may latch on to the external

features of performance without actually being involved in any worth-while consideration of the meaning. In some cases children may find it meaningless to repeat a sequence of acting-out. This is usually when they feel that they cannot recapture the original quality of their involvement, in which case they may not want to show.

## Performance by pupils

'Showing' involves the communication of dramatic statements to members of the class. The word 'performance' applies here to the more formal, planned presentation of dramatic statements to a wider audience (either pupils' own plays or someone else's). Refinement of the statement often involves greater use of technical media such as lighting and sound to highlight effects. 'Performance', for our purposes, also means a dramatic event that takes place in front of people other than the members of the class. In other words, pupils are using drama to communicate to others in the community. This means that more emphasis may be placed on the physical and verbal forms of representation and the impact that these make on the audience.

Working towards performances often involves lengthy processes of rehearsal. Adequate forms of expression need to be found. Sometimes (as seen in the Cato Street example) pupils are able to portray characters more convincingly by first exploring them in their own work. At times they will concentrate on various voice and body skills so that they can communicate as clearly and efficiently as possible. Preparing for performances usually involves an amount of repetition and polishing, leading to improvement not only in terms of acting-out, but also in terms of the overall production of a performance. A value of the exercise is that a large number of people, often of different ages, with various tasks, are challenged to co-ordinate their activities in such a way that the performance runs smoothly, efficiently and effectively. Timing, behaviour and team-work become essential, not only for the actors, but also for those concerned with stage management (lighting, props, sets, sound, costume, etc.).

The same advantages and disadvantages mentioned about showing apply to performance. Emphasis, however, is placed not so much on the process of arriving at and expressing ideas (although a number of plays performed in schools are a result of the children's and teacher's own work), but on the presentation of plays to a wider audience. The dramatic experience becomes a special occasion and acquires more importance in the eyes of both participants and spectators. The social and personal value of working for performances can be significant, as shown by three very different examples of successful school plays.

*'Charlie and the Chocolate Factory', based on a story by Roald Dahl. (primary school)*

This play was about five spoilt children who entered a special chocolate factory and what happened to them when they disobeyed the owner's orders. It was performed by third- and fourth-year pupils in a primary school. Although the performance was watched by parents and 'residents of the estate' on which the school was situated, the high point was in giving a performance to old-age pensioners. About 240 children and some of their parents were involved, either taking part or making sets, etc.

The staff and the head fully supported the play and its value. The teacher's aims were: 'To provide an opportunity whereby we can contribute to the life of the community of which we are part; to give confidence to some children and to provide a vehicle by which children who will become leaders within the school will emerge; to get all the children of the third and fourth year engaged in a project sharing their own experiences and finally sharing them with other people; to involve as many children as possible through drama, music and mime in a creative project.'

Songs were written by staff members for a large chorus. During rehearsal new ideas were being contributed right to the end. When the play was in its last stages, it still had a quality of invention and immediacy. Rehearsals took place during the mornings or after school for the main parts, when other year teachers either contributed or took children who were not involved at the time.

Members of staff and the head suggested pupils whom they thought would benefit from being given the responsibility of major parts. Examples of two reports indicate the teacher's reasons for suggesting particular parts. The first is about a fourth-year boy: 'He is a non-reader and has little idea of phonics. I selected him for a major part in the play because I hoped it would boost his morale. He felt a failure and school offered little whereby he could succeed. He can find success in drama because it is non-academic but creative. As the play progressed his confidence developed. He had a very shaky start and felt out of place and awkward. As he got to know the story better he became less worried about forgetting what to do and just concentrated on enjoying himself. The result was a truly remarkable experience for him. He was a huge success and even at the end of the improvisation he was creating new situations and thinking up lively things to say. According to his teacher his creative writing work has improved and our remedial teacher informs me he has taken to reading with a new zest and drive.'

The second description concerned 'a very lively boy who is often put in a secondary role by his friends—his real ability is masked by his friends. He finds it difficult to express himself without halting or getting confused. One result of the play was that this teacher got to know him better and established a more relaxed relationship with him which is resulting in him achieving more in the classroom. To say that it drastically improved his language usage would be too much, but it certainly helped.'

The staff and pupils echoed the teacher's comments about the overall effects of the play. 'The main general result was the great feeling of a sharing of an experience—children and staff, and children and children.

All of the staff were involved as indeed were many parents.'

*'The Bluebird' by Maeterlinck. (Twelve-year-olds in a grammar school)*

The school had a reputation for traditional performances with good standards of design, costumes and lighting. This play which involved all the second years in a grammar school was organized along very different lines although the same kind of care was taken over casting. All the second years had had experience in improvising plays. The teacher thought that he would like to experiment with using a script as he had two new teachers with no experience of drama except adult amateur drama. Each of the five second-year classes prepared one act during drama lessons over a term.

The teacher's aims included such things as 'encouraging children to work as a group, mixing sexes, inspiring confidence and a sense of achievement, encouraging other methods of expression, better use of space, dramatic shape, concentration and helping children to shoulder responsibility'.

One of the main motivations in working in this way was to encourage a sense of identity for the second years. The teacher explained, 'After the second year the children in this school move to another building at the other side of town where the senior year-groups are housed. The senior school is much bigger, more impersonal. It is important for children going there to adapt quickly to the new atmosphere. This is where a healthy group identity can stand them in good stead.'

Rehearsals were mainly concerned with memorizing lines and movements and putting the whole act into shape. This created difficulties for some of the children who had to learn to keep quiet and wait while other children were working. Some also found the discipline of constant repetition taxing. The teacher felt that the content of the play (although suitable for his purpose) posed problems. 'This is a very difficult play to put across with young children as they find the sentiments rather sugary and sentimental. They admit to the truth of the underlying philosophy, however ("You'll find your happiness lies right under your eyes") and are keen to take part in the play.'

In most performances there are parts of varying sizes and importance. This means that the experience will have different values for each participant. The following comments by children about the play are a reminder that working towards performances is not always enjoyable, although the end product can be worth while.

When we were rehearsing the play I found it very boring for we had to go over and over different parts again and again. I was also bored and angry for I had nothing to say but I suppose if you don't have the less important people you cannot make a play. The play became much more interesting when everyone had learnt their lines.

The part I played in the drama-play called *The Bluebird* was quite enormous. I was on stage right from the word go to the curtain. The rehearsals were worrying at times . . . Every Tuesday we would be given scripts and told to work on them. We slaved away for two months getting the play up to standard . . . When we had our first rehearsal, all the second forms, in the hall, I was worried I would make a hash of it in front of my girl friend but in the end I came off great.

At the first rehearsal I felt a proper idiot, as my part was Milk, and all I had to say was "I feel I'm going to turn". Well, what's wrong with that, you may say? To tell you the truth, I thought it was soft, and as I said it—I felt as though God would open the floors of the stage and swallow me up. Then, we were given our costumes to try on, and after that I didn't feel quite as embarrassed, as mine was one of the nicest.

Other children can get a great deal of enjoyment out of working in this way.

I thought it was fun doing *The Bluebird*. During the rehearsals everybody wonders if they will remember the lines and are tense. It is exciting working by script. It was my first time. I think *The Bluebird* was better than when we did our own little scenes.

### 'But There Ain't Nothing To Do'. (Third to fifth years in a secondary modern)

This play was done after school with a group of volunteers who worked with the teacher in making and producing their own play. It is an example of how pupils' dramatic work can end in a performance which is meaningful both to them and to the community they are communicating with.

It is also useful in as much as it illustrates the value of workshops after school for children who wish to do drama work in their spare time. Not only did children volunteer, but they also worked with pupils across an age-range with whom they might otherwise have had no contact. They worked together to create something which was valid to them. As the teacher said: 'This is your chance to communicate something that matters to you to as many as one hundred adults.' The teacher felt that the effort of working towards a production was valuable. 'Once it starts to fall together—they feel "wow we are saying something". They have given it a try and stuck with it.'

The play was about the boredom and frustrations teenagers experience on large council estates. It concerned gang warfare and a boy who was paralysed as a result of a fight. Various ways were used to present ideas including a film made by a group of boys who lived on the estate which showed very clearly the boredom of their life. Slides were projected and taped sounds were used to highlight and create effects. A group of boys made slides which dramatically portayed the incident in which the boy was paralysed. All pupils played teenagers and adults' voices were taped because the pupils felt they could not represent them without caricature which would have affected the power of their statement. Much of the boredom and violence was stylized. At one stage members of the team fantasized about what they wanted to be when they grew up—including a comic scene in which a brain surgeon goes through a farcical situation (string pulled out of the head, etc.). The teacher felt that the experience allowed them to 'start understanding what theatre means. It is a statement of communication in real time.' The audience was moved by the experience and rewarded the pupils by their obvious appreciation of the play. This was echoed by a woman who lived in the neighbourhood who wrote to say that it was one of the most touching she had witnessed.

The last three examples illustrate some of the values of working towards performances. They are a form of communication to others; and it is valuable for a group of people to work towards a common, tangible end, the success of which depends on everybody involved.

# Experiencing other people's drama

One of the values of acting-out in performances is the feeling of communicating something of mutual interest to others. As a member of an audience, you are being communicated to. This has its value as well. Through watching a performance the audience can experience other people's feelings and attitudes about aspects of human nature. Getting the most out of a performance requires powers of concentration, identification and the ability to comprehend differing levels of meaning portrayed during the performance. As members of an audience, pupils may become aware of the aesthetic quality of the play as a whole and, within it, the physical, verbal and spatial relationships of characters to each other as the meaning unfolds. It is a useful way of showing children the effectiveness of verbal and non-verbal language to express ideas. Live theatre has the advantage of direct interaction between the audience and performers. This means that performers respond to the mood of the audience and the audience are aware of the influence they have. Because of this and the vivid impact that live theatre can have, being present at a live performance gives a sense of occasion and urgency which can highlight the significance of the experience.

What children get out of performances depends on their receptivity at the time; their capacities to identify and understand; the quality of the meaning represented; whether it has been effectively expressed and communicated; whether they were expected to participate and what kinds of follow up, if any, there have been. Some teachers feel that a good theatre experience would be spoilt if discussed. Others wish to use the experience as a starting-point for reflecting on various issues raised by the performance.

Live theatre is not the only medium in which drama occurs. More people are exposed to drama every day through the mass media of television, radio and film. However, the same kinds of criteria can be used for judging all drama performances. They have to do with the quality of the meaning expressed, the adequacy of forms of representation and the overall quality of presentation.

Effective presentation can often have a powerful emotional and physical impact on the individual which can be remembered a long time after the event. The following examples of live presentations show the kinds of effects other people's performances can have on children. One shows the value of experiencing 'traditional theatre forms', and the others are examples of Theatre-in-Education teams with work specially geared to particular age-ranges.

*A visit to the theatre by sixteen-year-olds*
The impact that theatre can have is illustrated by a sixteen-year-old's reactions to a performance of *Macbeth*. This example shows how a theatre experience can stimulate and provoke thought long after the event.

This girl who went to an urban comprehensive in a working class catchment area had never been to the theatre before. She didn't want to go and used the excuse that she couldn't afford to pay for the ticket. She grudgingly went when money was provided. After commenting that the three witches were silly and 'talk rubbish', she settled down and became increasingly involved—sitting on the edge of her chair when Macbeth asked the witches to predict the future. When Macbeth ordered Banquo's death, she shouted 'No, don't' and started crying when the soldiers came for Macduff's wife and children. At the end of the play she remarked that she had hated Lady Macbeth because she 'would do anything to get what she wanted. I mean, like, kill a baby. That's too much.' When asked by the teacher whether she enjoyed the play and what she had got out of it, she replied, 'It's great. Can we go again? It really shows how horrible people were in them days.'
It is interesting that during her examinations five months later, she chose to discuss Lady Macbeth as a character, making the observation that 'Shakespeare showed that you really can't get away with doing wrong. Even if you get what you want, like Lady Macbeth, your guilt works inside you and you really suffer like Lady Macbeth went mad. At first I thought she deserved all she got but thinking more about it, I really felt sad for her.'

Theatre visits can be vivid and enriching experiences. In cases where plays are part of set texts a theatre visit may bring them to life and not only make them more exciting, but more memorable as well. Many children have no experience of theatre except through school. It is the school's responsibility to introduce children to an important form of cultural expression in which ideas about people and their situations are communicated through live performances. Not only can these be valuable experiences while they are happening, but they may also encourage children to use the theatre for their own future enjoyment.

Children do not always experience other people's drama through theatre visits. Most often, work is presented to them by teams who visit the school. When this happens it is not unusual for children to be invited to participate in some way. The following examples of Theatre-in-Education teams indicate some of the values of experiencing and participating in someone else's drama.

## Theatre-in-Education

### A Theatre-in-Education visit for ten-year-olds

An environment was set up in which the hall was blacked out. Three tunnels (through which children arrived) gave access to a space. Lying about the hall were large chunks of painted polystyrene. The play concerned an organization called the World Task Force. Three explorers from the force had gone to an unknown country and had failed to return. Children were called upon to help two officers of the force to get into the country, build bases and find the explorers, dead or alive. They were given a box with a tape-recorder, cassette, decorated arm bands, a torch and photographs of the missing men. Acting-out began with the officers preparing children for the mission—preparing codes of group discipline, signals, emergency drills, etc. The next stage was getting into the country by stealth and building bases (with the polystyrene). A beam of light came out of a huge painted eye, flashing on groups of children. A voice warned them to leave. Children dived behind barricades away from the flashing light. In the darkness, messages went from one group to another.

The major element in this section of the work was a 'dumb-show' in which the three lost explorers ('it's them—the ones on the cards') appeared and mimed a series of movements related to their arrival and capture in the country. Finally the Eye's voice rasped a warning to the rescuers that they too would become his slaves if they didn't get out while there still was time. To reinforce this threat, black cloaked and masked minions, armed with white poles, emerged and menaced the rescuers, hiding within their bases.

The rest of the section was taken up with rescuing the explorers. It was discovered that the Eye could not do anything when people were arranged in threes. The children, with the aid of the officers arranged themselves in threes and by communicating with each other through messages, managed to rescue the explorers. They escaped by dodging behind the barricades when the Eye was not on them. A scene took place where the men were restored and the officers thanked pupils and gave each one a signed statement concerning the contributions they had made.

In this experience, various media including props, physical objects, lighting and sound were effectively used to create an environment. Children were transported from their normal routines into a world of make-believe where they were presented with a problem they were expected to react to. Here the actors provided the symbolic situation and the main characters around which the drama revolved. Throughout the afternoon, children were absorbed. They were given the opportunity to react to a frightening situation within the safe boundaries of an 'as if' situation carefully supervised by adults. Conversation at the end revealed their excitement. The experience not only had immediate impact, it also provided stimulus for later work such as painting, poems, writing, discussing and doing project work on the excitement and difficulties encountered by explorers visiting strange places.

Most teams contact teachers in advance explaining their aims and intentions. Often hand-outs accompany the programme giving information about the subject:

*'A hook, a bob and a four-letter name.' (A junior programme)*
*The title.* A satirical and humorous comment on the methods of employment in the docks:

a hook—passed from father to son;

a bob—a shilling to tip the taking-on foreman in order to get work;

a four-letter name—if your name was longer, the foreman could not spell it and you would not be hired.

*The programme*
*Visit one* covers approximately 1874-1889. It begins with a classroom session involving three actor/teachers. As the actor/teachers will be characters living in the latter part of the nineteenth century, the moment they enter the classroom it would be useful if the children are engaged in some quiet activity, e.g. reading, and that the company are left to introduce themselves to the class. It would be helpful to the children's involvement in the programme that they are not told beforehand of our visits.

*Synopsis.* Two dockers are pushed into a room by the taking-on foreman, to wait with the other dockers (the children) for work. The year is 1874. The two dockers explain the method of employment, working and social conditions of the time. During the visit 'gangs of dockers' will be chosen to work in the West India Enclosed Dock (the hall). Through a series of incidents, the grievances of the dock-workers are explained, leading to the strike for the 'dockers' tanner' in 1889 and the formation of 'the union'. The action having been successful the class is left with a warning about future developments.

N.B. The hall and the classroom should be available through visits.

Included in the notes was a short history of Trade Unions; some useful addresses, a book list, quotations from documents of the period and a summary of the events of the 1899 London Dock Strike which was the focus for this project devised by the Greenwich Theatre Company.

The next example is a programme devised for sixteen-year-olds about the Craig and Bentley Trial. The play was based on the original programme devised by the Coventry Belgrade TIE team and used as a basis for a programme by the Cockpit Theatre in London. It consisted of a performance and a workshop which took half a day. Each session accommodated up to a hundred pupils in the theatre.

*'The Craig and Bentley trial.' (Sixteen-year-olds)*
An overall frame of an inquiry into the case was devised by the team to
give the pupils an opportunity to question issues involved and investigate
the apparent need of society to make examples and the consequences of
such actions. A handout was given which included a summary of the case.

In 1952, two young men engaged in petty theft on a rooftop were
interrupted by the police. In the subsequent battle, a policeman was
shot. The boy with the gun, Christopher Craig, was 16 and therefore
could not receive the death penalty. His companion, Derek Bentley,
was 19 and was eventually hanged for his participation, although he
had an IQ of 66 and a history of epilepsy and had given himself up to
the police without a struggle some time before the actual shooting took
place.

We examine Bentley's hanging in the context of its period. The
situation in 1952—the era of the spiv, the coshboy and the juvenile
delinquent—was not dissimilar to today when headlines of football
hooliganism, muggings and teenage violence scream at us almost every
day. Looking back on the event, it is easy to say that Bentley should
have been reprieved, if not found innocent. But at the time, the
population of England was all too ready to allow its judgement of the
facts to be distorted by what it wanted to hear, by the need to make an
example of somebody.

In addition a transcript of the trial was given including speeches from
the Prosecution and Defence, extracts of cross-examinations and the
Charge to the Jury by the Lord Chief Justice. There were also extracts
from some of the post-trial theorists and letters to the press. Several
provocative statements were included to prompt further discussion of the
issues raised. For example: 'Criminals will only be deterred from crime
and violence by seeing an example made. We must make that example now
before it is too late.' Finally, there was a bibliography showing the source
material used by the team. The team followed up the project by a
questionnaire sent to teachers whose schools had seen the programme.
Below is a selection of the teachers' own comments and some about the
reactions of their pupils.

*Teachers' comments:*
'The rigorous nature of this research accompanied by the strong
performances of individual actors/actresses really made this a powerful
piece.'
'Of great value for our integrated humanities course which focuses on
contemporary issues. Teachers in other subjects have commented to me on
how the project has borne fruit in other lessons on connected questions.'
'My only criticism is the discussion at the end. It is absolutely necessary, I
believe, to bring in the teachers to lead the discussion.'

*Pupils' reactions:*
'Very interested. Incensed by apparent injustice to Derek Bentley. Heated
discussion in the bus and much interest afterwards.'
'They liked the idea of bringing back the characters for discussion rather
than actors.'
'Mixed—some were really moved.

The last examples show some of the many ways that teams can

work in schools. What then are the kinds of experiences which teams or companies visiting schools can offer? They include a range from the presentation of traditional plays, often examination texts and the dramatization of works of literature, to the presentation of programmes devised for a particular age-group around certain themes. Some programmes encourage active participation, and teams deliberately plan their work so that the programme can be used as a basis for classroom work after the performance.

It is important that those inviting teams into schools should find out what respective teams have to offer. All teams have literature about themselves and their programmes which are readily available. If teams are catering for specific age-groups, both teachers and teams need to find out what content may be suitable. Lengthy research is often done for programmes with specific social or historical content. Many programmes have relevance across the curriculum and can be of considerable interest and use to teachers other than the drama specialist. It is the follow-up that will be different for different teachers.

Drama-in-Education teams consist of teachers who work closely with the children using drama techniques, but who may use the resources of theatre and performance as a stimulus for their work. In schools where there are existing drama teachers, teams often give support to teachers who are usually isolated, and may provide them with new ways of looking at their own work. More important, they are extremely useful in introducing drama into schools with no drama experience, and in many areas they work as advisory teachers in helping the development of drama in schools where teachers are unfamiliar with this way of working.

What other questions need to be asked concerning whether schools should invite teams to visit or not? First, there is the question of quality. Low standards of performance and poor choice of play, often inappropriate for the age-group concerned, can be more damaging to children's possible appreciation of theatre than never having had the experience. Then there is the question of content. Some teams feel strongly that their function is to challenge children's preconceived notions about reality so that they can gain new insights into a number of topics and issues. This has resulted in a particular viewpoint being expressed. The school needs to be aware of this and to be prepared to accommodate and build on the reactions and questions the visit will provoke in the children. Most teams are aware of problems such as these and work in such a way that children are encouraged to make up their own minds. Issues are often raised and discussed rather than forced upon children.

A visit by a team is an exciting and enjoyable event. Children can learn about a variety of topics in a vital and dramatic way. How the experience is used educationally depends on the original purpose of the programme and the way that the teacher develops the ideas in the classroom. One aspect of its value, however, should not be underestimated—that is the pure enjoyment and excitement which these visits can generate. Theatre-in-Education teams can provide a provocative starting-point for the resourceful teacher to build on. Although the teams are responsible for the quality of the work they provide, it is for the school itself to exploit its potential.

# Conclusions

This chapter discussed the kinds of learning that can be achieved through drama and what differences in practice might result from teachers emphasizing particular aspects of the process.

Teachers may emphasize *mastery of the process itself*. In this case the outcome of the activity will be more open-ended. More importance will be placed on the ability of children to use their own ideas. Responsibility is placed on children to take most of the decisions during exploration. In some cases children may wish to crystallize their thoughts and feelings into some kind of dramatic form. This involves learning to organize ideas into patterns which express the understanding they have gained through acting-out. In encouraging children to learn to use the process, the teacher will need to know what stage they are at: they may be at the stage of defining what they want to explore; attempting to construct symbols or symbol systems; trying to shape their ideas, or find better ways of expressing themselves.

If teachers wish to emphasize the *understanding* of a *theme, topic or issue,* they are more likely to take responsibility for introducing content and structuring the lesson so that understanding is deepened in a specific way. Considerable importance is placed on how children reflect on the experience. Discussion is often used as a means of finding out what children have understood as a result of acting-out.

*Presenting statements to others* can be an effective means of communication, either by sharing ideas with the class or by performing to a wider audience. Children may be encouraged to improve their physical and verbal skills as a more effective means of communication. Rehearsal is also a component in this type of work. Children can learn the value of persevering with an activity until it is complete. In working towards presentation, they also learn to co-operate and co-ordinate with other people to produce as effective an end-product as possible. They become aware of the impact their statements can have on audiences. Successful presentations can give children an enormous sense of achievement and build up personal confidence.

*Through experiencing other people's drama,* children can appreciate how others communicate feelings and ideas about people. They become involved in the process of identification, interpretation and appreciation of other people's use of symbols. They can also become aware of drama in a wider context, as an effective means of communication in their culture.

This chapter has claimed that certain kinds of learning can be achieved through acting-out. It should, however, be said that the quality of learning is directly related to the quality of the teaching. It is essential that when teachers make practical decisions about their work, they should keep in mind the kinds of learning they want to achieve. The decisions they make during sessions will radically affect the nature of the work and what children gain from the experience. It is therefore important to consider the kinds of practical decisions that teachers should take into account when planning and conducting drama sessions.

# Chapter 3
# The Drama Lesson

The nature of the drama experience revolves around the kinds of decisions that teachers make. It is hoped that by identifying patterns of decision-making in drama a basis can be given for making judgements about the way in which drama lessons unfold.

## Decision-making

In planning a lesson teachers often ask: 'What can I do with the class today?' They then try to answer this by searching for a general theme or a particular idea, and/or by thinking up a series of novel, exciting activities to stimulate and sustain the group's interest and ensure a level of enjoyment. In our opinion a more profitable approach is for the teacher to ask: 'What kind of learning do I wish to encourage through acting-out?' In order to make this central decision a series of preliminary questions have to be asked about (1) the needs of the class; (2) the resources of the teacher; and (3) the practical circumstances. The teacher's assessment of these variables will inform and determine future judgements.

1.  Before it is possible to decide on aims and intentions for the lesson, or sequence of lessons, the teacher must consider the general development of the class and their state of readiness for drama. The variables will include age, ability, group dynamics, individual and group strengths and weaknesses, attitudes to drama and the teacher, their experiences of drama and their understanding of the drama process.
2.  The teacher is the stimulus for the drama session and the catalyst for the group's achievement and commitment. Since he is part of the process and not separate from it, it is important that he sees himself as a teaching resource. He must consider what particular skills and interests he can offer, what he knows about his own strengths and how he can capitalize on these.
3.  In formulating his aims the teacher needs to take into account the institution he is working in and the freedoms and restrictions that result from being a part of that institution. In view of this, consideration must be given to the facilities for drama. In what kind of space will the drama take place? Does it have physical resources of its own (lights, rostra etc.)? Is it

sound-proofed? Does any other activity occur in this space?
Can equipment be left out? Are there likely to be many
interruptions? The teacher also needs to think about the
context of the lesson. How often does he meet the class? How
long is the session? How long have they altogether (a term, a
year)? Does he know what lesson the pupils are coming from
and where they will go afterwards? Are there future school
events that he must take into account when planning the
sequence of lessons—outings, examinations?

Having assessed these variables, the teacher is given a basis for
deciding on the kind of learning that is most appropriate at this
stage in the pupils' and his own development, as well as what is
practically possible. With his aim in mind the teacher's next
question will be: 'How can I achieve it? What strategies are
appropriate to the realization of my aim?' This question involves
decisions about the structure and choice of activities; social
organization; and the teacher's role and relationship to the class
and the acting-out. The extent to which these three areas are
planned and controlled by the teacher determines the overall drama
experience. Sometimes the teacher controls some or all of these
areas tightly and dominantly; on other occasions he allows the
pupils to do the same. In between these extremes there is space for
varying degrees of negotiation between pupils and teacher which
will affect their respective contributions to and participation in the
process. In other words, a teacher may totally direct the lesson and
channel the pupils' responses or he may expect them to make all the
decisions and take responsibility for the lesson. His decision to do
this will depend on what he wants to achieve.

The teacher who wants to encourage decision-making in his
pupils should not take this to mean that he can sit at the side of the
room and expect the class to get on with it. He still has to consider
his role in relation to them as a class and to any acting-out that
might occur. The children might find it difficult to make any
decisions for themselves. Therefore, the teacher has to find a role
that will enable them to make whatever decisions are important to
them. In some cases he may deliberately structure a provocative
atmosphere to spur them towards decision-making.

Depending on the kind of learning being encouraged, the teacher
will plan in advance to differing degrees. Similarly, the area in
which decisions are most crucial may vary from lesson to lesson.
For example, a teacher wishing to promote understanding of
something will probably be more concerned with how to structure
the activities and the role that he will adopt, in order to offer the
children the opportunity of new perceptions and insights, than with
decisions about social organization. Although these are relevant to
achieving his objective, in this particular case they might be less

important than in a lesson where the teacher is concerned about the group's ability to negotiate meaning. Here one of his chief planning concerns might be careful balancing of manoeuvring of individuals within selected groups or the whole class.

Although a teacher may have some notion of how he wants to manage his role during the lesson, he also has to remain flexible within it. He must be sufficiently adaptable to seize opportunities to advance the learning objective, either as they arise naturally or by intervening in an attempt to create such opportunities.

In order to make effective decisions about the structure, social organization, and role, the teacher needs to be aware of the factors which influence his choice and their possible implications. The rest of this chapter will consider these three areas in turn, and some of the determining factors for teachers to take into account.

# The structure and choice of activities

What needs to be decided? Will warm-up activities be included? What kind and for what reason? Is a stimulus for the acting-out necessary? How will it be introduced? Have the pupils appropriate information/skills/resources for the task/activity? If not, how will these be introduced and/or structured? When will one activity start and another end? Is a separate and distinct period of reflection important to the intention? Who will decide on the medium for reflection? Is the encouragement of a statement important to the intention? If so, will performance be an element? What is the most appropriate overall structure for facilitating these decisions?

## *Games and exercises*

Games and Exercises are often an essential part of the total work of the drama teacher. Games offer an immediate way of working together and can quickly release tensions in the group. Sometimes they provide a parallel and a natural introduction to the main acting-out. Children can be asked to make up their own games and rules, and teach them to others. In this way they recognize the need to agree the rules, and engage in the process of negotiating, structuring and organizing both ideas and themselves. Games are fun; they can enliven the learning of certain skills and reinforce the need for concentration and co-operation. Exercises may be necessary in a lesson because the class need to master a new skill. They may need some physical, mental or vocal limbering to help them adjust from the previous lesson. Or they may need to be reminded of the resources of their voice and body and thus the control of the media of drama; to develop a vocabulary of movement and voice skills which they may draw upon during acting-out.

Exercises and games can help the class to trust each other and be supportive. In this way the confidence to work in increasingly difficult situations is developed. An exercise concentrates on a single aspect. The participants respond to an instruction and follow directions. Games and exercises isolate important factors or qualities necessary for sustaining and developing acting-out of quality.

Generally, it is more usual for teachers to include games and exercises when they are getting to know a class or trying to establish a working relationship and readiness for drama, than when they are in the middle of a sequence of work. They are essentially prerequisites for acting-out to occur and should not be confused with the exploration and representation of meaning during acting-out. While games and exercises can be justified in terms of a teacher's long-term aims or as an introduction, they are not automatically an ingredient of every drama lesson. The decision to include them must depend on how appropriate they are to the teacher's intention, and the pupils' states of development.

## Stimulating and structuring the acting-out

Depending on the kind of learning the teacher wants developed he must decide whether or not to provide a stimulus or starting-point for the acting-out. The stimulus can be literally anything: one word, a picture, sounds, an object, a situation, a poem, a newspaper article. The teacher may decide to choose a general theme for exploration or focus on a more specific issue. He may or may not want to select some or all of the situations/structures, roles/characters for the acting-out. To illustrate this, suppose he chooses a stimulus such as the following:

**Teacher:** A tramp is asleep on the only bench in a railway station.

The teacher has given minimal information and no real focus. Apart from the strong symbol of the tramp, he has given no other information about characterization. Apart from the mention of the railway station as location there is no indication of the structure being crucial. The teacher is in effect providing an opportunity for the participants to decide how they wish to explore and develop this subject. If the teacher's objective is to encourage them to make decisions, then it is appropriate that the stimulus should be deliberately open-ended. However, if the teacher wants the group to develop it for a specific reason he needs to introduce and subsequently structure it differently:

**Teacher:** A tramp is asleep on the only bench in a railway station.
An old man and pregnant woman stand nearby. When asked to

move by a regular commuter, the tramp refuses.

Here the teacher has restricted the open possibilities of the previous example. The pupils have been given four characters, two of them, the tramp and the commuter, have been placed in a position of confrontation. The other man is old and the woman is pregnant. These factors are bound to influence the confrontation and make the tramp's refusal more significant than a lack of courtesy. The old man and pregnant woman have been described in passive role—someone else has been told to articulate their needs. This may influence the perceptions of their character. The structure that this teacher has imposed on the acting-out makes it more likely that the attitudes of the characters involved will be explored. Although this may not happen, since what occurs is unpredictable, by limiting the avenues of exploration the likelihood is increased.

While the possibility for any stimulus is endless, the way that it is introduced and structured is likely to affect the outcome. Below are just a few possibilities to illustrate this:

1. To encourage story-telling the teacher might focus more on the tramp. 'One day a tramp arrived in a small village. Where had he come from and why did he stay so long?'

2. To explore the pupils' own attitudes towards tramps, the teacher might adopt the role of the tramp himself in a class play. Or the group might be asked to examine a range of society's attitudes towards tramps through the symbolic roles of, for example, a businessman, a parson, a housewife, a magistrate etc., who are waiting for a train on the platform where the tramp sleeps. This second option allows the children to distance themselves from the issue while allowing them the opportunity of expressing themselves through the characters.

3. To discover their understanding of why people become tramps, the teacher might ask each person to develop the tramp's character, complete with life history, motivation and personality. He might then ask them to work in pairs, telling each other about their lives. Or he might ask one of the pair to be himself or another character and to question the tramp. In this way they might discover something about each other's concept of a tramp.

4. To use the symbol of the tramp as a way of highlighting people's fears about the unfamiliar, the teacher might read an article from a newspaper, focusing on a particular story. He might, through discussion, establish the pupils' general reactions and then proceed to set up seemingly unrelated situations of a more general nature to try and understand those fears. This might then lead to an exploration of the 'stranger' or 'outsider' theme, and an examination of their own prejudices.

But suppose the teacher decides not to introduce a stimulus. Suppose instead he asks the class to decide on the general field of exploration. In this case he might enter the lesson and ask the pupils what they would like to work on or make a play about. If they reply, 'tramps', the teacher then has to decide whether he wishes to impose a direction on their exploration of tramps, or whether he will wait for a potential learning area to arise.

The amount of time a teacher has with a class and the frequency of the sessions will affect his decisions, since this determines what can be realistically achieved. The more flexible day of a primary or middle school allows more opportunities for developing areas of interest thrown up by the children. In secondary schools where teachers often meet a class only once a week this is not as easy. Finding common interests or waiting for natural opportunities to arise, and so advance the learning through drama, can result in a loss of valuable time. The teacher with very limited time might structure the lesson to create such opportunities and to ensure that the children feel a sense of achievement, though this may be at the expense of other learning.

If teachers decide to wait and see what happens rather than plan in advance, they must use what arises and attempt to deepen the exploration. It is difficult to understand the teacher who claims that any interference by him corrupts children's natural learning. By refusing to take any specific role, other than the one the children demand of him, he limits the ways that he might be able to help them and does not make use of the particular skills that are available to the drama teacher.

As well as the choice of activities, the teacher needs to decide how long activities like warm-ups or initial discussion will last, and when successive activities will begin. There are no models for deciding this, nor should there be. However, it is important to appreciate time as a vital factor in realizing aims. Do the class spend so long warming up that there is not enough time for the acting-out? Does the acting-out never gain momentum because the teacher is constantly interrupting the activity?

Sometimes a teacher does not achieve his aims because he does not provide the pupils with the tools they require for the task. If a teacher gives pupils a poem and asks them to express their reaction to it, he is assuming certain abilities on their part. It is the drama teacher's responsibility to provide access to necessary information, skills and resources. The way in which these are introduced in a lesson is important since they can affect the pupils' attitudes towards them and whether or not they are utilized.

A teacher wanted his pupils to understand something of conditions in a coalmine in the nineteenth century as part of a wider theme they had been working on. When the class arrived for the lesson they were exuberant and keen to continue working on the previous week's work. As the teacher's aim for the class required that they know certain facts about conditions down a mine, he decided to read them an account of a miner's daily routine. Despite his choice of material being interesting as well as informative, the majority of the pupils were unable to listen. They were so eager to start work that they fidgeted and could not concentrate.

The class failed to make use of the information during their acting-out because when it was given they had not been ready to receive it. The teacher's task was to introduce this information without dampening their natural enthusiasm. He needed to find a way of capitalizing on their energy and drive.

As it happened the children provided this opportunity later in the lesson. Having bounded off they eagerly started work. But after twenty minutes they had reached a point where they required more factual information, in order to go deeper within the acting-out. It was at this point that the teacher's initial material was most useful; they approached him and began asking questions.

It is also important that the pupils know what is expected of them and that they have the necessary experience in drama to be able to respond to what the teacher sets up. At certain stages in their development the teacher may need to define what it is they need to make decisions about.

A teacher wanted his class to be responsible for the drama experience. So he decided to enter the studio in a symbolic role and let the drama develop out of the pupils' response to him.

As the class arrived, they were asked to sit in a semi-circle. The teacher then went to the back of the studio, adjusted the lighting so that it fell mainly on a chair facing the class, and put on a strange robe. He then walked to the front and sat on the chair facing them.

At this point he had assumed a symbolic role. His intentions were (a) to arrest their attention in this role; (b) to encourage them to project into complementary roles; and (c) to initiate the field and focus of the exploration. But the group did not know this. They sat and watched the teacher, waiting for him to reveal the reason for his unusual behaviour.

After a while the teacher looked sternly at them and asked them a series of questions:

'Why are you here?

What do you want from me?

What are you waiting for?

Some of you know what this is all about!'

Although the questions were designed to give these pupils the opportunity to suggest reasons for their meeting and develop it, they reacted to him as 'the teacher' behaving strangely. At first their only response was smiles and giggling. Then they began to negate his questions, telling him they did not want anything from him and suggesting he might as well leave. When he tried to pursue this they became more belligerent and determined that they would not join in and 'play the game'.

One or two individuals did attempt to join in and a few positive questions were asked about his role:

'Who are you?'
'What do you do?'
'Are you the Messiah?'

But because the teacher was determined that the class should supply all the information he refused to answer their questions. This tended to block the lines of inquiry of the few who might have committed themselves and instead alienated them as well.

Towards the end of the lesson, realizing that he had failed to achieve his intentions, the teacher called the class together and asked for their reactions to the session. During this the children tried to find out if the teacher had been 'serious' or 'just kidding'. They regarded the session as a puzzle which they were afterwards invited to unravel.

In this lesson the teacher began with the aim of letting the group take responsibility for the nature of the drama. He interpreted this to mean that he must not take any initiative which was not directly prompted and subsequently supported by the class. As it happened the group were not in a position to make these decisions. The way that the lesson was initiated and structured prevented them from being aware of the decisions with which they were faced. Equally they were never fully conscious that they were expected to make decisions. Furthermore, by the teacher being so non-committal, the pupils' participation in this case became limited to trying to fathom out what was in the teacher's mind.

If a teacher's intention is understanding of a particular theme, topic or issue, then the pupils must have sufficient information of the right kind or be provided with new ways of examining the information they already have. If pupils are studying Roundheads and Cavaliers in history, the drama teacher may decide to use their historical knowledge as a basis for exploring their understanding of the nature of civil war. Although their historical knowledge might be sufficient for the pupils to engage in initial exploration or to create a play about events in the civil war, the teacher needs to structure the information differently if they are to appreciate the issue of civil war in a new way.

To afford the pupils new perspectives, the teacher might decide to explore a basic family relationship. He might do this quickly by giving them each a role-card with information about themselves and their relationship with other members of the family. Or he might take more time allowing them to explore and develop the relationships for themselves. Using this as a basis he might then act as a catalyst to stimulate events which tested the strength of that relationship (for example, threats from outside, rivalry with another family). As a result of this preparation, at a later stage the pupils might be more ready to experience the full implications of brother fighting brother or son versus father inherent in a civil war. Furthermore, from the experience they might gain new insights, not just about Roundheads and Cavaliers, but of a more general kind about comparable contemporary issues. The teacher might want to introduce a moment of dilemma so that the decision—whether to fight for what you believe in and in effect be prepared to kill your family or whether to safeguard your family bonds and in so doing sacrifice a part of yourself—comes as a surprise. To give impact to this the teacher might decide to structure and direct the lesson very tightly, feeding in and revealing new information gradually rather than all at once, until the moment of dilemma. After this he might build in a period of reflection in order to assess their feelings about the experience or their ability to put it into words. This might be a whole group discussion or a personal expression of each individual's private reflections through another medium—painting or a poem. The teacher may stipulate the medium or allow the individual to choose.

In another lesson where children are using the symbolic process to create their own statements, a period of reflection (as distinct from the moment-to-moment reflection which is implicit in the process of creating) may not be as important to the kind of learning encouraged. However, towards the end of the lesson, if the class have reached a stage of anger or excitement in the acting-out, the teacher has to decide whether they can be realistically expected to concentrate on mathematical problems or mastering the French language if they leave the drama lesson in this mood. Not only has he a responsibility to the children but also to his colleagues.

After substantial experience in exploration through acting-out, the class, group or teacher may decide that it is valid to formulate ideas into a dramatic statement. The intention may be the refinement and clarification of those ideas. It might be communication to others. Whatever the reason, if the main concern is the communication of ideas, the teacher must consider whether the pupils appreciate the full range and potential of the media in making statements.

Finally, in terms of the overall lesson, the teacher must decide whether his intentions can best be achieved by a tight structure or a more flexible one; whether all or some activities will be planned in advance; and the extent to which he is prepared to negotiate with the pupils.

As well as these decisions the teacher also has to make decisions about the organization of social groups. This involves some understanding of how groups function and how meaning is negotiated in a situation which has its own dynamic and unique source of energy. What considerations are called for in organizing this interaction so that this source of energy can be creative and productive rather than destructive and inhibiting?

# Social organization

Since meaning is negotiated through social interaction it is
important to understand how and by whom this is done and the
factors which affect an individual's contributions.

The process of negotiation has been defined and discussed in
terms of 'real' and 'symbolic' roles (see pages 18-19). The following
examples are intended to illustrate how peer groups negotiate
meaning and how they move in and out of these roles.

### Soul for sale

At the start of the lesson the teacher defined the task: in small groups you
are going to have time to work out an improvisation for presentation to
the class. She then provided the focus: 'A stranger calls on people in a
familiar situation and has a powerful effect on them.'

The group of three girls: Mary, Mavis and Anna, all aged fifteen, sat
down together in a huddle and started searching for a central symbol
which embodied their individual reactions to the stimulus.

**Mavis:** Any ideas?

**Mary:** Confidence trickster.

**Mavis:** A devil comes to buy your soul off you.

**Anna:** Have you read 'Ghost Upstairs, Downstairs?' It's about . . . (she
explains).

**Mavis:** So what's the problem we have? It'll have to be something serious.

**Anna:** The Devil would want good souls?

**Mavis:** Not necessarily.

**Mary:** Let's throw lots of ideas in a pool then.

**Anna:** Someone's expecting a baby. No one knows whose it is. Then a
stranger arrives and says he'll provide money for its keep if they give it
to him at fifteen.

**Mavis:** We could have a pilot on a plane and a hijacker.

**Mary:** Or a crash . . . and the Devil says if you sell me your souls I'll
prevent the plane from crashing.

**Mavis:** Lots of soul-selling isn't there!

**Anna:** Shall we have that then?

**Others:** Yeah.

**Mary:** It'll have to be dark.

**Anna:** He can come from the back of the plane and say he knows what's
going to happen.

**Mavis:** We could then later show the effect on their lives.

**Anna:** Without souls they'll have no morals and people will think they are
mad!

**Mavis:** The third person could be a doctor who wouldn't believe it possible
to sell souls.

**Mary:** What is a soul anyway?

There was a momentary pause. No one attempted to answer this. Then
they continued talking and decided to start their acting-out in the
aeroplane itself. Before actively exploring their ideas in symbolic role they
agreed that there must be a reason why the plane was crashing. Engine
failure followed by fire was decided.

Three chairs were set up to represent the plane, and a metal frame which was lying on the drama studio floor was used as the steering and control panel in the cockpit. During the first acting-out, Mary and Anna were the co-pilots, Mavis the Devil. The following extract from their dialogue shows the difficulties they were having. It also illustrates an initial stage in the acting-out.

**Anna:** I don't know what to say.
**Mary:** (*suggested*) We're losing altitude. Velocity is increasing . . .
**Anna:** (*to Mary*) You can say all the technical bits, I'll just say 'Damn it!'
**Mavis:** What shall I say? What's that word . . . (*pause*) Missionary?
**Mavis:** No . . . emissary!
**Mary:** We don't want words they can't understand.
**Mavis:** Yeah, but we want it to sound old!

Very soon they were working half in role, half as themselves, making comments about each other's contributions.

**Anna** (*to Mary*): I think I could do with a cup of tea.
**Mavis** (*laughing*): You wouldn't say that!
**Anna:** Yes, you would.
**Mavis:** This is meant to be dramatic!
**Anna:** Yeah, but not yet.
Then later:
**Mary:** God! The engine's on fire!
**Anna:** You wouldn't say it like that!
**Mary:** Wouldn't I? How would I?
(*Anna demonstrated*)
**Mary:** You say it, you're better at it than me.

Eventually the girls abandoned this structure. Their representation was shallow and melodramatic and it embarrassed them. It was not allowing them to explore the ideas that they were really interested in—the effects of selling your soul. So they agreed not to represent this part of the story, but instead discussed what would happen to those who sold their souls. It was felt that if they related their experience to others no one would believe them and therefore they would be declared insane. This led them to the second structure for acting-out—a mental hospital.

The teacher intervened at this point and asked the girls to decide why the Devil had picked them. They sat apart, quietly thinking about this. When the teacher returned she initiated the acting-out by adopting a symbolic role herself, as head of the mental institution. She introduced Mavis (a new doctor) to the two psychiatric patients (Mary and Anna) and then left them.

The acting-out started again. Mavis interviewed the patients who related their individual versions of the meeting with the Devil and of the threatened plane crash. Anna and Mary were now beginning to develop their symbolic roles. Their language, behaviour and mannerisms were of people suffering from immense shock—they stared glassy-eyed; let sentences trail off before completion; wrung hands together; hung heads on to chests; stammered. Mavis, as doctor, first took the role of questioner then she confronted the patients with the news that she was really the Devil in disguise. She had come to collect their souls.

The dialogue that followed had a bizarre, rambling quality. The doctor taunted and teased the patients who became increasingly frustrated and

responded by threatening to kill her. She simply sat and smiled—a gesture
which conveyed her strength and their helplessness. Anna's and Mary's
conversation then digressed; an element of madness crept in. They talked
of going to the market square to buy another soul; discussed what kind of
soul they would buy—good or bad and how much it would cost.

To an outsider the conversation was surreal in character. The girls
earnestly discussed buying a soul as housewives might discuss the price of
eggs. They were very involved in the acting-out and sustained work in role
for many minutes before Mavis announced that she would have to kill
them in order to take their souls.

From this point on the group spent the time deciding how they would
represent the taking of souls. With the lesson nearing completion they
decided that the Devil's hands would be placed on the patients' heads and
that this would be the end. However, they were not happy with this and
explained to the class before presenting their work that this was an
unfinished statement that they wished to work on further.

This example illustrates how three girls arrived at a joint
statement as a result of their interaction. They had all had previous
experience of drama and this work was part of a CSE course which
they had opted for in the fourth year. The girls were friends and
used to working together. Their contributions to the negotiations
were roughly equal. They listened respectfully to each other and on
the whole accepted criticism of ideas. Disagreement was confined
to discussions on a symbolic level. Their 'real' social relationships
did not intrude, although it might have been a factor in their
embarrassment during the scene on the plane.

The example indicates the way in which the process of
negotiation can work in small groups. When the size of the group
increases, the way in which meaning is negotiated changes. It is
unlikely that this way of working would occur in groups of more
than five or six. A class of thirty involves people in different
methods. Below are two different examples of how meaning was
negotiated in a class of thirty. The first illustrates how children can
negotiate actively within the acting-out and get ideas accepted
without discussion.

The class of thirty twelve-year-olds were creating a play about a professor
who had a powerful wand that controlled and threatened the lives of
fellow villagers. The class were looking for a way of overpowering him but
could not overcome the wand itself, since it had been established that
anyone who touched it fell ill or died.

During the acting-out one of the villagers, Graham, rushed over to a
piece of newspaper tucked between two chairs and, holding it carefully,
approached the professor's wand. Wrapping the paper round the wand he
picked it up and carried it triumphantly back to the other villagers. There
was a momentary pause as everyone weighed up the effects of Graham's
action. Then several rushed forward, without discussion, and overpowered

the professor, thus reinforcing Graham's action and accepting his idea that the wand could only overpower you if you touched it with bare hands.

Graham rarely spoke or offered ideas during class discussion, although it was not unusual for him to initiate action in this way. He was obviously pleased with his contribution at the end of the lesson as were the rest of the class who could be heard congratulating him as they left the hall.

Not all proposals are so readily accepted though. A child initiating action in this way has to be prepared to accept that his idea may not be incorporated. While he is free to introduce an idea, others are free to ignore it; not necessarily verbally but by not reinforcing or building upon this action. The second example shows how canvassing for support before trying out an idea can increase the chances of its acceptance.

The class were involved in creating a play where several people at a football match were accused of possessing drugs. The acting-out at this point in the story became somewhat confused as police and supporters jostled with pressmen and guard-dog patrols. Two boys (a) whispered quietly together away from the crowd. Another two boys (b) were also whispering. Couple (a) then noticed couple (b) and approached them to involve them in their plan to advance the action of the play. But both couples were annoyed to find the other had ideas which conflicted with their own: (a) 'But I'm going to find it—he's going to arrest me.' (b) No, I'm going to find it when we take him to the police station.' They had to resolve this conflict before either of them could initiate further action.

In structuring a lesson the teacher might also consider whether there are moments within it when pupils can rest. Expecting pupils to be actively involved for the duration of a drama lesson is unrealistic. Everyone needs moments to rest, reflect and evaluate. A teacher should not suppose that a physically or verbally non-participating child is necessarily not involved. It is important that children learn to opt in and out within the process.

How do the dynamics at work within the group affect the amount and kind of contributions offered by individuals? Sometimes a teacher relinquishes control over a group to give them the chance of being collectively responsible for their own work, only to find that one person, or a handful, is directing the class even more tightly than he was. The process of negotiation necessarily involves an ability to listen, articulate ideas, make and take suggestions, give opinions, withstand rebuffs. Not all children find these abilities equally easy to acquire. Some learn to give ideas and opinions long before they learn to listen; others cannot cope with criticism and therefore prefer not to make suggestions. There are several general factors and many individual ones which can affect the amount and kind of contribution that an individual is happy to make.

## General factors affecting individual contributions

These can be divided into four broad categories: personality; context; the 'real' social network within the class and the individual's estimation of himself within it; and interest, confidence and ability within the drama activity.

### Personality

Not all children like drama—this obviously affects their contribution. Equally, some children are more naturally extrovert than others. Therefore some children are very actively involved and tend towards leadership roles while others prefer to stay on the perimeter, perhaps fantasizing privately. But both types are involved in the drama process. While drama cannot change personality types, the drama teacher can attempt to give everyone the opportunity to contribute without unnecessary fears of blocking or rejection. This might involve encouraging reticent children or curbing the overpowering enthusiasm of others. One of the dangers in drama is that it can simply reinforce the social behaviour of the peer group, thus denying some individuals the opportunity to contribute, and boosting the ego of those already dominant.

### Context

Context refers to both the general and specific environment that the individual is expected to relate to. In a general sense the physical environment can be an encouraging or inhibiting factor determining response. The drama space that doubles as a dining-room may have connotations for a child, affecting his attitude. The fear of his peers walking through the drama space when he is in a potentially vulnerable position, as far as the 'real' social network is concerned, may alienate an individual completely. In a more specific sense, 'context' refers to the group of people that an individual works with. The size of that group is of considerable importance to the individual's ability to contribute. While a child may find it easy to offer and receive ideas in a small group of three or four, that same child may not have sufficient confidence to speak out in front of thirty. Consequently, if his teacher always expects pupils to work together as a whole class, this child may never or rarely contribute. Conversely, a child may prefer the anonymity of a large group and feel that he is contributing to it, even though this may not be a verbal contribution. This child may feel exposed in a small group where a more overt contribution is expected of him.

In small groups more talking tends to take place and there is

more chance of everyone having a part. In groups under six, one or
two children often cast and direct the rest—'You be . . . I'll be . . .
Then you say . . .' etc. Often they have the loudest voices or they
have not learnt how to listen. Disagreements at the 'real' social
level are aired more frequently in small groups and these have to be
resolved before agreement is reached on the 'symbolic' level. In
larger groups these disagreements are no less real, but they seem to
be more frequently expressed through symbolic roles during the
acting-out. Large groups tend to favour those children who always
contribute and those who rarely or never do. In between these
extremes are those children who are eager to contribute but who are
perhaps inhibited by sheer size of numbers, or their small,
indistinct voices, or the apparent and for them frightening lack of
organization.

An important factor affecting an individual's participation is the
question of parts which is further affected by the size of the group.
All the children interviewed by the project team, whether naturally
inclined to be dominant or passive, mentioned the importance of
having a part. This did not mean that they all wanted the same size
parts. Some admitted that they liked a big part because, 'You get
your talk', 'You speak out for yourself'. Others were happy with
smaller parts: 'I don't like saying things in front of everybody'. But
what everyone demanded was a sense of significance:

**Jill:** I was a servant and I was bored.
**Interviewer:** What part would you have liked?
**Jill:** I just like a good part, you know. Anything's something anyway.
**Derek:** I like my part. I don't just like standing in a crowd. I like to do
something separately.

**Heather:** I'm not very good at doing drama so I just get left out and feel a
fool.
**Interviewer:** What do you mean when you say you aren't very good at
drama?
**Heather:** Well, I don't take an interest in it.
**Interviewer:** Have there been any drama lessons you've been interested in?
**Heather:** Well, last year I was interested in that one.
**Interviewer:** Why?
**Heather:** Well, everybody had a part. Everybody had to do something
then.
**Interviewer:** If I'd asked you last year, would you then have said 'I'm no
good at drama'?
**Heather:** I don't think so.

As far as the choice, size and significance of parts is concerned,
small-group work offers more children a chance to carve
themselves out a part that suits them. In fact because there are
sometimes not enough people in the group, some of them play
several small parts. Whole-class work offers some children the

opportunity of demanding parts that stretch them, but often leaves many children as part of the crowd or as an audience. After weeks of rehearsing for the performance to parents of a scripted play, one girl wrote:

At rehearsals I didn't see why I was needed and wasn't going to bother going on the night. After all I had nothing to say (I would have liked to have had) so what was the point. But I felt it was my duty so I played my minor part as well as I could.

And a boy echoed this:

I felt I was part of it, but not a big part because they could easily just miss me out unnoticed.

There are two aspects involved in having a part. First, that the child personally feels he is important in some way to the acting-out. Secondly, that he also sees the symbolic significance of the part he has been given. If he cannot see why his character is present he is less likely to contribute in role—for example, being a guard or servant may prevent him from contributing because a guard or servant would not speak in front of his superiors.

Different size groups offer experiences in different methods of negotiating. Although some children prefer small groups or pair work, others prefer whole-class activities. A teacher can only please them all and give each one the best personal opportunity for making or accepting a contribution by continually varying the size of group.

## The 'real' social network

The process of negotiation never operates entirely on the symbolic level. However high the level of involvement there is still the existence of the 'real' social network in which everyone juggles for status and recognition. Sometimes the real tensions are so urgent that they prevent the symbolic level from functioning; at other times they are its motivation.

A group of nine boys were exploring the potential of the newly delivered rostra blocks. They decided to build a fortress and 'have raids'. So they quickly and amicably assembled the fort, discussing as they went where the 'barricades', 'tunnels' and 'living quarters' would be. When it was assembled they chose two sides, agreed on the rules of the game—'No rough stuff' . . . 'If you're killed count up to ten, then you can come alive again'—and started. During this initial acting-out they took delight in dying dramatically from the ramparts and in using their voices to create explosions and gun sounds.

The teacher intervened to try and deepen the work by asking them to think about the reasons they were fighting and why there were two sides. The boys considered this and were in the process of elaborating their work when three latecomers arrived in the lesson.

The latecomers were truants from school who had been detected and brought back. They came in silently and sullenly and sat down. At first nothing was said to break the uneasy silence. The nine boys continued their acting-out, ignoring the truants who sat watching. Then the accusations started in an attempt to discover who 'split'. Very quickly the friendly co-operative atmosphere at the beginning of the lesson was destroyed and the nine boys started arguing among themselves—'Oh shut up! Just 'cause I built a better camp than you'; 'You can't tell me anything!'

The three truants started calling individuals over and asking them directly, 'Who split?' The boys quietened down. Activity on the boxes ceased. Bob, the most popular and respected member of the group and a natural leader figure, decided to take the initiative. 'Come on. Let's get on with it.' At first he was ignored. So he went over to where the truants were sitting and suggested they join in. 'Go on. It'll be more fun.' The truants did join in and the acting-out started again. This time the group outside the fort planned their strategies before approaching. Then the attack started. But it was no longer just a symbolic attack, half of them were really fighting to settle their real differences.

This example also reveals how status within the group can affect how others listen to or value an idea. During the earlier part of the activities, before the truants arrived, the boys were discussing how they would modify the fort they had built.

**Mark:** What we ought to have is a tunnel leading to a camp.
**Roger:** Let's make a maze.

During the discussion Roger repeated this three times. Eventually Bob, who had been listening to all the ideas, said: 'Let's make it a tunnel that is like a maze.' The idea was agreed on almost immediately when Bob suggested it. No one seemed to hear Roger or Mark.

Sometimes the real group relationships act as the motivation for the symbolic roles during acting-out. The following illustrates how real social relationships were explored through acting-out.

A class of thirteen-year-olds had been working on the theme of coalmining in the nineteenth century in social studies as well as drama. In the previous lesson they had explored life in a mining community in small groups of their own choosing. This lesson the teacher wanted to focus attention on the conditions down a mine. He was intending to structure the activity and feed in factual information, and give them the experience of working in narrow passages and shafts.

However, the class arrived unexpectedly at the beginning of break and excitedly announced that they wanted to continue with the previous week's work. During break they eagerly constructed their sets and asked if they could use the studio lighting. They started work straight away as if there was not a minute to lose.

One group consisted of six boys and six girls. They divided themselves into six couples (as decided the previous week) and began acting-out. Each couple was involved in a domestic scene at breakfast. There was little attempt at characterization since they were chiefly concerned with the typical stereotyped husband/wife roles and, of course, their real relationships. The climax for each couple was the man's departure for work, as this involved kissing the wife goodbye.

Yet, although this was the real motivator, it did not prevent the group from exploring other areas, such as working in the mine and the women's life at home, which they did with as much involvement. Towards the end of the lesson they sat down together and discussed the work, which showed that they were equally concerned to pay attention to details of the period, as well as role-play couples.

**Pupil 1:** There's too many families.
**Pupil 2:** Let's make it better.
**Pupil 3:** The kids used to work.
**Pupil 1:** Yeah, you be our kids.
**Pupil 3:** I don't want to be a child.
**Pupil 4:** Neither do I.

One of the most important developments for this group was working in a mixed group. This was the first time that they had elected to do so. Although there was concern about realism this did not override their concern to play adult roles. No one was prepared to play a child and said so indignantly. This would have been in direct conflict with the real relationship demands.

Group pressure affects the negotiations so that composition is a factor to be considered. If children are always given the chance to choose who to work with they tend to work with their friends. This can be inhibiting as symbolic roles may conflict with real roles. This may prevent a child from being taken seriously or force him to agree with something because the others do. These kinds of pressure are more apparent when children frequently work in the same small group. On the other hand, small friendship groups allow confidence to develop and provide many children with the opportunity of acquiring skills of negotiation before tackling more challenging group situations.

When asked whether they preferred working with friends, children were divided. Many said that they wished teachers would mix them up more often. This would help them to 'get to know how other people's minds work' and teach them to work with other people; 'When you work with your mates they prevent you from taking it seriously.' Although these children said they wanted to work in a variety of groups they were not able to say this in front of their friends. Many others felt that it would be 'no fun' without friends.

**Mike:** You'd be sitting there like a stuffed dummy. Well like, there is this kid called Norman. Sometimes he don't get in any group and he just goes over and sits on the boxes all lesson, doesn't do nothing.

Mike's fear of not being wanted by the group highlights the

problem of the isolate which is more marked in small-group work. When Mike was asked why *he* did not invite Norman to join his group, he replied, 'Yeah, but the others chuck him out', indicating the pressure on Mike to conform.

The following conversation between five fifteen-year-olds illustrates the barrier of assumptions erected by the peer group before the drama starts. These have to be dispelled before some individuals are given a fair chance.

**Sharon:** In drama you adjust yourself to the people you're working with.

**Peter:** We're all good friends anyway.

**Sharon:** We've got an open opinion to people. I feel I can give them a chance . . .

**Meg:** Yeah! As soon as someone walks in a room you don't say — 'Ugh, don't like her'. You try and make friends. Fair enough if they don't want anything to do with you.

**Sharon:** Yeah, you try.

**Interviewer:** What about some of the quieter people in the drama group?

**Peter:** I don't think drama is for these types of people. If they're not going to join in I don't think that's right.

**Sharon:** It spoils it for other people.

**Peter:** At the beginning we felt we had no right to leave them out of it, but you can't urge them on if they don't want to.

**Meg:** Yeah, but if they're shy. Because I'm shy.

**Andy:** Yeah, you're shy, but you'll do the work won't you?

**Meg:** I wouldn't have done though. It's only because everyone kept saying: 'Oh come on'. If they hadn't have done I wouldn't have been able to do it.

**Sharon:** Yeah, but we know you . . . and we know that with a bit of goading on . . .

**Meg:** Well then, we should have tried to get to know those others who couldn't do it. I mean Alan hasn't been there that long and he won't do much really.

**Sharon:** Because he's embarrassed.

**Meg:** I know, well you've got to help him not to get embarrassed.

**Peter:** I don't see him to be the type who does drama really!

**Meg:** Well, looking at you, if I didn't really know you all that well I wouldn't think you'd be the type to do drama!

## Interest, confidence and ability

These factors are related and influence a child's perception of himself within the drama activity, the contribution that he is able to make and his ability to take risks. Although many children said they liked drama they often qualified this, like Richard: 'It depends on the project you are doing. Sometimes you get 'orrible dreary things like the last one about broken homes and drop-outs and things. Not much fun! It was too sad you know—people committing suicide and that.'

Teachers should consider the impact of content on children. If the kind of learning being encouraged can be achieved irrespective of the field of exploration, then it is worth letting children choose what interests them. This might avoid embarrassment or boredom sometimes caused by the teacher's choice of content. When an eleven-year-old boy, John, was asked in an interview if there was anything that he wanted to say, he replied:

I think the drama teachers around the country should remember that the children are doing it and not just them. I mean—well—I'm not criticizing our teacher but some of the teachers I've known, they give you a subject and you've got to do that. He says 'build on that'. I think you've got to remember it's the children who've got to do it and if they're going to like it they may as well have a good subject.

Ability in drama is linked with experience in drama. It is to do with the ability to imagine, assume symbolic roles convincingly, speak clearly and fluently, respond quickly. Yet equally important to the child's perception of himself and his participation is the ability to develop ideas and confidence to articulate them. This is often the most difficult area, since it involves taking personal risks. It partly explains why during whole-class discussion in particular, a few tend to offer most of the ideas.

**Interviewer:** Why do some people find it difficult to speak in front of the class?
**Gwen:** They're frightened.
**Interviewer:** What of?
**Gwen:** The results. What other people are going to say about what they said. For example, someone might give an idea but nobody else might like it and they give comments. And you just feel as though you have given an idea. I've put some thought into the lesson. I'll not just bother.

Having the confidence and resilience to continue offering ideas when they are rejected is difficult to cope with.

**Interviewer:** How do you feel when people moan at your ideas?
**Jill:** A bit put down.
**Interviewer:** Is it the same in all lessons when you give an idea?
**Jill:** It's more so in drama.
**Ann:** People are not so concerned in other lessons because if you give a wrong answer the teacher's just going to tell you it's wrong. But in drama the teacher says nothing's wrong, it's just an idea.

In some schools children are rarely asked for their ideas or opinions. They grow up believing that 'teacher knows best'. When doing drama in schools like this the first step for the drama teacher is getting the children to realize that they have got something to say. The second step is helping them to distance themselves from their ideas so that rejection of an idea is not interpreted as rejection of self. Not all children in a class have John's attitude or confidence.

Everyone wants to have their idea and nobody else's. I'll be perfectly honest, I like to show off and I shout sometimes. It's just like a sort of urge inside you—everyone not saying anything and you saying something and everyone saying, 'Oh that was good John'. I like that sort of thing . . . But when you make a bad idea everyone turns to you and says, 'Oh, why did you do that?' Well, you've just got one answer, you say, 'Well, it's an idea isn't it?'

In small-group work there are not so many people to comment on ideas but it can still be a struggle getting others to listen. At worst: 'There is such a racket when you're trying to talk, you can hardly hear each other. You're bellowing at each other and someone's going on about one idea when you're going on about another idea and it gets a bit out of hand.' Many children need guidance and a structure before they are able to make progress in their negotiations and regard it more highly than a free-for-all. So that as Paul says: 'You're talking to other people and trying to get them to understand the plot or whatever you are doing in the play. So you've got to get them to communicate and not just say: "Right, I want this idea and this idea and that".'

Sometimes in small-group work one person is regarded as the leader and looked to for providing the ideas and direction. While many might envy this role, Andrea felt differently.

**Andrea:** Normally in a group I say 'Yeah' and that goes. It's like Penny, whatever she says goes.
**Interviewer:** Does that annoy you?
**Andrea:** Yeah, because then nobody else is doing anything. You see they're not doing *their* work, they're doing whatever I say, even if they don't agree they do it.

This last section about organizing social interaction has ranged from descriptions of how the negotiation process works to the factors affecting individual contributions within it. To summarize, the main recommendations are that teachers attempt to discover how groups of different size and composition negotiate; those individuals who contribute easily and confidently and those who need appropriate help in skills and experience; what the hidden tensions are within the peer group and how they might help or hinder the negotiations. Above all, teachers should appreciate the value of working in a variety of different contexts.

So far aims and intentions, lesson structure and social organization have been discussed in terms of decision-making. For discussion's sake they have been divorced from the role of the teacher during the lesson. This separation is of course an artificial one. The teacher relates to and affects all these areas through his choice and management of role.

# The role of the teacher

Once a lesson is under way a teacher makes spontaneous decisions according to its progress and in so doing assumes many roles. One moment he is a guide, or helper; the next he is devil's advocate. The ability to be flexible about his role is essential since this is the way that the teacher deepens the learning experience, teaches new skills, improves the quality of the work and offers constructive criticism. Since the teacher is a part of the symbolic process, he must use his knowledge of it to assume a variety of appropriate roles. This means he must be prepared to take risks.

Basically the teacher has the choice of assuming one of many teacher roles or one of many symbolic roles. Both role types afford endless possibilities but depend on what he is confident to handle in the given situation, and what is appropriate to the children's acting-out.

Confidence in role is partly determined by personal experience and partly by knowledge of the class and their ability to cope with a limited or infinite number of roles. For some children, at a particular stage in the pupil/teacher relationship, the teacher will always represent authority irrespective of the role he adopts within the acting-out. Pupils' expectations will influence their response so that trends in pupil/teacher relationships within the general school ethos will also determine this.

An appropriate role is one which attempts to satisfy both the teacher's aims and the unfolding symbolic interaction. Returning to our example of the tramp:

The teacher wants the children to understand something of the realities of being a tramp. So far they have only been working with a romantic notion of the freedom to travel without working. The class are enjoying themselves and happily creating a play about the tramp's freedom. They are working well together and there are no major conflicts within the group.

The teacher could let them continue. In one sense the lesson is going well and the children will probably leave with a sense of achievement. But the teacher's intention is to challenge their romantic notions in order that their view of freedom will also include the freedom to starve. So in this example the teacher has to find a way of intervening and presenting a different attitude for them to consider.

The following are just a few of his alternatives:

1.  He might stop the acting-out, call the children together for a discussion and directly challenge their personal assumptions. He can do this either in teacher or symbolic role.
2.  He might enter the acting-out in one or several symbolic roles and actively force the children to consider new elements—for example, as a policeman moving the tramp on, as a hostel

warden telling him there are no more beds for the night, as a
fellow tramp with a tale of woe.
3.  He might set up a new focus, seemingly removed from the
    tramp, and test their willingness to give up material possessions
    and comforts, before returning them to their original work.
4.  He might introduce the script of, or extracts from, *The
    Caretaker* by Harold Pinter and so force them to consider a
    view of Davies, the tramp, as a parasite, impinging on
    another's freedom.

If, however, the class are involved in presenting their ideas of
freedom, using the symbol of a tramp, to each other or an outside
audience and the teacher's intention is an improvement in
communication skills or the use of the media, then he will intervene
differently. Suppose:
1.  The children are not using their potential physical resources
    and are relying too heavily on verbal communication. He might
    stop the activity and temporarily impose a constraint on the
    work—making them continue working in silence. Once the
    pupils are conscious of the power of body gestures and
    movements, he might return them to their original acting-out.
2.  He is concerned about the superficiality of their representation
    of a tramp. He might enter as a tramp and accuse the
    pupil/tramp of being an impostor, following this with a series
    of questions designed to make him think more broadly or
    deeply about his characterization.
3.  The children are not aware of the heightening effect of spatial
    relationships. The teacher might divide the class into small
    groups and ask them to build several statues to depict given
    themes, such as war, friendship, poverty. The teacher might
    then ask all or some groups to demonstrate their statues in
    turn, and guide the perception of those viewing to a
    consideration of spatial relationships.
4.  The language used in the acting-out lacks clarity and precision.
    It rambles or takes short cuts, preventing direct comm-
    unication. The teacher might introduce an exercise to try to
    make the children aware of the importance of clarity. He might
    ask for a volunteer to teach the rest of the class something
    apparently simple — such as walking, or clapping hands — the
    rest of the class being told that they must follow every in-
    struction absolutely to the word. Since this is very difficult to
    do, the point of the exercise is to draw attention to the need for
    precision and clarity of expression.

If the teacher wants an improvement in the class's ability to
interact socially, his reasons for and methods of intervention will
be different again. His concern in this case will be how and by
whom ideas are negotiated. Consequently the teacher might accept

that the content of the work and the children's understanding of the underlying issues is superficial. Also he might be aware that their ideas would not be communicable to an audience. But as he wishes to improve the social interaction of the group, his intervention will be specifically related to this.

1. He might intervene when asked for help or when conflicts arise.
2. He might suggest a number of different ways that the children can listen to each other's ideas and organize themselves, or set them this as a problem to solve.
3. He might use his vantage point at the side of the room to assess individual contributions and general group dynamics and plan the next lesson in the light of his observations.
4. He might stop the acting-out and suggest some people change parts, or set up a hierarchical activity with some of the passive members in dominant roles.

So a teacher may intervene at any point in a lesson or not at all—that is the theoretical scope of his choice. So far, many of the examples discussed in this section have been hypothetical, to suggest some of the reasons for, and methods of, intervention, given specific intentions. Although a teacher's role is always the result of the unique interaction between him and his class, it is possible to generalize about reasons for intervening: to inspire, stimulate, initiate; to inform, instruct, teach; to encourage, suggest; to question, challenge; to focus, generalize, clarify; to discuss, reflect, evaluate; to modify, prevent, stop. Stopping the activity may be as positive as stimulating can be negative in a given situation. Although it is possible to say *why* a teacher should intervene it is impossible to say when and how. What follows are three brief examples of how individual teachers responded in their unique situation. It is hoped that the examples will show when, why and how these teachers intervened and the results of their intervention.

*The fashion show*
During this lesson the teacher only intervened once in the pupils' negotiations. What effect did this have on their acting-out?

The teacher's only stated intention in this thirty-five-minute lesson was to allow the pupils 'the opportunity of exploring the potential of the newly arrived rostra blocks'. She had not decided on a focus for their exploration but had instead decided to wait and see what happened. She had decided, however, to allow only ten minutes for this activity and told the class of twelve- to thirteen-year-olds this at the start of the lesson.

Two groups formed: boys and girls. The group of eight girls made a simple rectangular stage out of their rostra blocks. Then some of them twirled and danced around on it excitedly. Someone shouted, 'A beauty competition', and the dancing and twirling changed to parading and posing. After a moment it was decided that the stage was the wrong shape. To parade effectively it needed to be linear, so they changed it to an 'L' shape, which gave rise to the idea of 'A fashion show'. This suggestion was agreed by everyone and they drew closer together to decide on roles. There were four models, a commentator and three audience members. Everyone seemed happy with their part and the first acting-out began.

During this the commentator did almost all the talking. She described the models' clothes and the asking prices. The models paraded up and down self-consciously and giggled often. Any comments by them were in 'real' role to cover embarrassment. The audience sat watching passively. When each model had paraded once the show ended. The girls suggested doing it again.

At this point the teacher, who had been watching the activity of both groups from the side of the room, approached the girls and intervened. She called them together and, after hearing from them what they were exploring, asked them if they knew what went on backstage at a fashion show? They talked about this. She also asked the models if they had dressers and hairstylists. Before leaving the group the teacher informed them that the most important people at a fashion show were the buyers.

Lots of ideas and suggestions followed about how to develop their initial idea. It was decided that they would explore the atmosphere and relationships backstage, and follow this with the show itself. The models said they needed dressers and hairstylists and asked the 'audience' if they would play two parts. The commentator suggested that these three girls should also be the buyers at the fashion show.

The acting-out started again. Backstage the models were getting ready. They mimed putting make-up on, and began to develop characterization. There was a sense of urgency and tension in their preparations and evidence of some rivalry and jealousy between them. They also gave instructions to the dressers/hairstylists who responded accordingly. The commentator did not contribute much to this scene, except to hurry the girls up and announce that the show was ready to start.

The commentary was more detailed and imaginative the second time. The buyers were involved by being asked if they would like to feel the cloth or ask any questions about the clothes. The buyers responded by asking questions and chatting among themselves about the merits of each outfit. The models walked more sedately and seriously and in some cases extended their range of movements. The backstage rivalry continued as three models indicated their dislike for the fourth. At the end of the show the buyers discussed with the commentator which clothes they would buy. They developed the 'rivalry' further by choosing the clothes of the unpopular model and the commentator compounded this by rewarding her with a holiday.

The acting-out came to a natural halt. All the girls were pleased with what had occurred. The teacher asked them if they wanted the boys' group to see what they had done. They did not; but asked if they could repeat the whole thing once more for themselves. The teacher agreed.

In this example the teacher decided 'to wait and see' what would happen. She had also decided to curtail the activity after ten minutes if there was no obvious development. In the event the children were given the full thirty-five minutes.

When the teacher intervened in the pupils' acting-out they had already agreed on what to explore—the fashion show. But there was no real focus. The reasons for her intervention were that she wanted to suggest a focus for the acting-out, and to involve the three quiet girls who were passive members of the audience. In these respects her intervention had positive effects. The girls' work shifted from the external features of a fashion show to the relationship of the people involved, and the quiet girls were more actively involved as dressers/buyers and given the opportunity to contribute. This might not have happened if they had remained audience members because their symbolic role did not easily allow active participation; their real roles and status within the peer group were passive and as individuals they were generally lacking in confidence. By focusing on the relationships between models, dressers, buyers and the commentator, the girls were able to develop their symbolic roles. This allowed them to participate less self-consciously, their confidence developing through the symbolic roles. The real social network was momentarily suspended.

The commentator controlled the work through her role—announcing that the show was ready, telling the models their parade order, inviting the buyers to ask questions, and finally rewarding the successful model with a holiday. At first the buyers were in a subservient role as hairstylists/dressers, running around at the models' request. Later, they became the most important people, not only in symbolic role as buyers deciding the outcome of the show, but also because they were in a position to observe the models' behaviour and rivalry backstage and later make comment on it by commending the least popular model. The models used their symbolic roles to explore their real desire to parade and 'show off', originally sparked off by the building of a stage.

### The mad professor
This was the beginning of a new school year in a middle school and only the second time that these children, aged eleven to twelve, had worked together as a class in drama. They had all had two previous years' drama experience with this teacher, but in different teaching groups. The teacher's aim was to see how well this class could work together and discover something of its group dynamics. His specific intention was to see if they could respond to an open stimulus.

In the first lesson he had entered with three objects: a crown, a cloak and a wooden stick and placed them on the floor. He hoped to be able to stand aside during the lesson and intervene infrequently. But he had decided that if this did not work, he would structure the lesson and explore the objects as symbols of power.

In the first lesson the class had responded to the stimuli and they began to create a storyline. Therefore this second lesson was a continuation of the previous week's work.

What were the teacher's possible reasons for intervening? How did his intervention affect the acting out?

At the start of the hour's lesson lots of ideas were tried out in action by groups or individuals but the story lurched from one suggestion to another with no central focus. For example, a girl picked up the stick and announced that it had Italian writing on it. Some others showed interest in this and discussed it, but most ignored it. Later four boys brought chairs and placed them round the objects, announcing to everyone that they were sent to guard them. All reacted favourably to this focus which led to the boys' attention being diverted, while the objects were stolen. A search followed until interest waned.

The teacher called the class together for a discussion. He wanted to know how they felt about what had happened so far. There were lots of answers—most of them expressing some frustration or disappointment. They were all concerned that a storyline was not emerging and tried to suggest why this was—'People weren't listening'; 'We need to agree things about the objects now'. The teacher extended this and suggested that he pick a volunteer, whose responsibility it would be to give the class sufficient information about one or all of the objects as a stimulus for continuing the story. When this volunteer entered the acting-out, whatever he told them they were to accept. The class unanimously agreed to this suggestion.

The acting-out started again. Individuals and groups went back to being villagers and engaged in mimed activity and conversation in symbolic roles. The volunteer entered the village carrying the stick. He said he had found it in the woods and that it had blood on it. The villagers crowded round to look and ask him questions about it.

Four boys stood slightly apart from the rest, whispering. Then one fell down. The others lifted him up and carried him towards the village. As individuals saw this they followed until all interest was on the injured boy. They began questioning him. From the questions it was established that the boy had touched the stick. Also, that whoever touched it would be overpowered and fall ill, perhaps fatally. This caused great excitement and consternation.

Everyone was involved in this new focus except for one boy, Danny. He picked up the stick and walked away with it. Noticing this the others warned him of the harm he would come to, but he ignored them and taunted them by playing with it irreverently. A group of boys became particularly angry with Danny and tried physically to take the stick away from him. Danny ran away from them, refusing to acknowledge that the stick had any power over him.

The teacher approached Danny and quietly asked him if he had some special power over the stick that the others did not know about. Almost immediately Danny asserted himself and announced to the surprised villagers that he had power over the stick. There was a few seconds stunned silence.

The teacher stopped the work and called the class together. He told them what he thought they had established and asked for opinions and suggestions for building from there. All approved what had happened and there were several ideas for developing it but the most frequently suggested were linked with 'wizardry' or 'mad professors'. Danny offered to be the mad professor. The others agreed. At the teacher's suggestion the class went back to the acting-out and consolidated what they had agreed so far before the end of the lesson.

This teacher intervened several times. Once the lesson was under way his first intervention was to halt the acting-out and impose a period of reflection. The children were not progressing and their enthusiasm was waning. He chose discussion and asked for their comments and opinions of the work. In this way he discovered the conflicting interests and frustrations. Many of the children felt they were floundering because of a lack of focus or direction so the teacher took this opportunity and offered them a way of organizing themselves. This had largely been their problem. While there had been no lack of ideas, they had not established a way of agreeing on them. In suggesting that they pick a volunteer who would tell them something about the object/s, the teacher gave them a structure. This still allowed the children to decide the reason and focus for the acting-out. In this way the teacher was also reinforcing the lesson that during improvised acting-out, it is necessary to a large extent to accept rather than negate ideas during exploration, modifying them later if necessary.

The second time the teacher intervened it was a spontaneous decision made in the light of one boy's actions. By quietly asking Danny if he had some special power over the stick, the teacher turned a potentially disruptive action into a positive one. In this case the teacher had the choice of intervening in the above manner or of stopping the activity and reprimanding the boy. His knowledge of Danny—a boy who wanted attention but who had little status within the peer group—might have influenced his choice. Certainly giving Danny the opportunity to make a significant contribution meant that he became totally committed to the work and, it appeared, went up in the class's estimation as a result.

His intervention also had an effect on the acting-out though, since the suggestion was accepted by the class and incorporated into the story. The teacher called the class together after Danny had announced his special power over the stick. This gave the class a chance to evaluate the action and reject it if necessary, ensuring that they did not accept the idea just because it had been endorsed by the teacher. His final decision to suggest they consolidate their work to date meant that the children left the lesson with a clearer memory of the established events for future development.

### Arrival of the Aliens

This was a sequence of lessons that developed from an initial stimulus by the teacher. He had asked the class of twelve-year-olds to consider the effects on natural order if the sun's properties were to change. This led to a discussion about stars and galaxies and later a movement sequence representing first, the natural order and secondly, the disruptive effects caused by a meteorite.

In subsequent lessons the class explored the idea in a variety of ways: in pairs as astronomers noting the disruption and discussing it; as groups of individuals whose lives were affected by the change in the sun's properties; as individuals fleeing from the cities to take refuge in the countryside, and living in caves and banding together for security.

A disagreement between eight girls and the rest of the group about the future direction of the class play influenced the teacher's decisions about and intentions for the next lesson. The teacher's intention was two-fold: to modify the behaviour of, yet accommodate, certain individuals in order that work as a whole class continue; and to enable the class to pursue the story they had created. While the teacher was prepared to negotiate with the eight girls, he was not prepared to allow Tina, a dominant and forceful member of the eight, necessarily to have her own way. 'Tina is a difficult girl—she always wants power. I don't know what to do about it. I used to think that if I gave such kids a big part they would get over their bossiness. But with Tina it falls to bits if she takes over as leader.'

The teacher intervenes on several occasions during the lesson, for a number of different reasons. What is the effect of his choice of role and methods of intervention on the acting-out?

All those who were happy with their parts were asked by the teacher to remind themselves of what they had established by repeating it. Meanwhile he talked to the eight girls who told him they had decided to be an alien race of superior intelligence from a planet outside the galaxy. They had come to Earth to recruit an army for their inter-galactic war. In return they would promise to reverse the effects on the Milky Way. The eight girls decided that they were government ministers. Two of the more dominant girls, Susan and Jane, cast themselves respectively as General of the Army, and Minister of Defence, and Tina announced that she was Prime Minister.

The new work was to start with the arrival of the Aliens and their first meeting with the Earthlings. The teacher addressed the class before the acting-out began and told them that their confrontation was to be verbal only. He then drew an imaginary line on the floor and added that no one was to cross the line. The Earth people stood on one side, the Aliens on the other.

The acting-out started with the Aliens asking for recruits for their army in return for restoring natural order in the universe. This resulted in a lot of ideas and a lot of noise, both sides shouting at each other. One girl suggested that they 'speak one at a time', but her voice was drowned in the excited confrontation.

The teacher intervened and stopped the acting-out. He asked the class if they could think of a way of allowing each side to speak in turn and so be heard. Spokesmen were suggested and both sides attempted to elect someone. In both groups the election was undemocratic—one girl shouted, 'I'll be spokesman'; another said, 'I'll second her. She's got a loud voice.' A plea from someone else for there to be a boy and a girl representative was ignored.

Susan, Jane and Tina spoke for the Aliens and Marion for the Earthlings. The Earthlings refused to believe the Aliens' claim of superiority and demanded proof. The Aliens noticed that one of the Earthlings was wounded and asked him to be brought forward. They then proved that they had healing powers by mending his broken leg. (The boy was prepared to accept this without discussion, thus registering his vote that they should be allowed their claim.)

Having established that the Aliens had superior intelligence, the Earthlings wanted some proof that they could trust them to keep their side of the bargain. Someone from Earth suggested taking a hostage.

The teacher stopped the activity and asked the class if they could think of 'a better way of giving their word'. There were several suggestions— 'Shake hands', 'Make a pact'.

The teacher asked how pacts were made. Someone answered, 'In blood'. The teacher informed them that this was not always so and went on, 'It's like swearing an oath. Can you invent an oath?' Negotiations between the pupils and teacher continued about an appropriate oath and a suitable ceremony. When it was agreed, the acting-out continued with the ceremony of swearing an oath. A Bible had been brought from another classroom and each Earthling in turn approached the Aliens and repeated the oath. At the suggestion of the teacher the five Aliens, who had so far been silent, took part in the administration of the oath-taking and the ceremony.

When the ceremony was over the Earth people were taken to the Aliens' planet. Once there the Aliens attempted to train them into a fighting force. They were lined up in twos, given uniforms and drilled by Tina. The Earthlings reacted individually to what was happening to them—some obeyed, some questioned the orders, some refused to take it seriously. Tina was having trouble getting the Earth people to 'stand to attention' and the other Aliens were resorting to poking, pushing and kicking to get them in line.

The teacher intervened and spoke to the Aliens. 'Are you sure they're standing as you want them? Do they know what "attention" is?' He suggested the Aliens might show them by setting an example. He then turned to the Earthlings, 'Can I see how straight you can stand? I'm going to count quietly to twenty, then I don't want to hear anyone's voice except the general of the army.' The general addressed the now quiet army of Earthlings: 'You're going to be given food and water to nourish you. It might not be what you're used to because it's in pill form.' Another Alien handed out the pills and the Earthlings swallowed them submissively.

The teacher intervened almost immediately: 'So you've got an obedient army. What are you going to do now?'

**General:** Train them.

**Teacher:** Will you be taking suggestions from them about how you can best train them?'

**Minister of Defence (Susan) to Army:** We're going to train you in groups of six to use our weapons.

Six of the army were taken to another end of the room by Tina, Susan and Jane. The teacher called after them: 'What are the rest of us going to do while you're at the training ground?'

**Tina:** They can just talk.

The three proceeded to train the six; the rest talked with the teacher or among themselves. The teacher again called to them, 'Is this really the best idea? Someone here has suggested that the Aliens each take some of the army to train.' The teacher suggested that they come back and discuss alternative ways of tackling the problem of training.

A discussion followed in role. Susan asked the Earthlings if there were any generals or majors among them. Four boys stood up, and Tina, Jane and Susan proceeded to question them about their experience as soldiers. One boy suggested that the Aliens would get a better fighting force if they allowed the Earthlings to be trained by their own men—'they would take orders better'. Complaints about sitting on the floor for too long and being kicked by the Aliens were also aired in role. The teacher asked the Earthlings: 'Would it be a good idea for these four to train you next time? Would you be willing to take their orders?' The Earthlings agreed that they would. The hour-long lesson came to an end.

This teacher was involved in the pupils' negotiations from the start of the lesson although his role and method of intervention changed as the lesson progressed.

The two groups had emerged from the previous week's work: the Earthlings (a mixed group of about twenty refugees fleeing from the crumbling cities); and the Aliens (eight girls who had not felt able to find roles within the previously agreed situation). The girls' group, under the dominant leadership of Tina and the more popular influence of Susan and Jane, were to some extent refusing to join in because the idea that the class had accepted had not been their idea. This pressure group was trying to assert itself, not only through the roles chosen but also within the real social network. The teacher had the difficult task of trying to accommodate the eight girls in a way which was not too great a personal compromise for them and at the same time of modifying the behaviour of Susan, Jane and Tina so that the rest of the class could enjoy and develop what they had created. This was made doubly difficult by Tina who appeared to be directly challenging the teacher.

By joining the eight girls at the beginning the teacher showed that he was prepared to listen to and help them introduce their ideas. He was also in a position to veto, in private, anything that he felt would be counter-productive. It also meant that the larger group were prepared to listen to them because the teacher gave them his support.

He structured the confrontation, imposing two major constraints—the line they could not cross and the insistence on a verbal confrontation only. This had the effect of forcing them to listen to each other and attempt to communicate. It also prevented a physical 'bundle'—something twelve-year-olds find irresistible. By imposing constraints the teacher also established his role in relation to the acting-out. While they were responsible for the ideas, he was responsible for the structure and, if necessary, the organization. During the verbal confrontation one girl urged the others to speak one at a time. She was ignored. The teacher reinforced her plea by making them consider spokesmen. While this enabled everyone to hear the interchange, it also meant that only a few children were able actively to contribute. The dialogue became rather stilted because the conversants were having to speak to each other from a distance.

When a 'hostage' was proposed, the teacher quickly intervened, asking them to think of other ways they could 'give their word'. He did this because he did not want to split the focus of attention. Instead he reinforced the suggestion of the 'pact' since this provided a focal point for the whole group, and was a chance to involve everyone. During the negotiations about the form of the representation, the teacher took a fairly active role and deliberately selected the five Aliens who had so far played no part as a way of involving them.

Although the Aliens were giving orders through their symbolic roles and the Earthlings were disregarding them also in role, there was a danger that the real peer-group pressures would dictate and prevent further exploration. The Earthlings responded to the Aliens' kicking and poking by tripping them up. From this point the teacher's role changed and his intervention increased. He was an outsider with licence to question the motives and actions of both sides. As their teacher he also reminded them of the importance of commitment and standards in their work. Consequently, when having difficulty disciplining the Earthlings the teacher suggested that the Aliens show them what they meant by 'standing to attention'. Further to this he calmed the class by asking them to stand still while he, as teacher, counted to twenty. This allowed Susan to develop her role as the general and so further the acting-out. The teacher followed this up by asking the Aliens what they intended to do now that they had an obedient army. This prevented the Aliens from using the renewed commitment for excessive orders and drilling.

While some of the Earthlings were being trained, the rest were told they could talk. The teacher acted as their spokesman: 'Is this really the best idea? Someone here has suggested . . .' This was important since it was the first opportunity for some children to contribute. The structure of the acting-out and their roles within it had weakened their position in the negotiations, and there had been no opportunity for them to step out of symbolic role during the lesson. The discussion itself gave some children the opportunity of offering themselves as military experts. It allowed others to voice their grievances about their treatment during the lesson. Although the teacher had given the eight girls a chance to assert themselves, by the end of the lesson the rest of the class made it quite clear that they were not prepared to play a subservient part in future lessons, and elected their own leaders to train them.

The lesson may not have advanced the story of the class play very significantly, but more important was the real power struggle that was being projected and resolved through the symbolic action. After the lesson the class were asked to reflect on it by answering a questionnaire. Some of their comments support this observation:

**Tina:** In our last drama lesson, we as the Alien peoples came on to the planet Earth and wanted to recruit the Earthlings to our army. They decided to come so we swore them in. Then every time a suggestion was made (our teacher) nearly always opposed. In the end the bell went and we had done hardly anything.

**An Alien:** I was unhappy with my contribution to the play because there were three main people giving orders to the 'army' and so the rest of the officers really had very little to do apart from keeping everyone in line.

**An Earthling:** The most difficult thing I had to do was control myself from really shouting at everybody . . .

**An Alien:** The purpose of this lesson for me was to see if I could get other people to do things as I wanted them to.

**Teacher:** The value of this lesson was two-fold: in the story they were working on and their behaviour as individuals in the class. I think that some of them realized these two were linked. Their behaviour had to be modified before any work as a group could happen—even if only for a short time.

We have tried to show the importance of the teacher's role in affecting the nature of the drama experience by considering how decisions can affect the development of the acting-out. A further consideration of the teacher's role in relation to the quality of the drama experience will be discussed in the next chapter.

# Conclusions

A drama lesson involves the teacher in a series of decisions that starts with his knowledge of the class, himself and his practical situation. From his understanding of these variables he decides on an appropriate educational aim and a more specific intention. With this in mind he decides how best he can achieve it. He considers the overall lesson structure in relation to his objective; social organization in relation to the individual's ability to negotiate; and his role and relationships to the class and the acting-out.

Once the lesson is under way the unique interaction of class and teacher demands that he constantly reappraise the situation and its development, make immediate decisions about it and be prepared to take risks. The drama process revolves around individuals making decisions together, forming judgements and opinions and making statements. The process unfolds subtly, as the symbolic roles which individuals assume mingle with the real established relationships. It is hoped that a clearer knowledge of this process, and the decisions that can affect it, may enable a more positive realization of a teacher's educational aims and intentions and provide a basis for analysing and assessing outcomes.

# Chapter 4
# The Quality of the Drama Experience

We have been talking so far about what drama involves for those who take part in it; about the ways in which it can be used in education and about the demands it makes on the teacher who wants to set it in motion. But what is he working towards? How can the teacher recognize moments of arrival? What can be said about the crucial question of the quality of the drama experience? How can teachers recognize this and begin to move the children towards higher standards of work? We are not talking here about measurement or grading but about ways of knowing when work of value is taking place. Perhaps it should be said at once that there are no hard and fast, unchanging standards for judging the quality of drama work. This must be seen in the light of the group itself and the individuals who make it up. Nevertheless there are a number of general issues and questions to be raised when considering the overall problem of developing the quality of drama.

We have suggested four interrelated components in the drama process: social interaction; use of the media—the 'language' of drama; content; and forms of expression. We have seen that the emphasis in the drama lesson may shift between these, according to the kind of learning the teacher wants to encourage. The difference in emphasis will obviously raise different questions and suggest different criteria for quality. In the end it is the way in which these four elements are brought together and balanced within the experience which determines general quality. What then are the issues to be taken into account here?

## Social interaction

### Prerequisites for drama

The value of drama for the individual child depends on the depth of his involvement—particularly, we would argue, at the symbolic level. Children are not all readily involved in acting-out, for many reasons. For some the real social relationships in the class may be inhibiting—they may, initially, feel embarrassed about working in this way. Ensuring personal involvement is the first step on the way to work of quality and value. For this reason not all that takes place in a drama lesson is, strictly speaking, drama. Although acting-out is the central feature of drama, any lesson may involve a range of activities which lead up to or follow on from acting-out. The way in which acting-out emerges and develops in drama depends on the group's 'states of readiness'. The group need to reach the point where they are prepared to make the kind of personal investment in acting-out which will make it a potentially rewarding experience.

What are these 'states of readiness', these prerequisites for work of quality? Both the children and the teacher need to trust each other and to feel relaxed at the real level. Drama involves the exposure of attitudes and opinions in spontaneous response in acting-out. In effect this means taking risks—offering and building on each other's contributions as a way of developing understanding, both of each other and of the issues at hand. If the group feel secure and relaxed at the real level, they will be more prepared to take the necessary risks at the symbolic level.

The group need to develop a sense of co-operation in drama, in sharing ideas and in making decisions about their work. The ability to speak out and articulate a point of view, and to listen in return are fundamental. Some children do this less readily than others and may need encouragement to contribute, to make suggestions and criticisms, and the corollary of this, to accept criticism and withstand rebuffs. Not all children find it equally easy to make decisions affecting other people or to take on responsibilities within the drama process. They may not realize the range of decisions they can make in drama and may in any case lack the self-confidence to impose an opinion on the rest of the group. Others may impose opinions too readily and inhibit the rest. So a sense of co-operation and corporate responsibility for the work seem to be prerequisite. The ability to concentrate attention and focus energy is essential to acting-out. Even where there is co-operation and lack of inhibition, without sustained concentration the quality of the work may remain unsatisfying to the group.

All of these are attitudes to drama which need to be fostered in the interests of deepening the group's involvement. In the lesson itself the teacher may see a need to initiate exercises or games which prepare the group physically and mentally for the work in hand—trust exercises, games of concentration, and so on. Some teachers list the development of attitudes such as these among their aims in drama. We want to argue, however, that these kinds of development, desirable perhaps in their own right, need to be seen, within drama teaching, in terms of improving the quality in the discovery, expression and communication of meaning.

There is a further prerequisite for drama which has not so far been mentioned. It is possibly one of the most important. In order for the group to become deeply involved in acting-out, they need a 'sense of significance' in what they are doing. They need to feel that what they are doing is important for them. The group are more likely to commit themselves if they can see its relevance. In using drama the group are making an agreement to adopt different patterns of behaviour with each other and with the teacher. They are contracting to work together in a new way. If they do not approach their work with a sense of significance, if they do not develop this underlying 'contract' to work in drama, their commitment is likely to be nominal and the quality of their experience superficial and unrewarding.

## Use of media—the 'language' of drama

Words, sound, gesture, movement in space and time form the basis of the symbolic 'language' of dramatic expression. There is a double purpose in helping the child to develop skills in the media of drama: to extend his abilities in the use of the process itself for exploring problems of meaning, and to broaden his dramatic 'vocabulary' so that he may be able to express and communicate his perceptions in a more satisfying way. The more effectively he can control the media of drama, the more effective his attempts to use them in action will be. It may be appropriate for the child at certain stages in his development to concentrate specifically on the mastery of certain skills so as to improve his command of the drama process itself. Occasionally the teacher may see the need to structure exercises which focus particularly on voice, movement, and so on. Limited knowledge and abilities in these can affect the child's range of activity in representing experiences in drama. This in turn may limit the potential range of his understanding, by limiting his ability to find new forms of expression. In English a child does not learn to write just for the sake of doing so. He learns to write in order to do something else—to increase his range of thought and powers of communication with others. The medium is the vehicle which enables this to happen. Similarly in drama the teacher needs to supply the help and encouragement which the child will require in his struggles with the media. The ultimate value of this is in enhancing the quality of his work.

## Content

There can never be a list of guaranteed themes or topics for good drama. Yet the content of drama—the issues, topics, themes, concepts from which it grows—is crucial. The sense of significance in drama emerges to a large extent in relation to what the lesson is about.

The common dimension in the content of drama is that of interpersonal relationships and human response. Although in drama children may deal with abstract ideas, drama is not in itself an abstract symbolic form in the same way as, for example, music or visual arts are. Drama deals with the living symbols of human behaviour. What criteria can be applied then in selecting content to meet the practical situation?

A child may be obliged to take part in drama physically, but his subjective involvement cannot be forced. The individual is more likely to be drawn into the drama process if he finds something compelling in the questions and problems at the centre of it. The content must be within reach of the group, even though they may well have to stretch themselves to grasp and take hold of it. In other words, the problem of meaning must be appropriate to the group's state of development both in terms of not being too difficult for them or conversely too trivial. Of course this opens up an enormous question. How is 'appropriateness' to be defined? It is in fact too broad a question to be given a specific answer. It has to be narrowed down and answered within the limited context of each class.

The symbolic situations in drama need to involve some form of conflict, if new insights and perceptions are to emerge. This does not mean that the content of drama always has to be sensational or traumatic, nor that it should necessarily involve life-or-death confrontations. Rather there must be an inherent tension in the represented situation. For example, the concept of truthfulness may be better understood in terms of its opposite—falsehood. This conflict can be symbolized perhaps in the opposing behaviour of characters or groups of people, and then explored in the way the situation unfolds. The acting-out generally becomes more compulsive for the group if it revolves around a juxtaposition of attitudes, or an opposition of interests. It is this inherent tension in the acting-out which will draw the group into the problems of meaning. It is under this pressure of opposing and challenging responses that new insights and perceptions are forged.

# Forms of expression

We have defined drama as a process. But this does not mean that there is no end in view, no products. In drama there may continually be moments of arrival—moments when the group has new perceptions, reaches conclusions, makes statements. What is the relationship of these statements and the form in which they are made to the underlying search for meaning? What terms of reference can be drawn up for thinking about the quality of the statement? We are not using 'form' here just to refer to final, finished statements, but to the overall shape and pattern of the expressive act as it emerges from the interchange of ideas. Drama lessons, in fact, need not lead towards final statements at all. But it is important to recognize the interdependence throughout drama work of the form of the expression and the nature of the understanding it embodies. In drama, as in the other arts, the meaning actually becomes clear as the form of the expression takes shape. Often in ordinary conversation it is only in the act of searching for words, in phrasing a sentence, that the thought we are reaching for reveals itself. It is only in the act of expressing something that we fully understand what it is that we are trying to say. So in the arts meaning emerges and is crystallized in the act of making the expressive statement. The search for form begins with the search for meaning itself.

Groups may feel the need to have an initial structure for their acting-out in order to give it a sense of direction. But as soon as they begin acting-out, the interchange of ideas will almost inevitably begin to move them away from their planned destination to explore unforeseen areas of understanding. The group need to be flexible in the paths they choose when they begin to work. They need to be willing to take risks in exploring new forms of expression if they are to realize the full value of drama in action.

In considering the quality of the form of expression, therefore, the teacher needs to look beneath the surface, beyond what the drama looks and sounds like, to the deep structure of ideas, feelings and motivations which are giving it its shape. He needs to understand that the point of arrival may not be the final solution of the actual problem they are representing. Through drama they may not resolve the problems of overpopulation or the concept of truth. But they may have succeeded in discovering meaning in these things for themselves. In drama the resolution may not be of the represented problem, but of the problem of representation itself.

In struggling with different forms of expression the group may reach a statement which they find completely satisfying. They have clarified and crystallized ideas and attitudes through acting-out and have brought these together into a coherent pattern or shape. There is indeed enormous pleasure to be gained from the form of expression itself. This too is a moment of arrival in drama—a point when there is an inherent pleasure in the form itself, in 'saying it this way'. It is here that it becomes appropriate to talk in terms of the aesthetic response: a pleasure in form where the problem of meaning has been exactly expressed, where content and form have become indivisible.

## The drama process and creativity

There are opportunities for development and fulfilment within each of these four component aspects of the drama process. In judging the lesson, the teacher may see success in one of these components but not in others. He may be happy with the improved social relationships in the class but be dissatisfied with their use of the media and handling of the content.

We began by saying that the value of drama for the individual child depends on the depth of his involvement, particularly at the symbolic level. The possibilities for meaningful and fulfilling work in drama are increased when children leave their preoccupations with distractions and inhibitions at the real level and make an imaginative transition; when they become involved in the process of acting-out. They then begin to explore problems of meaning more intensively within the roles they have created. In the midst of this kind of involvement the group are pooling past experiences and current perceptions to develop their understanding of the issues. The individual is using what he knows to feel his way into the unknown. This is essentially a coming together of the various aspects of the process—social interaction, use of the media, content and form. It uses knowing and feeling as one force.

Below are two examples of drama experiences which teachers felt to have been particularly valuable in the context of the groups' overall work. They are not meant as models of good practice, but as general examples of the varied impact and vividness of drama at moments of absorption.

I began one lesson with a remedial group of about fourteen pupils by talking at some length about homeless families and showing literature from Shelter pamphlets. The discussion opened out to include the kinds of problem that people found with houses in the locality. We agreed to make up a play about a street with very poor housing conditions and a landlord who was ruthless in his exploitation of the property he owned.

I took on the role of Mr King, the landlord, and the group divided into families or units (for example, three Asian boys, very inhibited, shared a house together) and spread out around the drama room to establish the houses. I co-opted one boy to serve as my rent-collector and he went from house to house demanding rent arrears which the tenants were refusing to pay. There was a great deal of involvement, role-playing and interaction (within families and between families), but the moment in which the drama really took hold and swept everyone along by the nature of what was happening was in the direct confrontation of the tenants with the landlord (myself, completely in role) at a specially convened meeting in which they were allowed to voice their grievances.

Their role identification was being enforced by my 'open' role-playing in a direct situation of conflict. Their verbal thrusts as they leapt to their feet detailing the kinds of conditions they were suffering and their jokes at my life-style 'in my Rolls Royce with blond secretary' etc., was stretching me to think and react in a highly charged dramatic and intuitive way, which was the kind of experience they were engaged in themselves.

This example concerned a whole class of children. Their involvement was directly triggered by the teacher working in role. In the second example a small group is working by itself.

A boy was working with other sixteen-year-olds on an improvisation of the Easter Story. As Christ he was being scourged and vilified by the rest of the group. It was working mechanically but had no excitement within it.

The school choir was rehearsing 'Messiah' as part of the preparations for an end-of-term presentation. It was decided to try playing the scourging scene against the background of the choir's singing of 'Worthy is the Lamb'. The result was staggering. Not only did the improvisation become ritualized and climatic but the boy, in role, began to cry. Others watching him were similarly moved.

When asked about it he said that for the first time he understood how it was that a man who was being ill-treated could feel emotions other than anger and resentment. It would seem that the juxtaposition of the dignity and beauty of the music and the brutality of the event had, for him in particular and others not so acutely, highlighted a basic contradiction in man.

Moments of total absorption are rare and need to be seen in the longer perspective of the drama teacher's work. He needs skill and care in handling and building upon the child's commitment. In any case the value of drama in education does not rest solely on such experiences, however valuable they are when they occur. The drama teacher cannot legislate for work of quality in any of the four components simply in the way he structures the lesson. Creativity cannot be conjured up at will:

What about the creative state? In it a man is taken out of himself. He lets down as it were a bucket into his subconscious and draws up something which is normally beyond his reach. He mixes this thing with his normal experience, and out of the mixture he makes a work of art . . . Such seems to be the creative process. It may employ much technical ingenuity and worldly knowledge, it may profit by critical standards, but mixed up with it is this stuff from the bucket which is not procurable on demand.*

Involving the group will take time, skill and experience of being together. Carl Rogers, in talking about the problems of encouraging creative activity, comments:

From the nature of the inner condition of creativity it is clear that they cannot be forced but must be permitted to emerge. The farmer cannot make the germ develop and sprout from the seed, he can only supply the

* E.M. Forster, *Two Cheers for Democracy* (Penguin Books, 1974).

nurturing conditions which will permit the seed to develop its own potentialities.*

In the course of working through drama the group will encounter many problems. While it is possible for children to explore meaning in great depth without being satisfied with their forms of expression, it is equally possible for them to arrive at forms of expression without concern for the quality of the meaning. The group may feel unable to express themselves because of lack of confidence in the media, or in themselves. In the long term it is the teacher's responsibility to look at and develop the children's work, helping them to a greater involvement in all aspects of the process.

* C.R. Rogers, 'Towards a theory of creativity'. *ETC: A Review of General Semantics*, vol ii, 1954. Reprinted in P.E. Vernon, ed., *Creativity* (Penguin Books, 1970).

# Chapter 5

# Can Drama be Assessed?

Not all teachers are convinced that drama can or should be assessed. Some feel that it is difficult to make judgements about an activity that centres round the expression of feelings. Others feel that there are so many factors involved that it is impossible to assess them all. Yet others feel that if they were to approach their work too critically they would lose a great deal of the spontaneity necessary in creating vitality in drama. For many, to try to assess drama work is a misguided if not impossible task. We believe, however, that although drama is a flexible and creative process, drama teachers do intend definite learning to take place. Often they are not consciously aware of making judgements about pupils' work. But they do make judgements in order to be able to develop work both in a single lesson and over a period of time.

In this chapter we are using the term 'assessment' in this general sense of making judgements about work. We are not talking about grading or measurement. We intend to articulate what kinds of judgements are made to assess the effects of the lesson, and what criteria can be used to judge its value.

## Why assess drama?

There are a number of reasons for teachers to be critical about work in drama lessons:

1. If drama experiences are meant to help the development of children, teachers ought to have some notion of the kinds of learning they want to encourage and should be able to make judgements about what has been achieved in lessons.

2. Decisions teachers make concerning the structuring of lessons, and what roles they play within the lesson, help to determine the nature of the work. It is therefore important for teachers to be aware of the effect that their decisions and actions have on the lesson and whether appropriate strategies have been employed for their purposes.

3. One of the drama teacher's main tasks is to judge work in terms of the quality of the meaning explored and represented. In making these judgements the teacher needs to take into account the four main components of the drama process:

social interaction; use of the media; content; and forms of expression. In looking at any lesson the teacher needs to make judgements about development in all of these areas, although the importance he attaches to each of them will probably vary from group to group.

4.  It helps teachers understand the process better so that they can find more successful ways of working.

5.  It gives teachers a basis for deciding on future work.

# How can drama be assessed?

It would be impossible to give a tick-list for assessing drama lessons. Every lesson is unique and the drama process is used for many reasons with differing results. Judgements about work can only be made in the light of the teacher's specific intentions with each group. However there are a number of general factors to be taken into account.

1.  **Before the lesson.** Because of the developmental nature of the process, it is important to consider lessons in the context of what happened before the lesson—the pupils' states of readiness for drama. What kind of work is most suitable for them? This has been discussed in previous chapters.

2.  **The drama lesson itself.** This is our main concern in this chapter. What the teacher does in any session depends on his knowledge of how the process works and its various possibilities; what his individual philosphy is; what his pupils are like; and time and the space available. These will influence the way the teacher structures lessons and the type of work that can be done. The point or level at which teachers begin activities should be determined by their assessment of their pupils' states of development, which can be picked up by cues and signals as the lesson progresses. Sensitivity to levels of emotional and intellectual involvement is a basic necessity of all drama teaching. It is very difficult to ascertain accurately how ready pupils may be for various tasks or how they may respond. Teachers need to be flexible enough to cope with changes and to use possibilities when they occur.

3.  **Potential developments—both long-term and in the next lesson.** We shall be looking at this in the next chapter.

It must be emphasized that many other kinds of learning may take place in addition to those resulting from acting-out. The teacher needs to take these into account in assessing the lesson.

# Three drama lessons

Three examples are given of lessons taught by different teachers. These examples are not to be taken as 'models' for drama work. They are part of a normal day's work and to be seen in the context of the pupils' long-term development. Analysis and assessment of each lesson is based on team members' observation notes, and statements made by teachers at the end of their lessons.

It is hoped that by asking certain questions teachers will be better able to formulate appropriate aims, understand what happens in the lesson itself, and recognize how work might be developed in the future. In beginning to assess any drama lesson, the following questions might be asked:

1. What significant factors affected learning during the lesson?
2. Were the teacher's aims realized? If not, why not?
3. Were appropriate strategies and methods used for achieving aims and intentions, and for improving the quality of the work?
4. What was the value of the lesson?
5. How could judgements made about the lesson affect the planning of future work?

## Lesson 1: Difficult family problems

The school is an 11 to 16 secondary modern in a small urban area with a fairly mixed social intake. There are approximately 1050 children. Drama is taught within a separate drama department. Most classes in the first two years have one sixty-minute or two thirty-minute lessons per week. In the third year not all classes have drama; those that do, receive one thirty-minute lesson. In the fourth and fifth year, pupils may opt for an afternoon of non-examination drama. This class was of thirty mixed-ability boys and girls aged thirteen to fourteen. They have a thirty-minute lesson every Friday morning after break. The drama space is a newly-opened, purpose-built studio with an excellent lighting grid, sound room and facilities plus adjoining make-up/quiet work area. The studio is self-contained and without windows.

### The class

They are generally a difficult class and many teachers have trouble with them. They are very noisy and full of energy. They tend to form cliques rather than work as a whole group. There are three very sullen, difficult girls who truant frequently and are often on report for swearing at teachers, walking out of classes and generally answering back. In September there were two difficult boys; one has now left and the other has become more manageable.

In the first term of the year they were studying the Industrial Revolution in social studies. The teacher tried to link their drama work to the same theme but found it generally unsuccessful. They spent a long time working on conditions in coalmining during the last century, but because they only had thirty minutes for each lesson, progress was slow.

The class began to show increasing interest in drama lessons at the end of the first term. This increased in the second term, so that the majority of pupils were arriving at the start of break in order to have more time for their lesson. Although the lesson did not start until after break, the pupils often used this time to practise plays, set up rostra blocks, or explore the equipment.

## Background to the lesson

The lesson was part of a sequence of lessons on the theme of family problems. During the term the teacher had encouraged an understanding of family problems through structured exploration in which he asked them to explore certain situations through acting-out. He also asked them to devise their own situations which illustrated a particular kind of problem.

In the lesson prior to this one, the class had been engaged in making group statements about problems that teenagers experience within the family. They had worked from a single stimulus—the Beatles' group record; 'She's Leaving Home'. This was followed by a discussion out of which the teacher asked each small group to choose and represent a situation that might cause someone to consider leaving home. In this lesson, the teacher wanted to encourage the pupils' understanding of the problems each group had chosen to represent. The teacher commented, 'This is the third session in their second term and they haven't yet worked as a whole class.'

The teacher aimed to encourage pupils' understanding of the problems represented, to define them and find solutions, and to find a way of enabling them to watch each other's work seriously. His intention was to set them a problem-solving situation that they could tackle in small groups, but which had a common focus for the whole class.

## The lesson

The group arrived in the newly-built drama studio for the start of their thirty-minute lesson. Eager and excited they chatted both to the teacher and each other as they changed from their outside shoes to plimsolls. A group of four boys had been in the studio during break discussing and practising the play that they had made up the previous week and were

about to show to the rest of the class at the start of this lesson.
*10.55 a.m.*
Gradually, the teacher calmed the class down and asked for their attention. He then explained to them what the lesson would consist of and outlined their task as follows: 'You are going to see a play in which there is some kind of family problem. When you have seen it, the rest of you will divide into four groups seated round those tables and you will become an office/agency concerned with this family's problem. After the play each member of the family will arrive at your office in turn. You can ask them as many questions as you like before they move on to the next agency. When each agency has spoken to every member of the family, I will ask each agency to offer an effective solution to their problems.'

Before the lesson the teacher had set out, at intervals around the room, four rostra blocks. He now asked the class to take chairs and group themselves as 'agencies' around these rostra. They divided into four groups: (a) six girls; (b) six girls; (c) six boys; and (d) four boys. When everyone in the groups was seated, the other four boys, using the centre of the studio, presented their play.

The situation represented sibling rivalry between two boys. It involved a father and his two sons, Carl and Tom. Both sons received money from their father to go to a football match. Only Tom returned. Carl was brought home by a policeman. He was accused of abusive language and insulting a policeman. He denied it. Father and Carl argued; the brothers argued. Father was worried about the neighbours' reactions and compared Carl to his 'good son, Tom'. Carl claimed he was innocent and accused his father of favouritism and treating him unfairly. The play ended.

The teacher reminded the class once more of the task that he had set them. 'You have to find out as much as you can about the family. Whether or not there is a problem and the course of action that would sort their problem out.' Then he added a time constraint: 'You have about four minutes with each person.'
*11.00 a.m.*
One character from the play then went to each agency in turn where he was questioned by the group. Generally the questions were about age, family history, etc. although there were some questions like, 'Why can't you be more like your brother?'

*Examples of questions asked by groups*
**Group a (girls).** This group were interested and serious in their questions to Carl.
Were you adopted?
**Carl:** No.
Where's your mother?
**Carl:** She left us.
How old were you then?
**Carl:** One.
Why do you think your brother's better than you?
**Carl:** He's the brainiest.
Have you been in trouble with the police before?
**Carl:** No.
Has your brother?

**Carl:** Yes, but he hasn't told dad.
**Girl (to another):** Go on, you ask something.
On your birthday, did your brother get more than you?
**Carl:** He got a bike.
Do you have to work to get money?
**Carl:** Yes.

**Group b (girls).** There was a great deal of giggling with this group. One girl asked most of the questions. The teacher stayed with the group and made some suggestions about questions they could ask.
Age?
**Carl:** Sixteen.
Are you at school?
**Carl:** Yes.
Your brother said you're not.
**Carl:** I work after school and do a paper round.
**(Giggles.)**
Ask a question, Sheila.
Do you like your dad?
**Carl:** No, he's horrible.
Have you tried getting your brother into trouble?
**Carl:** No, I wouldn't get any money then.
Why did your mother go?
**Carl:** I don't know. She just went.
Did your father chuck her out?
**Carl:** No.
Do you like your mum or dad best?
**Carl:** Mum, she was softer, she gave me money.
Where is she now?
**Carl:** I don't know.

**Group c (boys).** This group asked Tom numerous questions very quickly.
Have you been to any away matches?
Do you like your brother?
Do you feel victimized?
Do you find your dad is always getting at your brother?
Do you mind being in trouble with the police?
How do you get in trouble with the police?
**Tom:** They always look for me.
Is it always the same cop?
Do you go to the same school as your brother?
What school?
**Tom:** I don't know.
You must know.
What do you do in school?
Who's the eldest, you or your brother?

Unfortunately there was only time to record some of Carl's answers to questions from Group c.
How old are you?
**Carl:** Sixteen.
Get your feet off my desk.
What school do you go to?

**Carl:** I've left school.
No you haven't.
**Carl:** I have.
Your brother just told us you hadn't.
**(Carl would not budge.)**
Do you often get into trouble?
**Carl:** No.
Why aren't you like your brother?
**Carl:** I don't know.
Do you like your brother?
**Carl:** Yes.
Do you like your dad?
**Carl:** Yes.

During this period of questioning as agencies, the members of the groups did not clearly define their roles, although there was a marked difference in tone and manner when they asked questions to the characters and when they spoke to other members of the agency. The boys from the play were answering in role, although they sometimes contradicted themselves. The teacher intervened during the lesson to remind the agencies of the time constraint and each character then moved on to the next agency.

*11.20 a.m.*

When each character had been interviewed by everyone the teacher asked each agency to decide collectively what the problems were and how they would solve them. They did this through discussion, while the four characters sat at one side of the studio.

*Example of Group c's discussion*

Do you think there's a problem?

**(They failed to agree.)**

His father should keep him away from football.
He should lock him in his bedroom.
What if he despises his father? He could kill someone next time.
He should go in the army.
No, he won't see his family. He would miss them.
He said he didn't like his dad.
Maybe, I don't like my dad, but I'd miss them.
I reckon the cops should lay off him.
Leave him in a cell overnight. Let him see what it's like.
(It is interesting to note that a boy who did not ask any questions made most of the comments during discussion.) In this group there was no attempt to arrive at a majority decision. There was no working concept of the spokesman representing the views of the group.

The teacher stopped discussions to ask each agency for its conclusion. A spokesman from each group told the class of their deliberations and offered a solution.

**Group a.** To Carl: 'You did have a fishing rod for Christmas, but you didn't know this.' 'The problem was that Carl was the favourite of his mum, but he got no attention when his mum left. So the solution is his father should pay more attention to him.'

**Group b.** 'Carl should get more money as he's older. The solution is that as he's seventeen, he should be at work.'

**Group c.** 'The boy should get interested in a job or join the army or cadets.

His dad should be more lenient and pay more attention to Carl. Tom
should share more.'
*11.30 a.m.* The bell.

## Analysis and assessment of the lesson

WHAT SIGNIFICANT FACTORS AFFECTED LEARNING DURING THE LESSON?
One of the main features of the lesson was that it was carefully
structured. In terms of content, the teacher defined what was to be
explored. He also told the class how it was to be explored—they
were to do this as members of an agency where they were given the
task of finding out what the problem was and how it might be
solved. Thus acting-out occurred in a strictly defined context.
Children were only responsible for finding forms of expression
through developing their roles and investigating the problem within
the teacher's given structure. The main kind of learning encouraged
was to try to interpret and understand a family problem by first
asking questions and then by discussing the matter. Emphasis was
placed on understanding the problem with the exception of the
original group who had responsibility for presenting their dramatic
statement to the class and then developing their roles by answering
questions. Towards the end of the lesson, the emphasis was placed
on social interaction and groups were given the task of arriving at a
decision about the problem and suggesting possible solutions.
Because of the structure, they also had to learn to make decisions in
a limited time.

Learning during the lesson happened within four distinct
activities: the presentation; the questions asked by agency
members; discussion; and feedback from groups.

THE PRESENTATION. The group showing their statement had to
recall what they had done in a previous lesson and present it in such
a way that they could be understood by others. They were learning
to communicate their ideas through drama. They also had to co-
ordinate their efforts so that the scene went smoothly.

The group's presentation was clear. However, although they
worked out what the situation was—boy brought back from a
football match—there was little sign of characterization and not
much evidence that the group had explored the relationship
between each other in any depth. This meant that the audience was
given an outline of a situation but not enough detail to go on.
During this time, the rest of the class were expected to interpret the
statement individually.

QUESTIONS ASKED BY AGENCY MEMBERS. The situation was elaborated
on by agency members asking the characters questions—thus
establishing more details and giving groups common reference
points for understanding and defining the nature of the problem.

Pupils were responsible for developing their own roles and methods of questioning.

The questions asked indicated a serious attempt to find out more about the characters and the problem. Some were interested in developing the relationship between the brothers and whether the father had a preference for the older brother—'Did your brother get more than you?' They asked about Carl's general behaviour—his life at school, whether he'd been in trouble before. Some of the girls placed importance on the absence of his mother—a detail established by questions. Most of the questions were concerned with establishing what the problem was rather than going deeper by developing a relationship with the characters or conducting their investigation in any detail. This might have been accomplished if there had been more time.

ROLE—PLAYING BY AGENCY MEMBERS. Although there was a marked contrast in tone and pace (sometimes aggressive) when group members questioned the characters and when they talked among themselves, there was little evidence of characterization or that they had decided what kind of agency they were working in. Pupils had not decided what the agencies were, what their personal positions in the agency were or what they were like as people. Except for a boy who told Tom to get his feet off his desk, there was little evidence that they had even established imaginary physical environments in which to work. They constantly slipped in and out of role—possibly because they found it difficult to identify with the situation they were in or because of lack of experience or embarrassment of one boy being interviewed by six girls. Although they were committed to exploring what was presented to them, they were not committed to their own acting-out roles. This meant that there were few or no areas of tension to generate emotional involvement in the issues concerned. This lack was especially felt by the teacher who commented on it at the end of the lesson. The method of questioning varied among the groups. Sometimes one or two assertive characters asked most of the questions. In one group, the more timid were encouraged to say something. In another, all members made equal contributions. The teacher stayed with one group who found asking questions difficult, influencing their work by his presence.

THE FAMILY. The boys had played in role throughout this time, and developed their roles further by adding more details when they answered questions. However, at times, they found it difficult to sustain their roles with any consistency and sometimes contradicted themselves. At one time Carl said that he went to school. At another he said he didn't. Because the group before the presentation had not developed any detailed background information, they sometimes gave contradictory information about each other. When this happened the boys found it difficult to respond adequately; rather than adjusting to new information and using it, they merely repeated their original statements.

THE DISCUSSION. Here more time was spent on establishing the situation. This was done by pupils making random comments about what they thought the problem was. There was no conscious attempt to reach a group decision. Discussion did show, however, that members tried to make decisions based on their understanding of what they had seen. For instance, Group c started by wanting to be punitive—'keep him away from football', 'lock him in his bedroom'; but after considering the situation further, attitudes changed—'praise him more'.

FEEDBACK FROM GROUPS. Here individuals needed to articulate opinions and give solutions. Interpretations were simple—usually one reason for the problem was given. Solutions given showed concern for the problem and were mainly practical—'he should go to work'. Reasons for how or why they had reached conclusions were not articulated.

So far comments and descriptions have been given in the light of what happened. These will now be discussed in terms of whether the teacher's aims were realized.

## Assessment

WERE THE TEACHER'S AIMS REALIZED? IF NOT, WHY NOT? One of the teacher's aims was to get the children to learn to watch each other's work more seriously—to develop a state of readiness for more thoughtful work. The teacher was pleased with their response: 'I think, knowing that they were going to be involved in the work might have been the reason they didn't lark about today.' From the manner in which the class listened to the group, and the kinds of question they asked, it was evident that they had paid attention to the presentation. From the questions asked it was interesting to note that pupils made certain interpretations about what they saw. For instance, although Carl denied doing anything wrong, all members assumed that he was guilty because of the way he reacted. All groups took the presentation seriously and asked questions about the family's relationships with each other. Even the group who giggled during role-playing asked questions about whether the father preferred one son and where the mother was. This showed some commitment to investigating the problem set by the scene.

The other main aim was for the children to define and understand the nature of a particular family problem and find ways of resolving it. To some extent this was achieved. By the end of the lesson it was clear that they had given some consideration to issues raised by the presentation. One group felt that the problem concerned the effect of Carl's mother leaving. They felt that his father 'should pay more attention to him'. Another group implied that the trouble was caused by Carl not having enough money and that he should therefore find work. A third group implied that he needed more interest in other things and that both father and son should change towards him, with his father being more lenient and his brother more generous. These solutions showed that they had considered the problem and come to conclusions about it. The teacher felt that 'they tended to see things more objectively; more balanced than I'd expected'. Yet how deep was their understanding of the problem? Although they took the matter seriously, the level of understanding was fairly superficial. For instance, most of the questions were concerned with trying to establish facts about the characters. Some questions did concern the relationships between members of the family and there was some attempt to establish motives, but they were crude: 'Do you like your brother?'; 'Do you like your father?' Some questions concerned the characters' background—'Have you been in trouble with the police before?'—but they were never followed up to find out more about what Carl was like as a person or what his motives may have been. In summing up what they thought the problem was, they picked on one particular reason rather than allowing for the problem to be complex or have a number of possible solutions.

There might have been a number of reasons for this. Because the presentation was not very detailed, they needed to establish more facts before working in greater depth. During acting-out members of the agencies had not established why they were questioning the family, what the agencies were, what their purpose was or what part they, as individuals, played in the agency. Although they took on mannerisms of authority through changes in tone, it was not clear that they had decided what their attitudes as individuals or agency members were to the family. Because of this they might have found it difficult to identify sufficiently. There was a certain lack of motivation in questioning members of the family, or indeed for members of the family to answer questions as they did not know why they were being questioned. If they had reasons for why they were there, questions might have been more concerned with going deeper into the problem. Another reason why understanding lacked depth might have been that agencies were given a limited amount of time with each character and very little time to establish relationships among themselves. Given the limited time available, the teacher probably did not expect more than this level of understanding to be achieved.

WERE APPROPRIATE STRATEGIES USED FOR ACHIEVING AIMS AND INTENTIONS? The teacher's intentions were 'to set them a problem-

solving situation that they could tackle in small groups, but which
had a common focus for the whole class.' This was achieved by the
teacher asking the whole class to watch a group's presentation,
work in small groups, and then come back together as a whole to
listen to the feedback. By structuring the lesson in this way, all the
pupils were involved in the problem because they knew that they
would have to work on it.

Throughout the lesson, the teacher's role was · mainly
organizational so he started the lesson by asking a group to show
their dramatic statement. By asking a group to present a statement
at the beginning of the lesson on a family problem he did two
things: (1) because the group had worked on the statement, they
started with an air of concentration which set a working
atmosphere from the beginning; (2) he focused attention on the
subject to be explored. During acting-out, he remained with one of
the groups to help them by suggesting the kinds of questions they
might ask. He was aware that one of the problems of small-group
work was difficulty in finding out what all groups were doing.
'Because I was anxious for the work to succeed and anxious about
Group b (who I felt might disrupt everyone else's commitment) I
stayed with them most of the time. This meant I didn't really get a
chance to hear the kind of questions other groups were asking.'

Apart from these two roles—that of organizing and of helping
one group—the teacher played no active part in the work. He only
intervened to remind the class that they had limited time for each
activity. By structuring the lesson with such clearly-defined time
constraints, he placed limits on how much in-depth work could be
done in any activity.

WERE APPROPRIATE STRATEGIES USED FOR IMPROVING THE QUALITY OF
THE WORK? The teacher did not attempt during the lesson to improve
the quality of the work although he had a number of opportunities.
For instance, he could have discussed the presentation in such a
way that pupils were given more information about the family. He
could have stopped the acting-out and done some work on the
nature and function of agencies. At the end of the lesson he could
have asked questions or discussed their assumptions and
suggestions.

His main problem was that of deciding what could be achieved in
thirty minutes. He had to choose between accomplishing what he
set out to do, or stopping at various points to develop and deepen
work. He chose the former which, because of careful planning,
gave children a sense of achievement because they had managed to
complete the task set.

WHAT WAS THE VALUE OF THE LESSON? The lesson was successful for
a number of reasons: Both teacher and pupils achieved the tasks
which gave them a sense of accomplishment and a good basis for

starting future work in the right frame of mind. Pupils took each other's work seriously and made a serious attempt to explore the problem. Because there was an emphasis on understanding, main kinds of learning involved interpretation, analysis and assessment of the situation. Learning therefore occurred mainly on an intellectual level.

HOW COULD JUDGEMENTS MADE ABOUT THE LESSON AFFECT THE PLANNING OF FUTURE WORK? On the real level, it seemed that pupils could benefit from more work on how to discuss things usefully and what is meant by making joint decisions. Although they mainly shared ideas, there was little notion of arguing points of view and coming to a general agreement. The main area for improvement was at the symbolic level. There was a need to work at a deeper level of involvement during acting-out. In the lesson, apart from the family members, pupils were not clear about what they were representing. This meant that they were limited concerning what they could explore on a symbolic level. More work needed to be done on developing roles/characters in more depth.

In deciding what to do in the next lesson, the teacher concluded, 'My general impression is that in the future it would be a good idea to develop their concept of an agency and the questions they ask.' This would then give pupils a better basis for questioning the next group's statement.

## Lesson 2: Looking at problems from different angles

The school is a 10 to 16 rural comprehensive with a mixed social intake of approximately 460 children. Drama is taught within an English department. All pupils receive at least one eighty-minute lesson per week for the first three years. Then they are offered drama as a non-examination option, for two years. The class is of seventeen mixed-ability boys and girls aged fourteen to fifteen years. All the pupils had this drama teacher for the first two years. In the third year, half of them had a different teacher. This group only started working together in September. This lesson took place in December. The lesson was 105 minutes long on Friday morning (11.0 a.m. to 12.45 p.m.). The class also had one other forty-minute lesson during the week. The drama space is the main school hall. This is a large, bare hall with a stage at one end. The group work in natural light. There are no black-out facilities or specialist lighting. In front of the stage there is a piano. Chairs are stacked in the corners of the room.

## The class

According to the teacher the majority opted for drama in their fourth year because 'they enjoyed it'. A few joined because 'their friends did' and a few because 'it was an easy option'. The teacher felt that a few had chosen drama because they had 'emotional problems and were seeking some kind of release in a pretend world'.

The teacher was aware of friction in the group between two or three members. 'They have to find their own way round this. It's my aim to see that their problems do not affect the development of the rest of the group.' One of her initial long-term aims stated in September was based on this: 'To develop a group feeling. They have to learn to trust each other as well as me.'

The teacher aimed in this lesson to encourage an understanding of tolerance and the dangers of forming hasty opinions through insufficient evidence, and to explore a problem by looking at it from different angles; for pupils to use the creative process to explore problems by themselves; and also to encourage a 'group feeling' and to develop an awareness of the difficulties of working together. Her intention was to structure carefully the first half to focus on the problem; to move into small-group work; and to follow this by discussion.

## The lesson

The group sat on the floor in an informal circle and the teacher joined them. She started by leading a very general discussion about village life, with particular reference to the distinctive nature of life in an inward-looking community. From this beginning she asked them to suggest 'character-types' that they might expect to find in a village. The group were relaxed and answered freely; smiling and laughing easily while at the same time listening closely to what the teacher had to say. The teacher asked each one 'to adopt a fairly crude character' that they would like to be and to think about that imaginary person for a moment. Then she went round the circle to find out the character-type that each had chosen. The roles were generally fairly prominent members of the community—publican, district nurse, local 'bobby', milkman.

The class then engaged in a game that involved meeting as many 'village characters' as possible and finding out about them. The teacher played the piano while the children milled around the room and when she stopped playing the villagers had to converse with the nearest person to them. A few were meeting and finding out about each other in role, but most at this stage were talking about their character as someone else. The teacher developed the game by asking them all to continue in role. The game and its development took about seventeen minutes, during which time boys and girls mixed and chatted freely and used most of the space.

At the end of this phase the teacher called the group back into a circle. This time the boys and girls were more mixed up when they sat down. The teacher pointed to individuals and asked them whom they had met and what they had found out about that person. No one was left out and all answered readily. There were some mistaken identities which caused amusement and laughter—for example, facts pertinent to the milkman were confused with facts relating to the postman.

At this point the teacher apologized for the superficial nature of the work so far but explained its purpose: 'It has given everybody an idea of who people are and the range of characters in the village.' She then asked the group to select a time and day of the week as part of the setting for a situation they were to explore. A girl suggested 'Saturday morning', and this, not being challenged, was accepted.

The teacher developed the basic elements from the previous game into an acting-out exercise by defining slightly more closely the context for their interaction in villager-roles: 'It's Saturday morning. Think about what you'd be doing as this character. I want you to go about your business, meeting and talking to people. Right, go.'

The class rose and started to circulate—enthusiastically for the most part. They were largely portraying stock characters and there were a lot of exaggerated country accents. After a few minutes the teacher stopped them and fed in some information as a focal talking point: 'Mrs Jones has run away with a single man and left her husband and two kids.' The class stopped and listened, meeting in groups and pairs to discuss the news. Generally they were gossipy and malicious, or outraged. Having allowed the 'villagers' to react to and adopt an attitude towards this news, the teacher stopped them again and fed in further information in order that they might take both sides into account. 'It seems that Mr Jones was a drunkard and used to get very violent. How does this affect your attitudes?'

The class listened intently to each new piece of information and then went back into role. They were still tending to form into huddles rather than use the whole space and they did not move from one person to another very quickly, perhaps because they were engrossed in lengthy conversations.

The third and final information fed in by the teacher during this phase was: 'It seems that Mrs Jones came back into the village. Mr Jones got very drunk and killed her!' There was genuine consternation at this news by some of the 'villagers'. The teacher therefore added: 'I want you to discuss this but to be aware of the changed situation. How will its seriousness affect your attitude and how you talk about it? Pause for a moment before you start.'

The conversations that followed took place mostly in groups, in areas that had gradually, during the exercise, been established round the hall—for example, the pub, the post-office/general store. Discussion in role was in earnest at this stage.

*11.35 a.m.*

The teacher halted this phase of the lesson and called the group back into a circle to discuss and reflect on the experience. She led the discussion by asking questions to explore the attitudes that had arisen during the activity. The pupils readily contributed and became quickly involved. The teacher began to channel their responses towards a more general consideration of difficulties encountered in marriage with particular emphasis on the question of tolerance. The discussion was structured to coincide with the successive stages at which information had been fed in—for example, 'How did you react when . . . ?' Then, 'Do you all agree with that . . . ?' When she asked how individuals had reacted to the news that Mr Jones was frequently drunk, the pupils seemed even more involved and anxious to explore this area. At this stage the teacher was not only structuring the discussion, trying to bring in the non-contributors and keep the speakers balanced, she was also contributing to the discussion herself. Although the general reaction to the killing of Mrs Jones had been shock, in discussion the pupils attempted to try to understand Mr Jones' motives.

After some minutes the teacher cut short the discussion, apologizing that they would 'have to leave it there'. She summarized and then concluded, 'We all hear rumours from time to time and we tend to form opinions very quickly without knowing all the relevant information.' This led the teacher and class into the second part of the lesson. She asked them to consider the effects of this conclusion by exploring it in small groups, in their own ways. They had to choose the situation, characters and structure. No questions were asked. Having stipulated that they should divide into three groups, the teacher left them to organize themselves. The class split into groups as follows: (a) five girls/one boy; (b) three girls/three boys; (c) three girls/two boys.

*11.50 a.m.*
The groups started talking and listening to each other immediately. There was an atmosphere of quiet concentration in the hall. The teacher visited each group to make sure they knew what they had been asked to do and ᴛhen left them alone. She stood at the side of the room watching, and although she left the room for five minutes, it did not affect the pupils' working atmosphere.

*11.55 a.m.*
All three groups were actively involved in working out their ideas. They worked mostly in role, interspersed with general discussion to evaluate their progress and make comments about individual contributions. They worked unselfconsciously and, with the exception of one group who could not decide what to explore, without needing help from the teacher. An example of one group's work follows. This group were involved in a story about a young mother driven through desperation to death by her child's persistent crying. They had spent about half their time discussing this problem and finding a framework for it, before actively trying out their ideas. Once the story was established they tried to find some way of highlighting the different ways people might view her death and the judgements they might make. They decided that the funeral would provide the structure they needed but spent the rest of their time trying to resolve difficulties that arose as a result of choosing this particular symbol, as they used exaggerated gestures and felt embarrassed.

*12.20 p.m.*
The groups were tending to stop working out their ideas through acting-out and instead were discussing their work and the problems they were encountering. So at 12.25 p.m. the teacher called the class back together and asked each group to tell her what they had been doing and the results. In turn the groups described what they had explored and the problems they had encountered.

**Group a.** The situation involved a young mother whose baby cried all night. The mother became increasingly upset and nervous. Her friend called the doctor who prescribed sleeping tablets. The mother took a couple but still could not sleep through the baby's persistent crying. She eventually took an overdose and died. Having established this, Group a spent most time improvising the mother's funeral. They found it easy to decide on an idea that interested them but difficult to portray the emotions felt at the funeral.

**Group b.** This group's acting-out involved two men who were rivals for promotion. One secured the coveted job and the other became bitter and jealous. That night he met some friends in a pub and told them of his anger. They agreed to help avenge him. They invited the successful colleague for a drink and then went on to a party. They succeeded in getting him drunk and then photographed him in compromising situations with two girls. Later they used these photographs to blackmail him. He felt so desperate that he committed suicide. The group explained that they felt some embarrassment about the 'sex scene', and were worried that the rest of the class would laugh and not take it seriously if they presented it.

**Group c.** This group could not easily agree upon an idea and so tried two different ones. In one a man moved into town. He was very rich and owned a mansion and several cars. One of the town girls had a reputation for being flighty. The man did not know this and married her. He thought that she married him for love. The town thought she married for money. She really married him because she was pregnant. In the other situation, a girl went out one evening with her friends and they all got drunk. Later she was taken home by a boy and the result was she became pregnant. They married, but as a result of married life the girl lost touch with her old friends. This group were unhappy with both situations. Some members preferred the first; others, the second. They could find no satisfactory compromise to allow serious involvement in the work—although as individuals they all wanted it to work.

Between each group's report the teacher invited comments and questions from the rest of the class but encouraged consideration of the general problems groups encountered, such as embarrassment and the difficulty of portraying emotions, rather than specific comments relating to the chosen situations.

This final discussion lasted for twenty minutes and concluded the lesson.

## Analysis and assessment of the lesson

### WHAT SIGNIFICANT FACTORS AFFECTED LEARNING DURING THE LESSON?

The lesson was in two distinct parts. The first part, consisting of a game and exercise, was carefully controlled by the teacher who, although she allowed pupils to choose their own roles, set the situation and fed in information concerning it. After asking them to choose their roles, the teacher made sure they had all decided on their parts and were ready to begin. By asking them to talk to each other about their roles, they were able, through interaction, to project into their adopted roles and start to build upon them. When the teacher asked them to discuss what they had found out about each other, she helped them further establish their roles and confirm what they had learnt about each other.

The decisions that pupils were able to make within this part of the lesson were limited to choice of role and reacting to the information fed in by the teacher. This meant that the teacher was able to control their response to the specific information—the gradual unfolding of the unhappy saga of Mr and Mrs Jones. This was done to explore and experience the dangers of forming too hasty judgements based on partial truth or insufficient information. By discussing various aspects with them, she was able to focus their thoughts and make as conscious as possible their understanding of the experience. The teacher was concerned to guide them towards the realization that 'tolerance was necessary on both sides'. Children were encouraged to draw general conclusions from the particular experience of acting-out.

In the second part of the lesson, the teacher asked pupils to explore a problem from different angles, to move from general notions of tolerance to specific examples. The way that the class worked changed significantly. Emphasis was placed on how pupils used the process themselves. She allowed them to select their symbols and symbol structures, to explore the topic through situations of their own choosing, and to represent their understanding of problems in dramatic terms. They were responsible for working together as a group and learning to use the process for defining, representing and exploring their problems. With the exception of one group they also attempted to modify and elaborate their roles through acting-out various aspects of the situations they had chosen—for example, one group acted-out the pub scene in which a man voiced his fury at being turned down for a job in favour of someone else.

The discussion at the end of the lesson enabled groups to share their work with each other and to discuss their difficulties. This gave the teacher opportunities for making decisions about how she would present ideas for exploration in the future.

WERE THE TEACHER'S AIMS REALIZED? IF NOT, WHY NOT? One of the teacher's main aims was to encourage an understanding of tolerance and the dangers of forming hasty opinions through insufficient evidence, and to explore a problem by looking at it from different angles.

The pupils discussed the relationship of Mr and Mrs Jones after acting-out, particularly the reasons for their behaviour. To this extent they were trying to understand both husband and wife in the light of information received about them. It was not easy to discern from their discussion how tolerant they actually were about what Mr and Mrs Jones had done.

In the second part of the lesson, pupils were asked to explore problems from different angles. What actually happened was that some of them reached the stage of defining and representing a problem, perhaps from one person's angle. The nearest any group came to looking at a problem from different angles was the group who worked out different motives for a couple marrying each other.

The teacher also aimed to get the pupils to use the creative process to explore problems by themselves. This they did in the second part of the lesson. Because the class was divided into a number of groups and wanted privacy, it was not easy to observe what they were doing during exploration. It was possible to have some idea of how they were working through discussions at the end of the lesson. Although all groups were involved, not all of them reached the same states of development.

The first two groups progressed from defining and agreeing an area that interested them to selecting roles and a situation through which they could explore it. For instance, the first group selected the situation of a mother who was driven to suicide because of lack of sleep. The pupils tried to explore the implications for other people by acting-out the funeral scene. The second group worked on an idea of revenge where a man was photographed in a compromising position and then killed himself. They acted-out some parts of this but found difficulty in portraying the 'sex scene' without embarrassment. Had they had more knowledge of the use of the media they could have found alternative ways of representing this.

The third group found it difficult to select ideas in the first place. They were unable to resolve differences in deciding what to explore. Two of the group disliked the first idea and roles that were proposed. They stated this from the beginning and although they said they would try it out anyway, there was no real commitment and involvement. The group then returned to the beginning and tried to re-define the issues they were interested in and to select another structure. Unfortunately the same thing happened again—the group could not all identify with the proposed representation of the problem.

The teacher's other main aim, to develop a group feeling and an awareness of the problems of working together, was the result of previous frictions within the group. During both large- and small-group activities there was no overt sign of friction. One group did fail to reach agreement about what to explore. This may have been because of genuine difficulty in finding something which interested them all. This group, like the others, had treated their work seriously and were obviously keen to make a success of it. By discussing their problems concerning work at the end of the lesson, groups became aware of the general issues involved in learning to use the process.

WERE APPROPRIATE STRATEGIES USED FOR ACHIEVING AIMS AND INTENTIONS? In the first part of the session the teacher attempted to deepen children's understanding by progressively feeding in information about the Jones family. By channelling the discussion, it was possible to encourage feelings of compassion towards both of them.

The reason why children failed to examine problems from different angles was twofold. First, the teacher failed to suggest how this could have been done. Secondly, even if pupils had had suggestions, it is unlikely that they could have carried them out. Within the time given, even the most experienced groups would not have been able to work on more than one problem. Had the teacher placed great importance on achieving this aim, she could have spent less time on the first part of the lesson and more time on this aspect.

In the second part of the session they were given about thirty-five minutes to work out problems by themselves. The only time the teacher intervened at this point was to help the group who could not reach agreement.

By starting the lesson with the whole class working together under her direction, the teacher was able to do a number of things. She was able to see that every individual was working by having to react to her instructions. By feeding information, each child was able to have a common reference point with the others. This mean: that they could all have their discussion on the same experience. By leading them into the work, the teacher helped them think seriously about the issue discussed so that they could start working on their own with positive attitudes. It is possible that the first part encouraged group feeling, but if her main aim was to unify the class she might have developed work in such a way that they achieved things together. As it was, each child in a role reacted with some other members to the information she provided. The second part of the lesson was concerned with small-group work where she achieved her aim of encouraging the group to create their own problems.

It is interesting to note that the first part of the lesson was longer than the second and to see how the first experience influenced the second. Through the first the teacher channelled activities towards more understanding of the Jones family, by giving information and directing discussions. Conclusions were reached about tolerance and the importance of basing judgements on information. How did this serve as a stimulus/barrier for small-group work? It is true that after acting-out and discussion, groups started work seriously. One wonders, however, whether it was really necessary for the second part of the lesson or whether a short discussion could have done as well. The main effect the first acting-out seemed to have on group work was in their choice of content. For instance, both groups one and two chose suicide.

The teacher's decisions concerning content (a wife running away and a drunken husband who murdered her) influenced the children's own work. Her positive relationship with her pupils meant that they were able to be frank with her and the rest of the class about their difficulties in exploring the problems. A working atmosphere was created in which children could freely discuss their own work in an objective manner and consider some of the implications of the relationships they were exploring. Through discussion the teacher was able to deepen their understanding of the issues involved and to help them become more aware of the kinds of demand made on them when using the process. The teacher was actively involved during discussions and for the first part of the lesson. She intervened only once in the second part when her help was needed. How did these decisions affect the quality of the work?

WERE APPROPRIATE STRATEGIES USED BY THE TEACHER FOR IMPROVING THE QUALITY OF THE WORK? During the first few minutes when the villager-game was played, the teacher apologized for the superficial nature of the work. The children were then asked to elaborate on their roles by working within a defined context—what each character would be doing on a Saturday morning. At that stage the characters being portrayed were mainly stereotyped with exaggerated accents. The teacher injected the information that Mrs Jones had left her husband, thus providing pupils with a chance to assume attitudes which were then modified and changed with each additional piece of news. Although responses were different each time, because the information was sensational and because the children mainly played stereotypes, reactions tended to be crude. For the teacher's purposes, it was not essential at that stage to produce work of quality. She merely intended to illustrate her point that attitudes would be affected by the information people have. The teacher took this point further and more seriously through discussion rather than exploiting the possibilities that other ways of acting-out might have offered. The role of the teacher then changed. She took little or no part in subsequent work and therefore took no direct steps to improve the quality of each group's acting-out which varied from group to group. However, all groups worked with a sense of commitment and quiet concentration. All were concerned with using the process for the task they had been given. Most of their time was spent in establishing a structure through discussion rather than in acting-out. One group did not get further than this. Having decided on storylines, the other groups experienced difficulties in finding adequate forms of representation. For instance, the group who wanted to explore different responses to the mother's suicide, found it difficult to portray emotions at the funeral. They had started by using exaggerated gestures that did not convey the real feelings of each character. Had the teacher wished to intervene rather than allowing them to work on the problem on their own, she could either have suggested ways in which they could have represented the funeral differently, or suggested that they did more work on building up details about each character and their relationships. None of the groups felt they had explored the idea in a satisfying way. This might have been because of insufficient time, their state of development in terms of acting-out, or because the children were more used to exploring through discussion than through acting-out. Because of the commitment and sense of purpose with which pupils worked, the teacher was provided with a good basis for enabling them to extend their use of the process in the future.

WHAT WAS THE VALUE OF THE LESSON? Although questions could be raised concerning the teacher's choice of subject (runaway wife, murderous, drunken, husband) and the difficulties for children of tackling emotionally charged situations, the lesson was valuable for several reasons: it allowed pupils to consider the complexities of emotional responses; it gave children the opportunity of using the process in exploring problems of their own choosing; it showed they were influenced by the teacher's initial choice of content. Because there was an emphasis on discussion, opportunities for using dramatic forms of expression were not fully explored. However, through discussion, the teacher was able to assess how groups worked together, what they had achieved within the process during that session. She decided to give them a variety of ways for developing the process for themselves so that they could be conscious of what it involved to work constructively together.

HOW COULD JUDGEMENTS MADE ABOUT THE SESSION AFFECT THE PLANNING OF FUTURE WORK? The teacher's attitude at the end of the lesson made it clear that she placed importance on how group members worked together. 'The main learning area arose out of the conflicts they experienced in the improvisations. Most of these related to problems of working together. The obvious course as the lesson developed, was to confront these face-on. The discussions threw out a great deal of useful information about the way the group relates to each other. Whatever specific problems they are currently experiencing they do seem to have the will to overcome them. My task is to help them do this by finding various approaches to drama which might facilitate this.'

## Lesson 3: Dangerous gas

The school, originally a mixed 11 to 16 secondary modern, is in the process of changing to a 13 to 18 comprehensive. The school is situated in a working-class urban industrial area and has an intake of approximately 940 children. Drama is taught within an English department. Most second- and third-year pupils receive one forty-minute lesson per week. In the fourth year drama is offered as a

CSE option to examination bands only. The third band, a non-examination class, receives one afternoon of drama per week as part of a general option. This class is of eight fourteen- to fifteen-year-old boys from the top two bands. (Most pupils in the school take CSE examinations.) One eighty-minute lesson is given every Thursday morning—forty minutes before and after a fifteen-minute break. Another eighty-minute lesson is given on Wednesdays (2.0-3.20 p.m.). The drama space is a large, bare classroom with blinds for black-out. It was converted during the summer holidays from an old science laboratory. There is some equipment within the department and some in the central school pool. There is very little lighting—only a couple of spots on stands. There is a limited costume cupboard.

## The class

One of the reasons why the drama option group was so small was its position in the option list. Many girls had shown interest in taking drama but it clashed with the only secretarial and clerical courses. Although all of the eight boys had worked with this teacher in the past, they first worked as a group in September.

One of the most striking features observed when visiting this school was the reluctance of the pupils to speak out in class. When they started drama in September, the teacher's overall aim therefore was to encourage these boys to believe in themselves and realize that they had something to say. In September his questions were often met with silence or nods. Boys sat with heads bowed, looked at their feet and, with the exception of one boy, only answered directly if asked by name. When they spoke they tended to mumble and show considerable lack of confidence.

Their general attitude towards the teacher and authority was expressed by one of the boys: 'Well, he's the teacher, en't he! He knows best.' In discussion, they explained to the observer that sometimes they wished that they could use a few swear words, 'because it's more natural like' and it meant that they were not always having consciously to check their words before they spoke to the teacher. Not only were the boys reluctant to speak to the teacher but, in comparison with the other schools in the project, they did not speak much to each other. The teacher's aim was for the group to create something on their own and to make decisions. He intended that individuals should select and adopt a role from a choice of role cards; and that they should make collective decisions within definite constraints.

## The lesson

*2.00 p.m.*
As usual the group entered the room quietly and without fuss. The drama

room had been recently converted from a science laboratory and therefore was basically a bare space with blinds and a costume cupboard. But on this occasion the boys were surprised to discover a considerable amount of sound and visual equipment set out in an elaborate design in preparation for their lesson. They peered cautiously at the equipment, gathered together and generally spoke in whispers.

After a brief chat to try to make the boys more at ease, the teacher explained their first task: 'I'm going to give you some cards that represent people. Look through all of them and then choose one that you would like to be.' He dropped the cards on the floor adding, 'By some mutual agreement you must each end up with one card.'

**Alan:** Are they real people?

**Teacher:** Why should I answer that?

The boys picked up the cards and stood forming a close circle. They read the role cards silently and passed them round. There were a few quiet comments to each other as the circle of boys grew tighter and tighter. There was no argument over the choice of cards; each boy found one that he preferred.

At this stage the teacher defined their second task: 'Now that you've decided on your role, go round the room and collect items of clothing or make things that fix that identity. You have ten to fifteen minutes.'

There were no questions although the teacher told them to ask if there was anything that they wanted or did not understand. Everyone seemed to understand. Alan, as usual, was the first person to make a move. He went to the cupboard and started to rummage; the others followed. Some concentrated on adapting costumes, others began to make props. Everyone was working quietly at something. They did not discuss what they were doing, although a couple of times one boy asked another to hold something while he fixed sticky tape to it. They only spoke to each other when they needed help.

The teacher stood at the side of the room watching and waiting. He tried to find things to do. 'It would probably be far easier when looking for things if you pulled them all out of the cupboard.' No answer. He went over and pulled lots of costumes out. The boys continued working silently. The teacher found a conical-shaped piece of cardboard resembling a hat. He went over and dropped it on Pete's table.

**Pete:** I'm making one.

**Teacher:** It'll save time.

Peter used it. The teacher reminded the class of the limited time they had.

It was now possible to see what some of the boys were making. Alan, whose role-card said 'Medical Consultant', had made a circular band for his head with a light on the front out of cardboard and cellophane. He had also made a stethoscope out of string and paper. Bob, whose card said 'Military Officer', was changing the colour of a white-peaked cap that he had found in the cupboard, by fixing black crepe paper over it with sticky tape. Paul was frustrated, because he was unhappy with his costume. He began asking different people if they could help him. Part of the description on Paul's role card was 'Visiting Foreign Research Scientist'. He had decided to be an Arab, but he could not get the headwear correct and spent ages tying and re-tying white sheets round his head. The other

boys tried to help but had no luck either. In the end as the time ran out
Paul put the costume away and worked without any props.
*2.17 p.m.*
The teacher, seeing that most were ready, asked them to stand quietly and
think about the person on their card. The instructions on the role-cards
that the boys had been given were as follows:
Bob: Military Officer—Brigadier General; A. N. Smith, commander of
the special unit administering gas and germ warfare; special work and
training with ZxmNo 3214AH (the gas in question).
Alan: Dr G.N.Jones, Medical Consultant on the effects and treatment of
gas/germ warfare when it attacks victims.
Pete: Government Scientist, working on the development and eventual
uses and controls of gas ZxmNo 3214AH.
Brian: A Miner, eye-witness to the effects of previous outbreaks of the gas
in question.
Paul: Visiting Foreign Research Scientist from the gas/germ warfare
department.
Keith: Personal Military Escort to Foreign Visitor.
   Two boys were away and the two cards that were not chosen were:
Secretary of State for Defence and Official Chauffeur to the state
authorities.
   While the boys stood thinking about their roles, the teacher spoke to
them: 'Now put on, wear or carry the thing you've made and get together
in that corner. When you're ready we'll start, or should I say continue.'
The teacher switched on a green spotlight then approached the boys in a
role. 'If you're ready, gentlemen, do be seated at the table.' The table was
laid with pencils, water, glasses and scribbling pads. They did so while the
teacher went to the projector and tape recorder.
   A slide of rolling moorland was projected on to a screen at one end of
the room. As the boys turned to look at this, the tape-recorded voice of the
teacher, in role, as Head of State, spoke to them and introduced the people
round the table. The boys nodded and smiled during this. The information
they were given was as follows: 'Gentlemen, you are gathered together
today because of your expertise in a very specialist and dangerous
field—germ warfare. It has come to light that somehow gas is escaping
from our top secret defence gas plant and scientific research headquarters,
in the north of the territory. Whether due to espionage, foreign infiltration
or merely old equipment, I need not stress the gravity of the situation, or
its implications—if it continues—to the community as a whole. In spite of
the fact that I am absent, attending a conference on world defence in
Geneva, I would urge you to act with all speed to remedy the situation'.
*2.25 p.m.*
The tape ended and the boys, sitting round the table, began acting-out.
Bob, the Military Officer and Alan, the Medical Consultant, contributed
most and took most initiative. The group spent some time trying to define
the exact problem—for example, 'the gas is polluting the rivers'; 'it's
affecting agricultural areas'. Sometimes statements were made, at other
times questions were asked such as 'How can you recognize the effects of
this gas?'; 'How dangerous is it?' Gradually, Bob assumed a leadership
role although strongly challenged by Alan. Brian tried to contribute but
was to some extent blocked. When he said he had seen something that

might have been 'a UFO', Bob immediately retorted: 'I'm sorry, I can't accept that.' After this Brian found it difficult to get into the conversation. The others contributed to a varying extent, except Keith who said nothing.

After five minutes the teacher entered the conference area and delivered a note. It read: 'A lot more people have been affected. Colour patterns have been noted. Your help is needed. Go to the observation post.' Bob now took charge and told everyone to go to the observation post. The teacher had set up an oil slide on the projector. These moving colours were accompanied by a low hum/drone on the tape recorder. At the same time the teacher intr duced a chemical which gave off an unpleasant odour.

The boys watched and discussed the slide in terms of 'one gas attacking another'. Alan, the doctor, went up to the screen and examined it closely with his stethoscope. He picked up a can—on the window-sill—and took the lid off very slowly and carefully. Returning to the group, he told them they should all stay away from the area. Bob reacted strongly: 'You mean you went there. You're mad!' Then, to the others: 'Get away from him'. From this point onwards Alan was excluded from the conference—he sat alone in the observation post. The others returned to the table. At the conference table the boys continued discussing the problem although they were no nearer to suggesting a plan of action. The teacher sent in another note to encourage them to arrive at a plan. It said: 'More trouble in the north. Have you got a plan?' They had not got a plan but Bob took further control and ordered that no one must leave the country.

Alan interrupted their conversations with a coughing fit, reminding them that he was still there. At first he was ignored but after a while Paul and another boy went over to him. Brian also left the table and went to the end of the room on his own. The teacher approached him and gave him a note which he took back to the table. The note read: 'People are dying while you sit around chatting.' Bob reacted angrily at this: 'I know that! But what do you expect me to do!' Paul and the other boy returned and announced that they were all now infected and that the doctor was dead. It was decided they needed to find an antidote to the poisonous gas quickly and moved to the end of the room where they started to carry out experiments. The area became a laboratory.

*2.45 p.m.*
The teacher stopped them and the group discussed the work. He asked for their comments and offered some himself. Their comments ranged from, 'We're not getting anywhere' to 'If we had time we could have worked plans out'. They discussed difficulties that arose—for example, 'The miner caused us a problem, he would not be there'. One boy was worried that he could not drop his accent, so that 'it didn't sound right'. The discussion lasted fifteen minutes and ended with the teacher suggesting that they go back to the beginning, but this time meet each other as people, rather than experts, before the conference starts.

*3.00 p.m.*
They started acting-out again. They followed the teacher's suggestion and then went into the conference room. Bob assumed chairmanship from the start, even taking it upon himself to introduce everybody. This time, however, the dialogue was quite different. Bob defined the problem straight away but was then strongly challenged by Alan, supported by some of the others, so that in effect Bob was being accused of negligence.

They were suggesting that it was his fault that the gas had escaped and attacked him for this. Conversation was fast and tense and most people were involved.

*3.10 p.m.*

The teacher stopped them and told them to write down their 'version of what happened, without discussing it'. Having done so the boys were asked to read their statements out. After this the teacher quickly summarized. He asked them if they thought that their written statements provided a starting-point for continuing the work next time. They thought so. The boys had to hurry off to mid-afternoon registration, but returned later to help clear the room.

## *Analysis and assessment of the lesson*

WHAT SIGNIFICANT FACTORS AFFECTED LEARNING DURING THE LESSON? This lesson was structured differently from the other two lessons as the teacher set up an environment for the pupils using visual and sound equipment. He also gave pupils defined roles to play. Before they started acting-out, he asked them to spend ten to fifteen minutes to 'fix (their) identity' by devising props or costumes for their roles. This allowed them to think about the kinds of roles they would play and to identify with them by using physical symbols.

The teacher role-played at the beginning of the session. As Head of State he defined the problem—escaping gas—and gave them the task of dealing with it. The slides and smell gave a tangible frame of reference upon which to base work; useful for them if they found it difficult to project into 'as if' situations, especially one demanding use of information. Because the teacher role-played, he was able to participate in the acting-out and intervene to speed activities up without breaking concentration by stopping the activity.

The pupils had to use their roles and develop them within clearly defined constraints. This meant that they had to select and develop what was significant to them from the stimuli they had been given. They then made decisions about what to do. This was different from the structured work in the second lesson where the teacher wanted to modify children's attitudes. In this lesson pupils were encouraged to define further how and in what ways the gas was dangerous so that they could devise ways of dealing with it. They were also able to develop relationships between the different roles in such a way that it affected their tackling of the problem—for example, during the last ten minutes the doctor accused the Military Officer of negligence.

WERE THE TEACHER'S AIMS REALIZED? IF NOT, WHY NOT? WERE APPROPRIATE STRATEGIES USED FOR ACHIEVING AIMS AND INTENTIONS? The teacher's main aim was 'for the group to create something on their own and make decisions'. This seems an odd aim in view of the fact that pupils were not given full responsibility for defining their own roles and were given a specific problem, of escaping gas, to solve. This means that they were only able to 'create something on their own and make decisions' within the strict limitations imposed by the teacher. Had the teacher wanted to fulfil his aims completely, he should have allowed the children to find their own areas of exploration.

The pupils were, however, able to make certain decisions within the constraints set by the teacher. They could elaborate—for example, they decided after looking at the slides that two gases were attacking each other. Individuals, in particular Alan (the Medical Consultant) and Bob (the Military Officer), took decisions about the development of the situation. Bob organized the meeting and gave instructions about what to do. Alan picked up a tin, pretended to be contaminated and died. This provoked consternation among other members of the group who eventually started a laboratory to counteract the effects of the gas. The teacher intervened on occasions to influence the course of action. Twice he gave them written instructions to speed work up and once he stopped and restarted work so that pupils would consider their roles in more depth.

If the teacher's aims were for the children to create something on their own, why did he take such an active part in their work? A possible reason was that these particular children found it difficult to project into imagined situations. The teacher gave them a starting-point by providing them with a structure. In addition, they did not find it easy to communicate verbally, either with the teacher present, or among themselves. Pupils were able to respond within the security of roles the teacher gave them. They also had a problem to solve so that they were given a sense of destination without which they may have floundered.

WERE APPROPRIATE STRATEGIES USED FOR IMPROVING THE QUALITY OF THE WORK? One of the teacher's tasks was to involve the boys so that they would be committed to developing the drama. He did this by providing them with a visual, sound and physical environment, as well as using costumes and props. Before acting-out started, he asked them to stand quietly and think about their roles. This gave them the opportunity to have something upon which to base their role-playing with the exception of Keith who found that his role as the Military Escort contributed nothing to the situation.

The teacher gave them the idea of escaping gas and throughout the acting-out tried to instill a sense of urgency. 'I need not stress the gravity of the situation.' At first the boys further elaborated on what the problem was and suggested ways in which it affected the environment—for example, polluting the rivers.

At this point, the way that pupils were responding to each other affected the quality of the acting-out. Two boys started competing for leadership. One boy, Keith, did nothing and Brian as the Miner found his ideas were being blocked and became less committed to participating. The teacher then intervened with the message that more people were affected and made the experience more vivid through the slides and smell. This increased the urgency and stimulated more action.

The first real moment of tension occurred when Alan, the Medical Consultant, picked up a tin and Bob, the Military Officer, insisted that he be isolated. They were still at a loss about what to do and were becoming uneasy so that the teacher provided another note urging them to make a plan. They were still stuck when Alan had a coughing fit and attracted Paul and the other boy's attention. Brian wandered away and Keith did nothing. The acting-out became fragmented and some of the pupils started losing attention. The teacher intervened by bringing Brian back with a note. Alan then died and Paul and the other boy contributed by saying that they too were infected and that something needed to be done. At that stage they decided to create a laboratory and conduct experiments. The danger of the gas had become significant enough to them to want to remedy it, but not without constant help from the teacher.

The teacher was not satisfied with their sense of commitment and stopped activities to discuss work. Reactions were mixed with discontent, 'we're not getting anywhere', to a request for more time to solve the problem. One boy was unhappy because he could not produce an appropriate accent for the role he was playing and Keith said that his role as Military Escort was not relevant so that he felt that he could not participate. The teacher then attempted to deepen involvement by asking them to start again more as people, rather than experts.

In the next ten minutes the content of acting-out changed from attempts to define the gravity of the situation to interpersonal conflicts between the characters involved. Most of the boys were involved with the confrontation between the Medical Consultant and the Military Officer, who was accused of starting the problem. Discussion was intense reflecting a greater quality of involvement. This could only have happened as a result of the build-up of detail and urgency throughout the lesson. Had the teacher encouraged them to do more work on the personalities behind the roles they were taking at the beginning of the lesson, they might have been involved earlier on.

WHAT WAS THE VALUE OF THE LESSON? A lesson such as this is useful in exploring the human implications of developments in science such as germ warfare or actual cases of pollution. By closely structuring the lesson, the teacher gave children a secure base from which to work. Through distancing themselves in role they were able to explore relationships within the group. The teacher allowed enough scope for them to make their own decisions within the situation. This meant that he could observe how individuals responded and the extent to which he could allow them to make decisions for themselves in the future.

HOW COULD JUDGEMENTS MADE ABOUT THE LESSON AFFECT THE PLANNING OF FUTURE WORK? At the end of the lesson most of these children were involved. This gave them a secure basis to work hypothetically. The teacher would in the future use a similar kind of structure and build on the level of involvement achieved in this lesson. The written statements at the end of the lesson could serve as a basis for reminding the boys next time what they had achieved in the last lesson.

The question of individual contributions is an important consideration in work like this. The teacher was able to observe what was happening at real as well as symbolic levels; it was possible that Alan and Bob were using symbolic roles to work out real power struggles. Keith made no contributions at all. In the future the teacher could ensure a greater involvement on the part of the more passive members of the group by giving them tasks or roles of greater significance.

# Conclusions

These three lessons have been described and analysed in some detail. Several factors have been taken into account: the kinds of learning that were encouraged and achieved; the quality of the work and whether teachers used appropriate strategies and methods to achieve their ends. The value of each session was discussed in the light of how future work could be developed.

Because there are as many criteria for success as there are lessons, it is not possible to give an exhaustive list of factors to be taken into account by every teacher. By describing three lessons, only a few aspects of the process have been examined. The following questions, in addition to those already asked, could form a basis for teachers who may wish to make a more detailed assessment of their pupils' and their own work. They are intended as a starting-point for teachers, who ought also to be able to devise their own questions relating to their own interests, criteria and ways of working. All or some of the following questions could be relevant to a teacher at a given time depending on what activities are and have been taking place.

## 1. Aims and intentions: the role of the teacher

What kinds of learning are being emphasized/developed?
How clear are aims/intentions?

Does the lesson structure allow meaning to be negotiated, in terms of the kinds of learning being encouraged?

Is the teacher sufficiently flexible to use unexpected learning possibilities when they occur?

What kinds of roles can the teacher play to achieve aims or improve the quality of the work?

## 2. Exploration, representation and negotiation of meaning through acting-out

(a) STATES OF READINESS. What are the states of development of the pupils? Do they have the necessary prerequisites for acting-out?

(b) CONTENT. Do pupils find the content significant? How committed are they to exploring certain content?

If children have chosen their own content, is the teacher taking into account the kinds of meaning they are trying to express?

Is he satisfied with the quality of the meaning explored? Is it superficial? Does it need to be deepened, challenged or changed?

What kinds of understanding have children gained through acting-out? Have they explored ways of extending this understanding as fully as possible?

(c) DEVELOPMENT OF ROLES AND SITUATION. When asked to create roles or characters, are children aware of the exact nature of the task being set—for example, whether they are expected to explore particular topics or issues, or to work towards developing the personalities of certain characters.

How aware is the teacher of each individual's capacity for creating roles? What help can be given?

If teachers give children specific roles to play, have they taken the particular personalities and needs of the children into account?

How is meaning being negotiated and unfolded at both real and symbolic levels?

What aspects of the process are being focused upon—for example, definition of content; selection, modification, elaboration and shaping of ideas; finding satisfactory forms of expression etc?

What components may need attention at any one time? Do these need different activities or changes in the role of the teacher?

(d) USE OF THE MEDIA. Are pupils aware of the variety of media they can use in representing meaning? How far does their knowledge and control of the media extend? Are they impeded by lack of necessary physical and verbal skills or knowledge of the possibilities of different media?

Is the teacher able to recognize and provide what is needed at a given time?

(e) FORMS OF EXPRESSION. Are the children aware of a range of modes/styles through which meaning can be represented?

If children are finding it difficult to express their ideas, can they be helped in the search for clarifying those ideas and finding alternative forms of representation?

Are children able to shape their ideas into an overall coherent form? How relevant is it for them to do so? Are they ready or willing to do this?

(f) NEGOTIATION OF MEANING THROUGH SOCIAL INTERACTION. Is the teacher aware of relationships within groups—for example, whether there are conflicts? If real relationships are hindering work, how can work be developed on a symbolic level?

(g) PRESENTATION. If children are acting-out to an audience, is the teacher sure that they are ready or willing to do so? How will children benefit by performing in front of an audience?

## 3. The pupils' perceptions

So far these questions have been directed at the teacher. There are, however, occasions when it might be useful for the teacher to ask pupils questions about their responses and what they gained from the session. It is suggested that the following kinds of questions, worded appropriately, together with the teacher's own questions based on the lesson, might give additional indications of the value of the session for the pupils:

What did you think the session was about?

What do you remember most about the session? Why?

When were you most involved? How?

When were you least involved? Why?

What kinds of contributions did you think *you* made?

What did you feel about working in this way with other people?

Did you find any part of the session difficult or impossible to do? Why?

What for you was the value of the session, if any?

Any other comments/suggestions?

As assessment which is jointly arrived at by both pupils and teachers is doubly advantageous: it allows the teacher to understand his pupils better; and it gives pupils a greater commitment to and responsibility for further work. The point to aim for is a position where pupils and teacher work as a team in assessment and evaluation.

# Conclusions

Not only can drama be assessed, but conscious assessment and evaluation is useful if both teacher's and pupils' work is to improve. Questions can be asked and answered about standards of work on a number of levels; whether adequate attempts are being made to stretch and challenge the pupils and deepen understanding and exploration in many ways. This can be done by the teacher having knowledge of how the process works and the state of development of his pupils. He needs to know what components of the process may need particular attention at any time. It is suggested that in considering criteria for assessment, it is up to the teacher to be clear about his own aims and intentions and to be able to make informed judgements in the light of them. The three lessons discussed in detail show that each lesson can only be analysed in its own terms. None of the lessons given was an example of a model lesson. They should be seen as part of an overall programme of a normal teacher's work in terms of a continuous attempt to achieve certain kinds of learning and development through drama.

# Chapter 6
# Long-Term Development through Drama

In the last chapter three drama sessions were analysed. The lessons were part of an ongoing programme for each individual teacher and his class. Rather than discussing individual sessions, this chapter will be concerned with what children can achieve when they experience the drama process over a period of time. In considering this, the following questions will be raised: Can generalizations be made about development in particular age-groups? What general comments can be made about long-term development in drama? What can children be reasonably expected to achieve through sustained experience in drama? What kinds of development might teachers work towards?

Because there are so many variables there are no hard and fast rules for development from the age of ten to sixteen. For any statement to be made on differences in development as a result of age, long-term research would need to be undertaken in which account is taken of contemporary theories of child development. Nevertheless it is possible to make some remarks about general features of development which appear to emerge between ten and sixteen, which teachers might take into account when planning work. These are based on teachers' comments about their pupils, and statements they made about the kind of work they would attempt with different age-groups.

At the ages of ten and eleven children tend to be less self-conscious about their work and to use unstructured drama as part of their normal play. They are extremely flexible physically and able to do a range of movement with ease that older children find difficult. But although they are able to project into situations, it is unusual to see forms of characterization that are not crude or stereotyped. As children get older and bigger they may become self-conscious in their physical movements. By the time they are thirteen some children are reluctant to do movement at all because they feel embarrassed. This of course depends upon previous experience in such work.

Until about the age of thirteen, children are interested in the story lines of plots and in working within them. By the time they reach the age of twelve and thirteen there is an increased awareness of how they relate to others. There is also an increased interest in subjects such as authority and sex. By the time children are fourteen to fifteen many are becoming more critical about the kinds of work which the teacher is asking of them. There is also an increased tendency for older children to be more objective in the way they analyse their own and the teacher's work. By the time they are sixteen they are more aware of their possible roles in the outside world and become even more conscious about how they, as individuals, appear to other people when expressing their feelings and ideas. They have a more complex notion of reality than the ten-year-old and this is often reflected in the complex way they portray characters, or in the depth of their exploration.

The point here is that if teachers are aware that children are going through certain developmental stages they can take this into account when structuring sessions. For instance, a teacher need not be too worried about failure to do movement exercises with a group of thirteen- to fourteen-year-olds if he realizes that they feel physically awkward and self-conscious. If he has discipline problems with a group of adolescents, it might help him to realize that they might be at the stage where they are questioning authority and that it might not necessarily be him who is at fault. If the teacher recognizes certain aspects of development, he is able to make possible for pupils the exploration of issues that they are personally involved in.

Generalizations about the kind of content used by teachers for different age-groups are equally difficult to make. A wide variety of suggestions were given by teachers, including simple stimuli for acting-out, fairy stories and myths and problems either relating to the family or to outside life. Script reading was used across the age-range as was the performance of plays. But as might be expected, sixteen-year-olds were more likely to be given adult scripts, both modern and traditional, than the younger age-group who more frequently used characters from myths and fairy stories. As children grew older, their teachers seemed to focus more on personal and family problems and issues of wider social significance. However, exceptions were always found to these broad tendencies.

What needs to be asked is how do questions about development apply to actual classes and particular age-groups? In considering the long-term development of particular classes two main factors need to be taken into account. The first is that not all children reach the same stages of development in drama. These are determined by factors such as age, ability, states of readiness for drama, previous experience and the amount of time and facilities available for drama. The second factor is that over a period of a year or two, if pupils have the same teacher, most pupils are likely to develop more along some lines than others. This depends on their teacher's specific aims regarding drama and whether they emphasize the development of certain aspects of the process more than others.

The problems of discussing development in terms of age arise from the fact that most children begin drama at different times in their lives. One drama teacher stated: 'The fixing of limits to the initial levels of experience is not arbitrarily related to chronological age, since the main aim of early activity is to introduce a new way of working: to provide security and an opportunity for easy involvement, two features of drama work relevant at any age.'

In starting with the class the teacher needs to be aware of the particular strengths, abilities and weaknesses of the pupils he is working with. For instance, a group of lively ten-year-olds might be able to go into flights of fantasy, and work without deepening their understanding in any significant way. If he wishes to rectify this, the teacher might have to start with more structured work to channel their activities into work with specific learning potential. On the other hand, a teacher could start with a group of intelligent fifteen-year-olds who have never done drama. They may be intellectually capable of formulating complex ideas and expressing them verbally but not have enough skills to express themselves through drama. They may be too physically inhibited to represent characters or roles adequately. The teacher may need to break down their physical and social inhibitions and attempt exercises or games requiring a spontaneous response before going on to more exacting work.

Once teachers have decided on their pupils' states of development—that is, where to begin—they can then channel children's work into particular kinds of learning by developing appropriate programmes of work over a period of time. The following two examples illustrate ways in which some pupils developed during a school year. The first example is of work in a primary school with ten eleven-year-olds, in which drama is seen as part of a general school experience. The second example with fourteen-year-olds shows how a teacher uses a variety of ways of working to develop a dramatic statement with the pupils which is then presented to members of the public. Both examples show different kinds of development as a result of the differences in teacher emphasis and pupil variables.

# Development in a class of eleven-year-olds in a primary school

## The school

The school was a central urban primary school. It was a red brick nineteenth-century building but had a cheerful atmosphere because of the way that teachers had arranged their classrooms. The predominant occupations of parents in the school catchment area were semi-skilled/skilled manual and unskilled manual. The most usual form of accommodation was a mixture of one-roomed or two-roomed flats or tenement flats.

All classes were unstreamed. In addition, within a class there was a slight difference in ages as children start school at different times of the year. Each teacher taught the same class in the older age-range for two years to ensure maximum continuity.

The drama teacher thought that the school aimed to teach as much literacy as possible' as well as 'to give the child an all-round education'. Timetabling of subjects was mainly the teacher's own choice although availability of the hall determined when more free activities could occur.

## The teacher

This teacher had ten years' teaching experience, and had been teaching at the school for five years. She was teacher-trained with drama as a specialism and had also completed an ADB Ed. course. (A professional in-service training course in drama run by the Drama Board of Great Britain. See pp. 199-201.) She was the only trained drama teacher in the school. Her main task was as a general teacher to her form. The amount of drama she taught was therefore limited. She also taught two classes of eleven-year-olds for one hour each week and a class of eight- to eleven-year-olds once a week.

As a general teacher, she saw drama as part of the pupils' general activities. She felt that there were many links with other subjects, for example, history or literature, that could stimulate drama. Drama in turn could feed back into writing or painting. Her drama methods were a mixture of movement, small- and whole-group work, with her occasionally role-playing. Vocabulary development and discussion played a large part in lessons as well. She usually started each class with movement—awareness of the body, space and weight—as well as building up trust, etc,, through physical contact. She felt this form of work was useful in building up concentration as well. In very general terms she thought that drama encouraged pupils 'to approach each other in a more co-operative way'. Drama could be useful in improving the child's vocabulary. In this sense, in the encouragement of oracy, she did not feel that the aims of drama were different from that of any other subject, which generally had to do with the development of the individual. Where drama did make a special contribution was in the field of 'social relationships' where co-operative group relationships could be encouraged. The use of movement was valuable for children's physical development.

In drama, she saw herself primarily as an 'introducer of ideas' but thought that children ought to be encouraged to extend their ideas and 'make things go deeper'. This meant helping children to be more 'thoughtful about what they were doing'. She also thought that it was more important to encourage children sometimes to practise what they were doing so that they could experience working towards perfecting something.

## The class

The class was of mixed ability. There was a large proportion of immigrant children, some with language problems. This was their final year at primary school. This teacher had been with them already for a year. They had therefore had a year's drama experience with her.

## Space for drama

The hall which was used doubled as dining-room. It had a number of other purposes, and was used for gym and movement by classes in the school. Classrooms led into the hall so that when lessons took place, there were constant interruptions and much external noise. The teacher felt that she would have benefited from an extra space which was only used for drama and movement, so that pupils could be freer than they were as they had to be quiet in the hall.

## Examples of work done over the year

During the first term, the teacher explored the theme of the Industrial Revolution. She did this in a number of ways including television programmes, books, writing, discussion, and pictures and documents on the walls. Drama was seen as one among many methods of investigation. Work included the creation of machines through movement, sound and art work. Attempts were made to 'understand the effects of machinery on a village way of life'. The children, armed with background knowledge, acted-out as villagers a situation in which they reacted to the arrival of a new weaving machine. The sessions ended with a meeting in which they agreed to give the machine a chance. The next series of lessons concerned exploring the 'effect of migration to the city'. In family groups children tried to persuade their parents to let them go to the city. They then explored the problems of finding accommodation and the kinds of rules landlords might impose on tenants.

In the second term they explored concepts of 'struggle and achievement'. Work included an examination of the case of Christie Brown, a cripple who learnt to paint with his feet. Children tried to paint pictures with their feet and mouths and then did group and individual movement work involving differences between struggle and achievement—for example, overcoming physical obstacles. The idea of overcoming obstacles interested the children so that the teacher played a detective who was frustrated in solving a crime because of confusing evidence fed in by the children. Later work concerned exploring differences between turbulence and peace through contrasting movements. The theme of war was considered and children were given photographs of various people and asked to act-out situations suggested by them. Some were statesmen arguing for war and others were victims. Discussion in role played a large part in acting-out.

Work in the third term included working on the story of Theseus and the Minotaur in a number of ways. Children in family groups talked about the possibilities of being chosen as sacrifices. A meeting was acted-out in which discussions were held about the criteria that could be used in choosing victims. In another lesson, the killing of the Minotaur was represented in movement.

### Kinds of development in the class over the year

The teacher's impression was that generally 'children were able to take what they were doing further over a longer period of time and to work upon ways of improving their work.' From the project's observations over a year the teacher seemed to achieve development in three main fields: movement; abstract conceptualization; and the ability to conduct reasonable and imaginative discussions. Her main emphasis seemed to be that of exploring social and cultural themes—for example, the differences between landlords and tenants and the story of Theseus and the Minotaur—and within that, of increasing children's involvement through acting-out and giving them circumstances in which to explore and develop their use of language, physical as well as verbal.

### Development in movement

Almost all her classes started with movement. At the beginning of the year she concentrated on trust exercises—for example, children supporting each other, mirroring each other's movements, moulding each other into shapes. This started with pair work but moved on to group work (a very successful session involved groups forming themselves into climbing apparatus of different shapes and levels and allowing individuals to climb over them). When asked which sessions they enjoyed most, a number of pupils mentioned this exercise. As the year wore on, she continued to do basic movement work, (for example, on differences in height and parts of the body). Gradually she started to ask pupils to work on movements that had some form of symbolic significance, for example, to do movements signifying bondage and freedom, or to create mythical animals in movements and sounds. Towards the second half of the term, movements were geared towards the exploration of particular content (the story of Christie Brown).

This teacher had taken the class for a year before the project's observations. As a result they were used to movement, and it was of a high standard. When they did individual work, their movement was fluid and flexible. Many were willing to explore a greater range of movements and to use different levels. A few made good use of space. None was self-conscious and all seemed to be enjoying themselves. At the beginning of the year individual work was good, but they found it difficult to work effectively in pairs. Some of them found it difficult to follow the teacher's instructions and therefore did not complete the exercises. It was interesting to note that when the teacher, for example, asked children to make up shapes that their partners could imitate, many children worked against their partners by making shapes which they knew would be impossible for their partners to copy. The teacher had constantly to ask them to simplify rather than complicate their work. This improved as time went on until groups of four or five children were able to work together constructively. Less time was taken to get down to work. General co-ordination was good and they developed definite group identities in the shapes or sequences they made together. Their sense of co-ordination and timing also improved. Boys and girls worked together and although some groups took longer to get together than others, the more mature groups started making very clear movement statements by the end of the year with full use of levels, space and movements. Towards the end of the year some of the larger children, especially the girls, became more self-conscious and less enthusiastic to do 'free' movement, although they still enjoyed working in groups. The teacher felt that at this stage of development it was important to structure lessons flexibly in such a way that they could experience a number of levels of involvement.

*Abstract conceptualization and appreciation of content in drama*
At the beginning of the year topics given to children were usually concrete, relating in some way to their own experiences (as in the relationships between landlords and tenants). Here, the children were concerned with establishing the details (who the tenants were and what the landlord was trying to get out of them) rather than going deeper into the implications for people being evicted. As they developed they showed a capacity for understanding abstract concepts and for putting them into dramatic and other forms. This indicated that they had grasped the intrinsic meanings of these concepts and were able to handle them. One group, for example, was able to represent forces of good against evil by making a statement about the killing of the Minotaur through movement (see page 29). Another group represented the 'difficulties of overcoming obstacles' by creating a difficult human climbing-frame that one person had to negotiate to reach the top. As the year progressed they were more able to translate their understanding of certain concepts (for example, the differences between 'conflict and peace') into other media, such as writing and painting, thus indicating a general conceptual grasp of what they were exploring.

*Developing the ability to discuss*
In the first term, when the teacher was talking to the children, the conversation was mainly in terms of questions and answers to those questions. By the end of the year children were discussing the pros and cons of various issues and were giving reasons for their statements. For example, in discussing why sacrifices should be given to the Minotaur, much discussion ranged around the importance of protecting the whole community. They were also able to put themselves into other people's positions and argue from the point of view of the characters they represented. For example, one boy volunteered to be sacrificed. He said that he was an orphan and that his only brother had been killed by the beast. He therefore wanted revenge and argued that he should go because he had nothing to live for and that his determination would see him through.

The quality of work that this teacher achieved was done through continually stretching the children in various ways. The teacher was not content with their movement work until she was satisfied that they had the control, variety and confidence they needed in order to express the feelings and thoughts they wished to portray. Her emphasis was often on the social nature of the aspects explored. Also she often encouraged specific ideas and skills through doing drama—for example, that in many cases, group work and decisions could not be made unless a leader was appointed, indicating that she placed personal value on developing groups' skills in leadership.

The quality of work achieved developed from a mixture of constant discussion and talk on the part of the teacher about the content and nature of the work and the fact that she built up to large-group work carefully by having children work on a theme in small groups first. This meant that all children were able to be involved at different levels. Those usually passive in large-group work had to take responsibility in small-group work, and those who were dominant in large-group situations had to take the opinions of others in small groups. In small-group work she often placed an emphasis on discussing in role. This emphasis on talk rather than the children being allowed to work and act things out at their own level clearly tied in with her general attitude to language development. For example, she often started off by asking children to give her the meanings or approximations of certain words relevant to the scene—for example, 'give me as many words as you can which could mean or describe "struggle"'. These were written on the board in the classroom and used for class work.

In general terms, this class improved their ability to act-out and talk about issues in role. The teacher commented that unless she was careful, children could approach their work with a great 'air of fantasy'. There was little evidence of in-depth characterization. Characters tended to be crude, often representing one aspect—for example, the landlords represented were all stereotype monsters, too hard and strict, assuming postures of aggression and belligerence.

The emphasis in this teacher's work was on movement, vocabulary and discussion. Although it is not possible to determine whether the development found in drama lessons was a direct result of the actual drama experiences (except perhaps for movement) or as a result of the children's general experience, drama was a useful way of seeing how far they could apply their understanding and ideas in concrete forms of representation.

# Development in a class of fourteen-year-olds in a comprehensive school

## *The school*

The school was a mixed comprehensive. There were 1500 pupils. It was founded in the 'twenties as a co-educational grammar school and the great bulk of the pupils were still examination orientated. The school had a reputation for being 'steadily successful'. It was not streamed and was structured in terms of house systems and academic departments led by directors of faculties. In the first two years the intention was to give children a wide range of experience. In the arts, therefore, the subjects rotated over a period of time. In the third year the emphasis was on more formal work in preparation for fourth- and fifth-year examinations. The school aimed at generally achieving flexibility and awareness to enable the children to cope with different situations, and at greater economy and effectiveness in communication on all planes. The school had a very good academic record.

There was a long-established department of drama within the school, and a lot of support for this work among the staff. Drama was compulsory in the first three years and optional in the fourth and fifth. One group was doing a GCE drama course. In the sixth year drama was part of a liberal studies course and was optional. There were two full-time members of staff teaching drama, and two probationers who were shared with the humanities department. The director of drama had a scale-five post with responsibility not only for his own department, but also for encouraging drama across the school curriculum. Various after-school clubs were supported.

The school had new and very good facilities for drama. The new theatre was 1200 square feet in size, open-plan with a balcony and first-class lighting. There was also one studio with lighting and sound and one other space/hut which had been converted into a studio. There was also an open-air theatre.

## *The teacher*

The teacher had had sixteen years' teaching experience. He had taught in a number of schools in different parts of the country. He was head of department in the last school he worked in and had recently assumed his present post.

He felt that the main approach to drama should be that of inquiry on the part of the child. He felt that drama is not about solving our problems, but about finding out what the problems are in the first place. It should be exciting; urgent. It should give children a sense of occasion, a sense that something exciting is about to happen. For children, there is a 'danger element', an element of confrontation that puts them at risk and challenges them. He also felt that it was possible through drama to give them 'a greater awareness of social commitment' as well as giving the individual 'a deeper reflection of their own resources'. 'It is often a circuitous route that leads me to ascertain the degree by which a child is using his personal resources. First of all I aim at achieving a situation whereby the individual child is apparently coping with me and with his peers, then comes the structure of the work so designed as to offer numerous opportunities for decision-making by the children. It might crudely be described as cornering the children, forcing them to cope with a series of obstacles—some of which are created by the teacher, others of which are related to the dynamics of the group. For instance, crawling through barbed wire, suggested by me, can necessitate the pupil to use his memory, physical acuteness, directly in relation to my structure but the moment he finds that he has also got to lead a blind comrade through that wire we raise the issues of inter-group negotiation.'

Over a year he would expect improvement in the teacher's ability to relate to a class; the class's ability to relate to each other; their awareness of 'where they were at in drama'; and individual development—seen by 'the speed with which pupils employ ideas' and manoeuvrability, 'the ease with which he translates ideas from one medium to another'. Other things included, for example, an awareness of style 'that which best encapsulates the statement you are trying to make'.

In the early stages the work was largely controlled by the teacher so that trust and confidence was built up. In the first year he helped them use and suggest stimuli. In the second year he was more exacting about the quality of work. As they grew older he encouraged a more analytical approach and a capacity to understand how various dramatic techniques could enhance the expression of ideas. He sometimes worked towards exposition which, if it was good enough, could be shown to others.

## The class

Members of the class opted to do drama on a termly basis. They were of mixed ability. Although some of the pupils had elected to do drama, for some it was their second or third choice. He found that a third were indifferent and a third 'unreasonably indifferent'.

Although they had all had experience of drama, this was their first time with this particular teacher. This might have affected some pupils' attitude to doing drama.

## *Aims for the class*

The teacher felt that he wanted to give children reasons for doing drama. He wanted them to be aware of how they could affect or influence other members of the group and the teacher. He intended to do this by starting with their interests, negotiating a 'statement' with them and working towards a performance. He felt that work leading to exposition could be valuable. Presentation and achievement in the theatre arts linked drama with other art forms. Working towards exposition gave children a 'sense of urgency and motivation'.

## *Examples of progression of work*

The teacher took the theme of 'fear' and the topic of 'people under stress'. The pupils suggested certain sub-headings which they wanted to explore—for example, the fear factor in activities, and group relationships with regard to stress. In exploring the fear factor, the teacher asked children to examine everyday activities they did and to discover the danger element in them—for example, spilling a cup of tea. The teacher encouraged them to examine the consequences of their work and to come up with general conclusions about the nature of the theme they were exploring. They decided that every activity contains a danger element, and that this element can be contained by correct handling. In social situations, the danger element can be contained through negotiations. Work continued in which both the teacher and pupils explored the consequences of negotiations breaking down and fear taking over. The teacher asked pupils to give examples of such situations in which they could work—for example, football matches. Chants and slogans were used to build up tension.

The teacher drew parallels between contemporary and historical issues—using background material. The children decided that they wanted to do a documentary. The Black Death was chosen as a dominant theme. After exploratory work the group decided that it wanted 'to put together a statement—to say the same thing all together to an audience.' The teacher devised a script which contained the main elements of the work done and which also won the approval of the pupils as being a fair representation of what they wanted to say. The statement was then rehearsed and polished. The children worked within the structure but also had chances to exercise degrees of personal choice in how they moved and sometimes in what they said. It was performed to the rest of the school, parents and other interested members of the community. As communication became a major factor of the exercise, an account by an independent outsider will be given of the impact that the play made on her.

## The performance

The drama department has been using the new theatre complex for six weeks even though the lighting rig and seating have yet to be completed. For the particular performance I was about to watch the central well had been cleared and there was a construction of blocks and stairs from the floor to the balcony, creating a spacious stage area. As the audience trooped and giggled in, I felt that if disruption was to take place, judging by the girls and boys splayed out around, this particular audience would surely be its instigator.

At 2.30 pm the members of the group, dressed in black and wearing white plimsolls, took up their positions on stage greeted by loud applause from the audience. The programme had already pointed out that '"With You Without You" is not a play in the conventional sense. There is no distinct story-line—the actors continually change their roles and time plays tricks on the audience—but that there is a theme throughout in that all action centres around people and their interrelationships. The third-year drama group has developed this theme, using a mixture of script and improvisation added to which we have the theatrical effects of stage, sound and light. Thus we present an experience rather than a formulated statement.'

The first scene moved into a busy market-place with the stall-holders clearly miming their wares, fruit, cloth, etc. Although verbal scripting helped the audience to appreciate 'a red apple', the peeling and eating of a banana could not be mistaken, even by me. A sudden change from hubbub and a commotion to silence, slow motion dramatized by lighting and then back to the normal busy market scene. My only criticism during this scene was my difficulty in understanding what the 'man with the poisoned cows' was saying. He spoke too quickly so that it sounded as if his cows had been poisoned with powdered milk.

Moving very cleverly into the 'Black Death' the audience became most engrossed by the female narrator's description of 'black spots' spreading all over the body and were further spellbound by the 'religious-type' chanting of the cure, which all the group proceeded to drink (with sound effects) and then collapse, covering every inch of the stage.

Again the audience were deathly silent waiting for the next move. Two boys stirred, while the rest of the group kept their 'freeze' positions, and began 'digging in a graveyard'. Yes, you could see the space Mike Parker was holding. Yes, you could feel him digging and really feel his jolt as he hit the coffin lid. I was quite unaware that the rest of the group had sat up before this stage and were drumming the floorboards to add to the eerie atmosphere already created by the lighting and sound effects. By this time I was fully engrossed—not one of the group had distracted my eye—I had no difficulty concentrating on the grave-diggers. The whole audience responded with 'ahs' and 'ohs' when Mike bit off the finger of his accomplice to remove his ring.

The ease at which the scenes interchanged was amazing. The group settled in nicely, all determined to make a success of their individual and their combined performance: each carefully considering the other.

I must admit I did get a bit lost at one stage. I could not quite understand what a scene was all about, and found the scripting difficult to follow. Two girls were concentrating hard on their lines and pauses, but I felt they were a little over-anxious to finish their piece as soon as possible. The rest of the audience had become a bit restless by now and odd groups of chatting could be heard. I feel this was due to lack of definition of the scene but it was only one weak part in an excellent performance. The audience showed their appreciation with whole-hearted applause.

I was most impressed and quite flabbergasted by this very mature performance from a group of fourteen-year-olds. Not one of the individual character parts was overshadowed by any other member of the group. They played as a whole for themselves and for the audience. There was an air of tension—a 'we want to succeed in what we're doing' atmosphere.

### Kinds of development in the class
Working towards presentation in this class involved four distinct phases of activity each of which encouraged development in a different way. The first phase involved exploration of ideas introduced by the teacher. The second phase involved shaping the ideas gained through exploration into a dramatic statement. This was partially done through suggestions by pupils but mainly by the teacher writing the script for them. The next phase, that of rehearsing for the presentation, included learning how to improve skills oi communication: how to make movements more precise: how to put ideas across more clearly and how to repeat and recreate each scene until it runs smoothly, and has the required impact. The presentation allowed children to receive live appreciation for their efforts.

In terms of the overall experience, the teacher felt that the pupils had developed in three main ways. They had experienced drama work of quality and would be able to recognize this in the future: 'what they did get was the "high" which is personal and at the same time part of a broader group feeling'—this would give them motivation for work in the future. By working together towards a successful presentation, children learned to recognize 'the potency of their action in that it affected a group of people and allowed each individual to lend his strength to a group to make a statement that enthrals and affects others.' Because of this the relationships within the group had improved. One boy who began the term reluctantly and unable to communicate with other members of his group, by being given an important part, changed his attitude to drama and to other members of his group. He was more confident and generally much happier, not only in drama but also in other classes. The teacher felt that by working at different levels with the pupils in exploring ideas, in using his own creativity to write a script for them, in working for performance, his relationships with the pupils had improved considerably. A number of children echoed the feeling that they had improved their relationships with others: 'You develop mutual trust. You can look at people from different angles—learn about people's real feelings—that people have more to show than what they show.' 'Drama teachers use self-discipline—especially working with other people.' 'You really get to know your neighbours.' 'You learn about other people and yourself.'

The teacher felt that there had been great improvement in the class's ability to know 'where they are at in drama'. He felt that they were more conscious about the different aspects of the process involved and able to follow his instructions more quickly. As one child put it, 'You have to be good at imagining—you have to think of the situation, to understand a piece of music so that you know what fits with it. You have to be in touch with everything around you, have different ideas about it. You then discuss your ideas with other people—work it out with them and then communicate.'

He felt that the children were better at playing with ideas, that they had improved their speed in translating them into dramatic media. Many children had improved their ability to work within and develop the dramatic situation. One girl said that the usefulness of this phase for her was the feeling that 'it's about juggling ideas together, opening doors to go through, things to explore'. In terms of shaping, one boy felt that he had learned that 'drama teaches you organization—organization of yourself and your ideas and the way people get together'. Because the teacher used the children's ideas in writing the script they were able to work towards presentation with a sense of commitment. This meant that although rehearsal was often long drawn out, and meant many moments of sitting quietly and waiting while other people did things, children were more able to sustain their interest.

During rehearsals development occurred in two main ways. The teacher tried to develop an awareness of the potency of style by helping the children to build up techniques such as pace, and to appreciate moments of silence. He worked constantly towards helping them make their movements more precise and specific and to control their voices so that the meaning would come across more clearly. For instance, he rehearsed with the children a routine of gestures and sounds showing the horror and fear of the Black Death, using different levels and different sound effects—pitch and volume. 'When you do something good, sharing it with an audience is wonderful, you feel, well, as though you really matter—what you communicate matters.'

The teacher felt that some children had gained confidence through the experience. Other children had learned to work better with each other. Some children had learned to express themselves verbally and physically more effectively. Two children felt that they had been helped with their own personal forms of expression. 'Drama helps everyone. It releases people to think and act. All people project images in front of other people. We should be aware of that and be able to control what we do and say.' 'It gives you confidence in yourself to express your feelings. Other subjects have to do with writing—drama has to do with action, how you move and speak.'

Although there was a general sense of euphoria at the end the teacher felt that it was important to be aware of the dangers of working in this kind of way. He felt that the problem about successful performance is that after it there is a sense of anticlimax. Everyday work seems less urgent. He felt that 'they sometimes resort to what worked last time—producing effects without a sense of internal significance.' There can be a danger of slick and superficial work.

# Long-term development

These examples show how particular classes of children developed over a year. The lines along which they developed depended mainly on the teacher's assessment of 'where they were at' in the process and the kinds of learning that the teacher wanted to develop. It is important to keep in mind the child's total dramatic experience through his school life and to ask, for example: what sorts of development should teachers work towards over a long period of time (for instance, from the ages of ten to sixteen), and what should pupils be expected to achieve at the end of five or six years' drama? If children are to derive the maximum benefit we would argue that they need to be exposed to a wide range of drama work over a period of time: to learn to use the process; to explore certain themes, topics and issues; to share and give dramatic presentation and to appreciate other people's drama.

## *Learning to use the process: exploration and representation of ideas*

As they have more experience in drama work children ought to be able to use the process of symbolization more effectively in exploring and representing meaning. This involves learning to *find appropriate forms of action.* Through experience individuals ought to be able to develop an increasing variety of roles. They ought to be able to move from crude stereotyped characters to a more complex understanding and representation of people with all the nuances of emotions and behaviour. Through the interaction between symbolic roles, they ought to deepen their understanding by developing situations in such a way that the particular idea or ideas that they are exploring can be elaborated upon, modified and further understood. One of the ways in which children develop through using the process is in an increasing capacity to extend and explore ideas further. This means that children should learn to use all aspects of the process. They should be able to define their own areas of exploration, decide upon symbols and symbolic structures in which to work, and be more easily able to get beyond the point where they are just discussing in real terms what they are going to do. This involves developing the capacity to select and reject ideas, to modify and elaborate them and to shape them into patterns or forms which adequately represent those aspects of meaning children are trying to express. Working at the symbolic level can allow new insights, into the *content* which the pupils are exploring, to emerge. For example, in the description of the performance given there was an episode in which 'Mad Meg' was cruelly teased by children. The pupils were trying to convey symbolically what it might be like for abnormal people to be made into scapegoats by normal members of society. They wanted to show how painful and frightening it could be for those concerned. In developing through drama children should be increasingly able to use, represent and express their understanding of people and their circumstances in a variety of ways.

Children ought to become more conscious about the ways in which feelings and ideas are expressed through drama. This means being able to opt in and out of role, and to be involved both subjectively and objectively, as part of an attempt to improve the general quality of the work.

Working towards a high level of involvement can take a long time. In the three lessons described in the chapter on assessment and evaluation, none of the children had reached this. Sometimes work had to be done to help them develop their own role sufficiently for meaningful exploration to take place, or the teacher had to improve social relationships before the acting-out could begin. In one case children were not secure enough to take major decisions. It is by no means certain that at the end of five years in drama, all children will have learnt complete mastery of the process. However, most pupils, given reasonable experience in acting-out, should be able during drama to select and develop their own ideas by creating interrelating roles and situations and, when appropriate, to shape and synthesize ideas gained through exploration into a dramatic statement.

Being able to use acting-out in symbolizing, expressing and communicating meaning involves increased command of *dramatic media*. This means that over a period of time children learning through drama ought to be given the opportunity to extend and vary their means of expression, both verbally and physically, so that they can draw upon these when looking for adequate forms of representation. In addition, by learning to use and control the media, the child also learns how to express himself with more confidence both verbally and physically in normal everyday communication. Through experience in drama it is hoped that children will be less inhibited and be more able to express themselves fluently and with confidence. It is also hoped that by being given a variety of dramatic roles and situations throughout their school careers they will develop a flexible approach to their use of spoken language, be more aware of how other people respond to them, and be conscious of the demands that different social situations create and their ability to respond positively within the situation.

The children in the 'Dangerous Gas' session (Chapter 5) started drama lessons at the beginning of the year without saying much either to each other or the teacher. Ten months later they were willing, in role, to talk fluently, to ask questions, to establish certain aspects of the situation and to use speech to solve problems. Through *social interaction* and by using the media of the whole person, children can explore aspects of meaning together and increase their understanding not only of the particular content they are exploring but also of their individual interpretations. Through drama children can develop an increasing awareness of the way that other people perceive reality. They can also explore and perhaps extend those kinds of symbols which are mutually accepted as cultural stereotypes. The child at ten who plays a difficult landlord doling out punitive rules to his tenants in an unrealistic fashion ought by the time he is sixteen to be able to portray a landlord complete with a personality and his own difficulties. He ought to be more aware of the problems involved in the whole question of landlords and tenants at a more sophisticated and complex level.

Through drama children can also learn to offer, accept and modify ideas, and build upon what has gone before; reach mutual agreement about how dramatic situations are to develop and work together in the organization and shaping of ideas which they, as a group, may wish to express. Drama enables children to be more aware and more effective in corporate decision-making. They should also learn to be more aware of how individuals react to others and the ways in which individuals contribute to the overall activity of the group. As children improve in working together in this way, development should be seen in terms of the speed with which they get down to work, how they form their criteria for the quality of their work and how as a group they assess the success of their activities.

Development through social interaction in drama is distinctive from other forms of corporate group decision-making because it focuses primarily on the simultaneous symbolic and real relationships of people, the roles they play, their personalities, feelings and ideas and the human situations in which they might find themselves.

## Understanding through drama

Children should become increasingly able to translate attitudes and ideas about various issues into dramatic statements which reflect their understanding. A teacher can deliberately structure a lesson to explore specific content. Children may be expected to generalize from their particular experiences. For instance, the group of children who were acting out a village scene of the nineteenth century, in which the introduction of a weaving machine affected employment, might be able to take from that experience an understanding of the general problems caused by mechanization. It is hoped that as children grow older, they will become more able to deal with more and more complex and sophisticated issues through drama.

If children use drama for this purpose it is hoped that they will develop an increasing capacity to translate their understanding gained from acting-out into other media, including writing and art. The most common aspect of reflection is the use of discussion both before, during and after acting-out. It is hoped that after a sustained period of drama, children will be more able, not only during but also after acting-out, verbally to express themselves more fluently and to state their opinions and feelings about the issues involved clearly and more thoughtfully.

Through drama, pupils put themselves in other people's shoes and may realize the attitudes and feelings underlying different points of view.

## Participation in presentation

Children given a balanced diet of drama over the years should at some stage become aware of the effectiveness of drama as a means of communicating ideas and feelings to other people. They can learn how to put ideas across clearly. They should develop an awareness of the impact that the dramatic statement can have. They learn the importance of sustained corporate effort in producing an end-product that is effective and which runs smoothly. They develop a sense of satisfaction from working over a period of time towards an end-product that can be shared and appreciated by others.

## Experiencing other people's drama

At the end of five or six years of drama pupils ought to be more able to appreciate other people's drama, to be aware of and critical of the drama they encounter outside their school lives. This includes television, radio and films. It is also hoped that they will be informed about the theatre as a basis for future enjoyment. It is hoped that over a period of time, either through English or in drama lessons themselves, children will be introduced to a wide range of playwrights and, by the time they are sixteen, have some knowledge and experience of professional presentations of plays by significant playwrights. It is hoped that by having experiences of other people's drama, children will be able to make the link between their own work and the cultural significance of this kind of communication.

Children should develop an awareness of the quality of their own and other people's work in drama. This involves learning about the process itself: being aware of how emphasizing different aspects can achieve different results. They should become increasingly aware of the levels of both intellectual and emotional involvement at which they are working and be able to appreciate whether adequate symbol systems and symbols have been found to express meaning. They should be critical about whether they or others have expressed themselves clearly and concisely and have used the media effectively in communicating meaning to others, be it simple or complex, trivial or profound.

# Conclusions

Levels of development reached by pupils over an extended period of time depend primarily upon the quality of the teaching. Each teacher needs to be aware of the previous experience that pupils have had and the states of development they have reached in their understanding of and capacity to use the process. Teachers need to be sensitive to what pupils are doing in terms of development on a minute-to-minute basis and be flexible enough to develop work as certain needs arise. They need to work purposefully so that children feel a sense of achievement at the end of each lesson. The teacher should see to it that each individual child is challenged and stretched by being asked to project into a number of different roles and situations. It is also important for the teacher to be aware of the variety of ways in which drama can be used over a period of time so that children are not limited to one form of development in drama at the expense of others.

Children, to derive the maximum benefit, need not only to be exposed to a variety of ways of working and to teaching of good quality; they also need adequate time and facilities for developing in the ways described. It is pointless to give lip-service to the value of drama and then to allow so little time for it that children are unable to reach reasonable states of development. If the educational validity of drama in the development of the child is recognized, it needs to be organized in such a way that maximum opportunities are given for development to occur. This raises questions about the place of drama in the curriculum and possible ways in which it might be organized.

# Chapter 7
# The Place of Drama in the Curriculum

So far we have looked at the possible functions of the drama experience itself. Aims, we suggested, are developed by the individual teacher to meet the demands of the situation he is working in. This leaves an open question for the teacher to answer in thinking about whether or not to use drama in his work. Are the developments which are likely to be brought about in children through drama compatible with his aims in education? We have so far been concerned with ways in which drama can be used in the classroom. But what kinds of place can drama occupy in the curriculum as a whole? How can it fit into the overall pattern of the child's experience in school? What is the role of the drama specialist, and what are the implications of this for the non-specialist? Before going on to look at the place of drama in the curriculum, and from there the ways in which it may be organized on the timetable, it will be useful to review briefly the main case we have put forward for its value in education.

We have argued that drama is an active process which functions as a way of exploring and expressing meaning in certain kinds of experience. We have looked at this in terms of the concept of symbolization. The arts as a whole are rooted in symbolic forms of expression of particular kinds, and it is in this context that their role in education can most clearly be seen. The potential value of active experience in the arts lies in the child's controlled attempts to explore, develop and express ideas and concepts which will help him to make sense of his subjective responses to the public world. Drawing from this we would argue strongly that the arts should be given at least the same status as other areas in the curriculum.

The distinctive contributions which drama can make in this process revolve around the experience of acting-out. This involves the child projecting into imagined roles or situations. We have defined acting-out as the exploration and representation of meaning through the medium of the whole person; this is done by and through social interaction. In drama the child negotiates meaning through social interaction at what we have called the 'real' and the 'symbolic' levels. As he explores problems of understanding in the represented situation, he is simultaneously exploring and deepening his real relationships with the other children involved in the work.

There are four inter-related components in the drama process, through which learning can take place: *social interaction*—at both real and symbolic levels; *use of the media*—the main media of dramatic expression are voice, language, body, space and time; *content*—the potential content of drama is enormous in terms of themes, concepts, topics (the distinctive feature of the content is that it is explored at the level of interpersonal response, and through human behaviour); and *forms of expression*—the search for meaning is closely associated with the exploration of different forms of symbolic representation.

The teacher therefore needs to be clear about the kinds of learning he wants to encourage through drama, and whether he wishes to emphasize: exploring the use of the process itself; understanding themes, topics and issues through acting-out; participation in presentation and performance; interpretation and appreciation of dramatic statements by other people. He is faced therefore with a number of decisions in the way he structures and organizes drama with each group. These will radically affect the nature of the learning which takes place.

We now want to move the centre of the discussion away from the drama teacher's work in the classroom into the wider context of the school curriculum. There is little point in discussing drama at a general theoretical level, or in terms of what happens in the lesson itself, unless some attempt is made to see its place in the school as a whole. Inevitably, in talking about its place in the curriculum, some thought must be given to its status there. Drama like the other arts, but perhaps to a greater extent, has tended in practice to be seen as peripheral. The reasons for this are not just administrative. They reflect an assumption that the arts are, in some way, less important in the child's school life than other curriculum work. We suggest strongly that this assumption is untenable in any system of education which purports to help the child to understand the society of which he is part and in which he is meant to take an active role.

The value of drama is intimately bound up in the individual's attempts to make sense of the world he lives in and the life he leads. If the case we have argued for this is accepted, then its implications for the curriculum must be carefully thought out. We recommend strongly that drama has a sufficiently significant role to play in the child's education to merit its inclusion at the centre of the curriculum—as a core activity. If it is to have its fullest impact, sufficient time and facilities need to be given for children to learn to use the process and its related skills. This is particularly important in the early years when long-lasting skills and attitudes are being formed. Moreover, sufficient opportunities should exist for children to develop and apply these in the later years of their school career. But saying this obviously raises a number of difficulties in relation to staffing and timetabling which can hardly be ignored. How can this be realistically accommodated within the practical pressures of the (increasingly congested) school day?

At the curriculum level a number of questions are in urgent need of clarification. What are the specific responsibilities of the drama teacher? What is the related role of teachers of other subjects who want to use drama as part of their general repertoire of teaching techniques? What is the relationship of drama to English teaching? What are the roles of drama in performance in the general cultural life of the school? How can drama best be blended into different kinds of timetables? What are the current patterns of organization? What practical problems exist in this respect and what are the alternative structures? Is there a case for examinations in drama and what issues need to be taken into account in considering this? Finally, what kind of facilities should be available for the teaching of drama?

# The role of the drama specialist

The first step in describing the role of the specialist is to define what a specialist is. There are a number of problems in the way of this. Subject specialists are usually so called because they have undergone a period of professional training in their chosen field. Drama is a comparative newcomer to the school and in some cases those teaching it do not actually hold a professional qualification in drama. On the other hand, there are still only a limited number of drama posts in schools, again because of its recent emergence as a specialism, which means that many of those who have qualified in a main course in drama are often employed to teach something else, particularly English, with drama as a second 'subject'. An increasing number of teachers in other curriculum areas have also become alive to the potential of drama in their own work and use it as part of the normal teaching, say in history or sciences. How then is a specialist drama teacher to be defined? For our own purposes we have chosen to define a specialist according to the terms of his employment. We include as a drama *specialist* anyone who is employed specifically to take drama work of some kind, although he may well have additional teaching responsibilities; and as *non-specialists*, teachers who involve themselves in drama work with children, but who are not specifically employed to do so. In saying this we acknowledge that some non-specialists may well have undergone a teaching course in drama.

Given then that a teacher is employed specifically to teach

drama, what is his role in the school? We suggested earlier (page 23) that the teacher's responsibility is twofold: to encourage the child to deepen and challenge his perceptions of himself and his world so that he gradually begins to make sense of the complexities and subtleties of his experience, and acknowledges, accommodates and reassesses his world-view in the light of new experience; and to do this through enabling the child to use and express himself through the symbolic process of the arts.

We can now elaborate this to take into account the differences in emphasis we have described in drama practice. The drama specialist has a general responsibility to deepen the child's experience in all areas of drama, exploring all its uses. He has a particular responsibility to develop their experience of drama in its own right. This includes helping children to increase their skills in the use of the media of drama, and to develop their ability to work together co-operatively in the negotiation of meaning.

If the versatility of drama, both as a creative process in its own right and as a way of learning across the curriculum, is to be fully exploited, we would argue that the appointment of drama specialists is essential. Drama is not easy to initiate or to develop. For many children who are new to drama, it is a way of working which makes unusual demands on them. It may take them some time to become used to relating to each other and to the teacher in this new way. If drama is to be used by non-specialists outside the drama lesson, the specialist teacher can provide the essential background and experience which will enable children to adapt more readily to drama work in these other contexts. The specialist can also play a vital part in advising non-specialists about how they can use drama in their own work.

# The role of the non-specialist

How then does the work of the non-specialist drama teacher relate to the work of the specialist? Broadly speaking, there are two types of non-specialist: the general class teacher (in the primary or middle school) who can use drama spontaneously during the day according to the work in hand; and the subject teacher in the secondary school who may also use drama as part of his general repertoire of teaching techniques. The differences here are mainly in the practical circumstances. Teachers in primary and some middle schools are seldom employed to take only specialist subjects. Consequently there are rarely drama specialists there, as we have defined them. These teachers will therefore have the opportunity to exploit all aspects of the drama process. A great advantage here is the comparative flexibility of the school day which will allow drama to emerge naturally from a range of work.

The primary-school teacher is in a position to develop drama work naturally from the children's play in the early years and can ensure an easy and uninterrupted transition to more demanding drama activities in later years. Apart from its intrinsic value in the primary school, this early experience of drama can provide an invaluable foundation in terms of skills and attitudes to drama work, which can be built upon in the secondary school.

The non-specialist in the secondary school usually works within a less flexible timetable and has more limited opportunities to develop work in drama. He is therefore more likely to concentrate on one use of drama—the understanding of specific content, themes, topics and issues related to his particular subject. When drama teachers are appointed, there is a tendency for other teachers to think they should 'leave it to the specialist' and not use drama themselves. In practice there is a close relationship between the work of specialists and non-specialists—although they do have separate and distinct responsibilities. The non-specialist's use of drama to explore specific subject-matter will be greatly enhanced by the complementary work of the specialist, helping the child to a greater facility in the use of the process as a whole.

If the work of the non-specialist is aimed at increasing understanding in specific topics, he needs to recognize the need for careful planning and structuring in the lesson in order to direct the energies of the group to the specific problems and questions in hand. In early attempts at using drama, the non-specialist may in any case feel more secure if the lesson is more closely structured. However, within this he needs to be flexible. He must be able to provoke an immediacy and spontaneity of response in the group through his questioning and control of the work and be able to seize upon the opportunities for learning which arise. It is in the nature of drama that the group may offer more valuable suggestions for approaching the work than the ones the teacher planned before the lesson. The teacher needs to be sufficiently responsive to build on this and not stifle it through too rigid an approach. Similarly he needs to be able to select those of the children's ideas which are most relevant to the task in hand.

The non-specialist must know what he wants to achieve in using drama. He must ask whether drama is really appropriate to the kind of learning he is concerned with. Drama can be an invaluable method of approaching subject teaching where the teacher's concern is with the human response to situations. Its main value is not in the teaching of facts as such, although the work may certainly encourage a deeper understanding of essential information. If the geography teacher wants the class to have a precise understanding of the physical features of Japan, drama may not be the best way of pursuing his aims. It would be more direct to show the group a film or study a map. But if the work involves an understanding of personal responses, and human experiences under particular conditions, if it involves the exploration of attitudes and opinions, or the representation of abstract concepts in more concrete form, then drama will come into its own. A teacher who is looking at the slave trade in the Southern States of America, for example, may begin by dividing the class into two groups, one group representing the attitudes of the abolitionists. By exploring the conflict in attitudes through acting-out, the group may be brought to a deeper understanding, through personal involvement, of the motives and philosophies underlying the actual events. In history, dramatic exploration can lead to a greater appreciation of the issues. Drama provides the form rather than the fact. Through drama the child may begin to see universal themes in specific events or topics. But he must begin by making the situation personal.

For the non-specialist to be effective he needs an understanding of the kinds of experiences the children are having in acting-out and of the demands it makes on them in both real and symbolic terms. He needs to pay particular attention to the selection and introduction of relevant information so that attention is focused on the content he wants them to explore. As his experience of using the process grows he might be prepared to enter the symbolic situation himself, in role, as the need arises. Using drama as a method of teaching does not simply mean providing a structure and observing the work as an outsider—the teacher is an integral part of the work.

The non-specialist is less likely to have time in his lesson to develop what we have called the 'prerequisites' for drama (see pages 87-9)—co-operation, concentration, use of the media, and so on. Once again the work of non-specialists will benefit enormously from the more sustained work of the specialist in the school, who has this as part of his specific responsibilities.

The crucial question then, for the non-specialists, is whether the kinds of developments which are encouraged in drama are part of his overall concerns in his teaching of a particular subject. Our own observations suggest that drama can play an invaluable part in enlivening the teaching of many subjects across the curriculum, particularly in the Humanities. This value is more likely to be realized where the children have a background in drama through sustained work with a drama specialist; and the teacher is sensitive to the demands of the drama work, and has a clear idea of the kinds of learning he wants to encourage.

# Drama and the English Teacher

In very many schools where drama is established on the timetable, it is organized through the English department and taught by specialist English teachers. This is not just because in many cases it is easier, administratively, to introduce new 'subjects' through existing departments rather than to create a new one. It is because there is, for many teachers, an obvious conceptual link between drama and English. This view of drama and English probably results from the tendency in schools to think of plays in terms of literature rather than in terms of performance. Most English courses include a study and appreciation of play texts as part of their work in literature, and possibly as part of this the study of the historical development of the theatre. A wider view of drama sets it more clearly in the context of the arts in education rather than specifically in the field of English teaching.

Drama needs specialist provision, in terms of teachers, and, as we will go on to argue, in terms of facilities as well. Drama may not have an exclusive relationship with English. But there are two major, overlapping areas of concern in both drama and English teaching which suggest the possibility of a particularly fertile relationship between them.

## Spoken language

Many of the far-reaching innovations in the teaching of English in the past twenty or so years have focused on ways of extending children's abilities in spoken language. A particular feature of this is the emphasis on increasing their skills of communication in a range of language registers. Spoken language develops through social interaction and is one of the prime media of dramatic expression. Different situations elicit and often demand different forms of linguistic response. Although the drama specialist is also encouraging pupils to experiment with their use of language, the English teacher with a greater knowledge of language development can specifically structure drama work which focuses directly on the appropriateness and effectiveness of language usage in varying situations. He can help children to develop their knowledge of, and ability to select from, a range of linguistic choices and registers, according to their appropriateness to different contexts and the roles of the individuals within them.* Although the drama teacher develops language as a medium of communication, the English teacher can help the children to examine the process of communication itself.

* For a description of a range of activities and exercises in exploring language usage, see for example, J. Seeley, *In Context—Language and Drama in the Secondary School* (Oxford University Press, 1976).

## Drama and literature

Although drama can now be seen in a much wider setting than the study and appreciation of plays, this does not mean that these activities now lie outside the scope of drama teaching. What has changed is the way in which they fit into the overall pattern of drama work. In discussing the relationship of drama and theatre we suggested that they should be seen as a continuum. Theatre as an art form has grown from and developed around the same impulses to explore and represent experience through role-play and characterization which are the foundation of the expressive process of drama. In practice there can be a rich cross-fertilization between the child's own expressive work in drama and his growing awareness of the themes, concepts and images of dramatic writing.

The drama teacher can draw on the vast resources of dramatic literature, its situations, characters and forms of symbolization, as a way of stimulating and enriching the child's explorations in drama. Equally the English teacher can use drama as a way of deepening the child's appreciation of, and sensitivity to, the work not only of the playwright, but also of the novelist and the poet. In this interchange between drama and literature, both in the drama lesson and the English lesson, the child is also brought into direct contact with a wide range of shared cultural symbols. Through drama the script can be lifted from the page and translated into the media which properly give it its life—sound, stillness, movement, space and time. This can be done in two ways. Through acting-out children can be helped to isolate the underlying themes and reach for a more personal understanding of them by exploring them through more familiar situations and expressing them in their own way. The English teacher can also enable children to see plays in performance in the theatre or by visiting companies. This is as much his responsibility as the drama teacher's.

# Into performance: the school play

We have maintained that performance work should not be seen as an inevitable or necessary goal of classroom teaching in drama. But performance work can make an enormous contribution to the general cultural life of the school and provide valuable and rewarding experiences for the children who take part. It can also provide an important link between the school and the community, particularly as a means of involving parents in the children's work. In many cases 'performance in school' is taken to mean the annual school play. A problem with such a limited conception of performance is that the traditional school play is often an isolated activity divorced altogether from classroom drama where it exists, and sometimes in place of it where it does not exist. We want to use the idea of performance to encompass a much wider range of events and experiences which may arise from classroom work or from extra-curricular activities. As well as allowing for the possibility of an annual event we would want to include: performances which develop from classroom projects with particular groups; performances which are devised with specific objectives—for example, to present set plays for the benefit of both audience and the children studying them; occasional productions for audiences drawn from out of school, from other schools or from other year-groups within the same school; small-scale lunchtime performances; presentations for assemblies, and so on. Performances may include: scripted plays; musicals; operas; reviews; multi-media events; documentaries arising from particular projects; interpretations of novels, short stories, poems; scripted plays, both modern and traditional. Any of these may include, or consist entirely of, the children's original material.

Such a wide conception of performance in the life of the school broadens the opportunities both for staff and children to participate as actors, directors, and in technical capacities. The question of who is to produce the performance need not be limited to single members of staff on a yearly rotation basis. Where there is a drama specialist in the school there is often an assumption that he is necessarily the best qualified or most enthusiastic teacher to take on the responsibilities of performance work. This policy of giving permanent responsibility to any one member of staff might well be reconsidered. An alternative is to have one teacher perhaps as the co-ordinator of a team of teachers who have interests in this, more than one of whom can be working on different performance material with the children or who can co-operate on the same production. This would certainly make organization of rehearsals easier and would allow for simultaneous rehearsal sessions with larger groups.

Some thought should also be given to methods of casting. There are two main ways of doing this. Sometimes the material is chosen first and the cast is then selected to suit the play. This is done either through auditions or by accepting all-comers through open invitation, or by inviting particular pupils to participate. Another starting-point is where the group is already together and either they or the teacher choose material which is appropriate for them. A drama group, a class or any combination of people can be involved.

Plays are often chosen to suit audiences. It is worth considering an alternative principle—choosing the audience to suit the play. This might include invited audiences of parents and staff; open invitations to the public; audiences from other classes or groups in the school or from other schools; audiences composed of adults and children from particular organizations. All of these considerations will affect not only the choice of material but also the style of presentation, the type of staging and the actor-audience relationship.

There are a number of practical considerations which have perhaps led to the 'once-a-year' approach to performance, such as the availability of pupils, and of rehearsal and performance space, at certain times of the year, and the examination schedules within school. Outside the timetable there are often problems with the Evening Institute using the school after 6.00pm. There may also be problems in avoiding clashing with events in other schools. This might be overcome by headteachers allowing blocks of time during the year to accommodate the rehearsals and the problems associated with large productions.

The organizational problems of performance work on a more occasional basis within the curriculum are less severe. Performances which are used to answer more immediate and precise demands arising out of curriculum work undertaken by certain groups in the school are equally valid and to be encouraged. Faculties or departments or specialist study-groups can benefit directly from experiencing performances around specific topics. Moreover, the opportunities are greatly increased for different groups of interested children to take part in a range of capacities.

In planning performance work the following general principles might be considered:

1.  Although performance work should aim at high standards of presentation for the benefit of cast and audience, any drama work, especially in performance, must have as a priority the quality of the relationships and general educational achievements of those involved rather than an exclusive preoccupation with theatrical finesse.
2.  Productions should be an enjoyable and satisfying experience for the participants.
3.  Original material created by the group should not be seen simply as a step on the way to 'proper' theatre work using established playwrights, but as a different, equally valid source of expression in its own right.

# The present situation

Before these potential roles of drama both as a specialism and as a non-specialism can be realized in practice, there has to be adequate provision both in terms of time and staff.

**What kind of ways are there of organizing drama in the school?**

## *Drama in the primary school\**

We noted earlier that it is rare for primary-school teachers to be employed specifically to teach drama. The primary teacher usually works with the same group of children for most of the day, with a responsibility for all general teaching. In practice this means for the most part that the teacher is free, within the overall aims of the school, to organize the children's day in whatever way seems most appropriate. This flexibility within the demands of the curriculum means, in theory, that there are many opportunities for drama to occur spontaneously, without the need for special timetabling (although limited space in the classroom may present problems). What it means in practice is that without a co-ordinated policy in drama in the school, the amount of drama done depends largely on the enthusiasm of individual teachers. It seems that, despite the amount of attention which has been given to the idea of the integrated day in the primary school, many schools still tend to compartmentalize the day fairly rigidly, dividing the teaching-time around the core subjects of reading, writing and number work. The primary-school teacher is rarely expected to take drama as a regular requirement. It is not recognized by many headteachers as being as valuable as art and music except in terms of productions. Yet the potential for drama here is enormous. This emphasis on developing children's play and learning through discovery can lead into, and be greatly developed by, a progression into more structured drama experiences.

How can this be done? What kind of starting-points are there for the interested primary teacher? One way is for an inexperienced teacher to work with a more experienced one. The following example illustrates how one teacher became interested in trying drama in his class:

*Q:* Given your lack of drama training at college, what was it that really made you interested in this type of work?

*A:* Well, on my final teaching practice I was at a local junior school and worked with a very good teacher . . . I watched him do a lot of drama work and was fascinated by what he was doing. I could see there was a great amount of value in his work. I realized that there was a lot more to this drama than I had originally thought . . . Having seen someone else making it work, making it relevant, and working in some depth with the class, I wanted to be able to do this with my future class. The whole atmosphere of his classroom seemed to have been influenced by this drama work. That was the sort of atmosphere I wanted in my classroom. His teaching was not split up into compartments through the day. His classroom was an environment for learning.

* A detailed account and analysis of drama in the primary school will appear in the report of the Schools Council Drama 5-11 Project, directed by Tom Stabler.

From this starting-point the teacher went on to develop work in his own way.

*Q:* Let's think back to your first session here. What sort of things did you try?

*A:* We started by playing some games . . . to get to know each other better and to get used to working in this large space. I suppose I was working on instinct rather than on training. Then I began to structure their ideas a little more.

*Q:* Where did the themes for your drama lessons come from?

*A:* We would often start by building something in the hall. Would you call it a 'set'? Perhaps an environment. Then I tried to get them to use their imaginations rather than impose my ideas, then we would decide what it was we had built . . . They would improvise in groups of about six. I was not yet ready to take the whole class together. What they were doing was very much an extension of play in the infant classroom.

*Q:* To what extent were *you* involved in their improvisations in the drama lesson?

*A:* Sometimes I joined in a group in role; sometimes I just eavesdropped; sometimes I would stop the activities and ask them questions about what they were doing. Occasionally I would ask a group to show part of their work to the rest of the class. The most memorable series of lessons this year was about a coalmine. We had seen a television programme about mining, but the children didn't really seem to understand what it was like to be underground. So in our drama session we built a long tunnel that all the children could go through to get the feeling of a real mine. We were talking about the difficulties of moving people in confined spaces if there had been an accident. This eventually developed into a whole-class performance for assembly, about rescuing people. It was also a tremendous stimulus to their writing and for encouraging them to read.

As this teacher developed the work in drama he came to recognize both the difficulties and problems of stimulating and controlling the work, but also the enormous pleasure and value of drama, when the groups imaginative energies have been engaged.

Sometimes, I admit, we did drama just because I was timetabled to do it that morning. Sometimes it was almost too forced. On these occasions there was nothing natural about the work—perhaps I wouldn't feel like it, perhaps the children wouldn't feel like it. At other times we would hit on an idea that sparked us all off, and then it became a great stimulus, not only for the drama sessions, but for all our work. That's what happened with the mining rescue project. They were already taken up with the idea in the classroom and from the television programme so that, given the opportunity to try it out in 3D so to speak, they leapt at the chance. It was a success from the word go. We could have gone on for a long time with that project, but I prefer things to be cut off when they are fresh rather than dying out.

This teacher was fortunate perhaps in that, for a term, he had the opportunity of working alongside a teacher who was skilled and experienced in the use of drama. In the course of this he began to develop the ability to ask questions of the children—so essential in drama—and to stimulate and advance the group's acting-out. In his day-to-day work, the primary teacher who has an understanding of what drama has to offer, is in a position to blend it into the overall scheme of work as the opportunities arise. Even though problems of space may limit opportunities for extended work in drama, teachers were quick to comment on the way that drama directly fed into their other classroom work:

Well, obviously, I tried out more things in the hall, but what I found fascinating was that it was affecting my teaching all of the time. In fact you couldn't really tell where drama ended and everything else began. I remember once we started off by playing some music and asking them what it made them think of and this eventually developed into a long story about some frogs and a queen who didn't want frogs in her palace and so the story grew and grew until it went on for over half a term. They made a huge picture of the story, and wrote more and more sections of the story. They were really living that story . . . In fact when it came to Christmas they even wanted to put frogs on their Christmas calendars.

In view of the long periods of time which primary-school children spend with their teacher, the kind of working relationship which is established is an extremely important influence on both the overall quality of their work and on the ways in which drama can be integrated into the day. In practice, the use of drama can help to influence and change the nature of this general relationship. An older teacher had taken his professional training after a career in the armed forces. He was asked directly about the way in which he started to teach drama in his school.

In this school you are given very little to go on and have to make your own pattern. The only thing that is timetabled for you is the use of the hall. Teachers do very little work together here—just assemblies. We do exchange classes occasionally in order to take advantage of our particular skills. I might be taking a class for drama while another teacher takes my class for French. I also do a lot of science work—that was my main subject at college, science.

*Q:* When you arrived at the school was there any drama work going on at all?

*A:* No not really. Just the Christmas pageant.

*Q:* So how did the drama work begin?

*A:* It just happened that one day a notice came round about a day's course in drama (at a local teachers' centre).

*Q:* Did you then come back and try things out with your class?

*A:* Yes, I tried games and short exercises. In fact, looking back most of my early work consisted of a series of short unconnected exercises.

*Q:* So did there come a time when drama was in the children's timetable?

*A:* Yes. Once a week, one hour's session in the hall . . . But we also do drama at odd times in the classroom. We clear all the furniture from the centre of the room and do drama there and then . . .

*Q:* How much carry-over is there from drama into other activities?

*A:* I don't push for this—the drama experience is enough in itself . . . But it's impossible to stop its carrying over. There is often spillover into writing or just into conversation. My drama work has certainly helped me to talk to children, and they to me. The relationship has become different. It's an easier relationship.

The way that drama is used in the primary school depends first, on the value which the individual teacher sees in such work; and secondly, on the opportunities for drama which he creates. As with any new way of working, the early attempts at drama may prove unrewarding and perhaps even worrying as both the teacher and the class adapt to new forms of behaviour and control. Given time and increasing experience, however, working through drama can help to invigorate the children's work across the school day.

Although there are, as yet, apparently few primary schools with a co-ordinated policy in drama teaching, there are some examples of schools where the initiative to develop drama, coming from the headmaster, has permeated the whole fabric of curriculum work. An account of the impact of drama in such a school is given below. The description of this small, rural school, and the influence of drama work upon it, was written by the headmaster himself as an illustration of his conviction of the potential of drama in the primary school.

*A view of the school prior to my appointment*

These are my impressions but are, I hope, supported by the views of the assistant teacher.

The school was organized in a very strict manner with a rigid timetable through to the infants. The authority of the teacher was unquestioned. In the playground there are four straight lines (now fading gradually) on which the children would line up at the end of each play session and come smartly to attention on the sound of the second whistle. The work done by the children, other than the infants, seemed to be mostly academic, mostly in exercise books and usually from some sort of textbook.

There were two basic attitudes to this organization from interested parents. One was supportive, since it was the same system (and the same school) they had been through. The other was strong opposition. The Parent-Teacher Association had originally been formed in opposition, not as a co-operative measure. The great concern of most parents with the new appointment was with discipline. Most significant and telling in the children was the way they addressed their teachers and other adults in the school. Every phrase was prefaced with a 'please Sir' and spoken with a distinct falling stress. It was a self-effacing pattern of speech and can still be reproduced in moments of stress.

It was this which forced me to throw caution to the wind in my first week and plunge into drama activity, in order to make the children talk about something sensible, and to generate something so exciting to talk about, that their stilted style of language would disappear. This was successful and repeated activity has served to eradicate it.

I believed that drama, its associated activities and the attitude of a drama enthusiast was bound to have a profound impact.

It is an attitude I know which can be easily established without drama. However, in my opinion, drama, its attendant activities and attitudes, demands and dictates this emphasis because, more than other activities, it is essentially involved with the sympathetic interaction of people.

The condition of this particular school could not have been so radically and effectively changed without the use of drama.

### Problems incurred in beginning drama as a specific activity

Generally the children took to it readily. They identified it with PE, since it involved the moving of furniture, and much of the early work was concerned with balancing, group shapes, trust games etc. This was most refreshing since no specific attitude was adopted when drama occurred. However, as we progressed to producing stories in groups, the group dynamic put pressures on the children which they had not previously experienced.

They had not previously been asked to work co-operatively and some who found that their group was forcing them 'to do something' took the option of excluding themselves. This I found was a very necessary safety valve for some individuals, otherwise the whole activity could have foundered on bickering, tears and distress. The dominant characters had a hey-day initially, but as the others saw things working they would rejoin, and as time has passed the previously dominant personalities have had to meet the increased confidence of the other children.

It was very confusing for some of the children at first. They had not experienced this kind of activity. It seemed like play, and this was not the sort of thing they expected in school. Verbal cues on my part became crucial. Whereas previously children would interpret my cues with their own judgement, in this school they followed them to the letter. This in fact proved very valuable, since we had, by necessity, to be very structured in our work—only by firm structuring were any initial results achieved.

The greatest obstacle was the pressure which drama activity puts on the child. He has to do something, make a contribution, verbalize in some way. Previously the children had been very secure with exercise book and pencil in a seated position, knowing when the task was completed. Now they had to invent and express virtually in the same process. It was very different for them. What was also strange for the children was that there were no wrong answers and no completely right answers. They floundered at first . . . But later they found new security in the confidence of their own actions within the boundaries of a particular story or theme.

### Drama and its impact on children's language

The way in which the children addressed their teachers was most amazing. Their stilted speech reflected stilted language in written work. It was difficult to get the children to talk in an expressive manner. Once drama had been introduced, once there was sufficient stimulation, the development was rapid and is still continuing. This, I feel, says a lot for drama and language development generally. Once the children had played out an experience, they were eager to express what had happened. The accounts of occurences and stories which developed were soon expressed with enthusiasm and vigour. /

The way in which the children talk to each other has also undergone a change. The co-operative work in drama has made it possible and easy, in fact quite natural, that their other work should be co-operative. A class discussion can now take place with most people contributing and respecting each other's ideas, often without much stimulation . . . I felt that the isolation of their former work had prevented such linguistic activity. I claim that this is the result of drama as a specific activity, since so much verbal activity takes place that it provides the children with skills and confidence.

Writing has remained a problem. 'Oh, I hate writing' has remained to some extent. This is probably because this has traditionally been their main vehicle of learning and an extensive amount was done.

Their ease in verbal expression, however, has shown a marked influence on other expressive media. Art had previously been a one-day-a-week affair with paint and paper. New media and techniques were easy to introduce and the children took to them readily—mainly, I believe, because through drama they were given a meaningful stimulus and a refreshed way of looking at things and the confidence to launch out with unfamiliar materials.

Perhaps the final word on the effects of drama in this school should come from one of the parents:

Drama would seem to encourage freedom of thought, individuality, stimulate the imagination and release a general sense of fun and laughter. The introduction of drama into the school has had a wide-ranging effect. I would say that a more relaxed attitude to school in general is the most noticeable effect amongst my own children. They also enjoy the added interest of a new experience which gives them more to talk about and think about. It may help them to communicate more easily with each other . . . a diffident or self-conscious child may take some time to adjust to such a different medium.

A child who will usually produce predictable and even mundane writing is jolted into doing something more original and exciting. My daughter who professes to dislike drama and is rather reserved in public has certainly seemed more sure of herself and is much more imaginative in her outlook.

Clearly it was not simply drama itself as an impersonal concept which brought about such sweeping changes in the atmosphere of the school, but the general attitude of the headmaster and his teachers to the children, and their willingness to break down the barriers which a rigid timetable had set up. Drama was a process through which more relaxed and imaginative relationships could be established. The introduction of drama in such a whole-hearted way across a school is still fairly unusual. In this case it was the result of particularly strong conviction and sense of purpose on the part of the headmaster.

In the majority of primary schools the children's experience of drama is likely to be more intermittent. This presents particular problems. Sometimes children will encounter challenging drama work early in their school life only to find it excluded from their curriculum activities in later years. This lack of continuity can mean that each time they enter a new 'drama phase', usually through meeting another enthusiastic teacher, they have to return to preliminary work once again. This discontinuity of drama work is most likely to make itself felt during and after the all-important transition from the primary to the secondary school.

## Drama in the middle school

Middle schools vary a great deal in their structure and organization—some are organized in a similar way to the primary school; other schools correspond more closely to secondary patterns. For this reason only we will not discuss middle schools as a completely separate category, but intend that the general points raised under the primary and secondary headings should be applied to the middle school where appropriate.

## Drama in secondary education

In the secondary school both the teachers and the children work in a very different situation. Subject specialism suddenly becomes the norm rather than the exception. Instead of spending most of the day with one teacher, the children may now work with as many as eight teachers a day. Similarly, the teachers themselves often see as many as eight classes per day—maybe 240 children. Planning a course of work may have to take into account week-long gaps between short periods with each class, and also the fact that the same working spaces will be used by many different groups. Planning a timetable which has to take into account a broad circuit of subject teaching and larger numbers of children of different ages and abilities is bound to present enormous logistic problems. The job is often complicated by limitations of space and facilities. With the increasing congestion of the secondary-school timetable there are obvious difficulties in fitting in any suggestions for new curriculum work without a broader look at the whole timetable. Otherwise, new types of work can only be accommodated at the expense of time available to existing subjects.

So how much drama is there at the secondary level and how much time is generally allocated for it? The regional surveys of the project's working parties give the following general picture of its allocation in the secondary school—a picture which is broadly supported by a national survey of drama in the secondary school.*

Although drama is now taken in all types of school throughout the British Isles, the total number of such schools still appears to be fairly small—396 schools replied to the national survey, out of an initial sample of 1775, to say that they actually organized drama as part of timetabled work in the school. The majority of these schools were new or recently reorganized comprehensives (46 per cent of a final sample of 259 schools). The survey did indicate a growth of drama in grammar schools (15.4 per cent) and independent schools (14.7 per cent). The opportunities for curriculum innovation are greatest of course in the comprehensive schools with more possibilities for reorganization of the timetable.

The reports from the working parties illustrated that the general development of drama varies from region to region. A questionnaire sent to 83 schools in the Devon area showed that drama was established on the timetable of 48 of them (59 per cent)—in most cases as a compulsory activity, particularly in the first three years. In the Leeds Metropolitan Area 107 middle, high and secondary schools were contacted. Of these the working party found that 75 had a 'definite drama policy throughout the school (as distinct from it being casually taught if an individual teacher chooses to teach it)'. These are quite high figures taken nationally. The working party did comment, however, that drama 'was not always being taken by a trained drama teacher'. This is characteristic of the national situation. The numbers of drama specialists in schools, trained or otherwise, are still quite low when compared with specialists in the other arts. In the national sample there were overall twice as many specialists in both art and music.

Generally speaking, if drama is actually on the timetable, it is usual for the school to employ one drama specialist. It is common for there to be two specialists. But it is exceptional to find three or four specialists in the same school. Groups of drama specialists tend to be confined to the large comprehensives. It is interesting that almost a quarter of the schools in the national survey, all of which participated because they organized drama on the timetable, had no drama specialist on the staff. This all points to a situation where drama has tended to be taken for the most part by non-specialists. There were in the sample schools over twice as many non-specialists as specialists. In a large number of cases these were working within the schools' English departments. In 56 per cent of

---

*K. Robinson, *Find a Space*, A report on the teaching of drama based on a survey of 259 secondary schools, prepared for the University of London School Examinations Department, 1975 (mimeo).

the 259 schools, drama was organized through the English department. Approximately 40 per cent of schools have an independent drama department. Over half of these (59 per cent) only had a staff of one. In most of the remaining schools (1.4 per cent) drama was organized through a faculty of creative or expressive arts. It is worth noting that of the total of 294 specialists working in these schools, almost a fifth (17.7 per cent) had had no specific training in drama teaching. One of the underlying reasons for this situation is the tendency to appoint teachers as English/drama specialists, spending a proportion of their time in each area.

The pattern of specialist provision varies, once again from region to region. In the Devon area there are 36 specialists working in 28 schools—although there are 48 schools timetabling drama. Although there is a comparatively high proportion of trained drama teachers in this area, many of them are not able as yet to work through their own departments. In all, 130 teachers were named in the area as spending some part of their week—from one period to a full timetable—teaching drama. In Leeds the numbers of trained drama teachers are shown in Table 1.

Table 1. *Numbers of trained drama specialists in Leeds middle, high and secondary schools (educational year 1974-75)*

|  | Type of school | | |
|  | Middle | High | Secondary |
| --- | --- | --- | --- |
| Number of schools | 52 | 28 | 27 |
| Schools with a 'definite drama policy' | 34 | 21 | 20 |
| Trained drama specialists | 19 | 13 | 20 |

So far as general provision for drama is concerned, even where there are specialists on the staff—appointed specifically to teach drama—it is unusual for them to teach a full timetable of drama. In the view of many teachers this is not altogether a bad thing. Teaching drama continuously can be tremendously exhausting, particularly if there is a large and fast turnover of classes. Some teachers welcome the chance to take other subjects as part of their workload in order to ensure freshness and vitality in their drama work. When there are a number of specialists in the school, the actual amount of teaching time given to drama may be reduced without affecting the children's opportunities in drama. This is not so, however, in schools with only one specialist. In some cases even single specialists are teaching drama for less than 50 per cent of their timetable. So how much time on average can the secondary-school child expect to spend on drama activities in the present situation?

As we have seen, the majority of children can expect to spend no time on drama at all—because there is no drama in the school, at least not within the terms of our inquiry. The general pattern which emerges from the available statistics is that in those schools where drama is timetabled, it is usual for there to be one single period or (in a smaller number of schools) one double period of drama for all children in the first year of secondary school. Slightly fewer schools make drama compulsory in the second and third years. If it is compulsory, once again it is for one or two periods a week. This means in practical terms that the average child may have between 35 and 80 minute of drama per week, until the fourth year. Then the picture changes considerably. The figures in Table 2 give a fairly typical profile.

Table 2. *Number of Leeds middle, high and secondary schools where compulsory drama is established on the timetable for children between the ages of 10 and 16 (educational year 1974-75)*

| Age of pupils | Number of schools | | |
|---|---|---|---|
|  | Middle | High | Secondary |
| 10 + | 34 | — | — |
| 11 + | 34 | — | 20 |
| 12 + | 34 | — | 20 |
| 13 + | — | 21 | 17 |
| 14 + | — | 0 | 1 |
| 15 + | — | 0 | 1 |
| 16 + | — | 0 | 0 |

The Bullock Report also found that:

Improvised Drama was taken by over one-third of the twelve-year-olds but only 17 per cent of the less able fourteen-year-olds. Fewer than 10 per cent of the 'examination' fourteen-year-olds spent time on it, which suggests that it was not considered to be truly 'serious' work. Those children who spent time on this activity tended to have about half an hour on it, the remedial children of both ages marginally less.*

The reasons for this sudden change is, of course, the beginning of the option system in the fourth year. The children now have to decide which subjects to 'keep on' during the two years leading up

* Department of Education and Science, *A Language for Life*, Report of Committee of Inquiry appointed by Secretary of State for Education and Science under Chairmanship of Sir Alan Bullock (HMSO, 1975), p.435.

to the public examinations at the end of the fifth year. To return briefly to the national survey, of the 259 sample schools, only 147 continue to offer drama in the fourth year of the secondary school. It is compulsory in only 41 of these (16 per cent of the total sample). In the fifth year 110 schools still have timetabled drama (compulsory in 21 of these) and in the sixth year, the number drops to 80 (compulsory in 10).

During the first three years the secondary teacher is likely to be working with whole classes of children—between twenty-five and thirty-five pupils. One of the advantages of the option system is that from the fourth year onwards the size of groups falls to between ten and twenty in most cases, and the actual time these children spend on drama effectively doubles to perhaps two double periods per week. The major disadvantage is that for the majority of children starting the fourth year, their brief experience of drama is now over.

# Practical problems within the current situation

A teacher working within this pattern of provision for drama, whether he is a specialist or a non-specialist, faces a number of very real problems in his attempts to realize the value of drama, both for the individual child and for the school as a whole.

## *Time*

Many difficulties arise from having large groups of children for only one or two periods per week each. As one teacher put it:

The problems of working the system which I faced and the weaknesses in my own practice for coping with them, were only too apparent. It was possible that within a given day I was going to have to face eight different groups of about thirty kids, making a grand total of approximately 240 contacts within a day. On that basis alone it seemed to me as if I was fighting a losing battle. With those sorts of numbers it was clearly difficult to build up any meaningful relationships with more than a handful of kids. They didn't know me and I didn't know them—and we were never likely to know each other. They arrived . . . knowing that just thirty minutes later something else would happen. It would seem understandable that children in that situation should start to anticipate the end of the lesson almost before they arrive. There is nothing special about the lesson—there can't be, it only lasts for thirty minutes. They know only too well that you can get away with doing very little in that time when you are part of a group of thirty.

This teacher's reaction is typical of many, highlighting the real problems of working with a continuous succession of different classes. It is difficult to build a working relationship with a group when there is hardly time to learn their names. In addition there is often little time for adequate preparation of the work.

Much of the quality of drama work, as we have seen, depends on the group and the teacher having time to adjust to a new way of working in the lesson, and on developing 'states of readiness' for drama. As this teacher points out, with such limited amounts of time, and set in the context of so many other forms of learning during the day, the group barely has time to adjust before the lesson is over. Consequently, it is often easier to withhold any commitment to the work. This pattern of organization can also directly affect the kind of content the teacher can tackle with each group:

Any attempt to pursue a theme or an idea ran up against the problem of a particular line of development never being completed within the course of one lesson and having to be picked up the following week. This fragments the work . . . it never seems as if you are getting anywhere, nothing ever gets finished and ideas that might have been successful under a different system are abandoned simply because everyone gets 'fed up' with it dragging over a period. Work cannot be done in depth and so the lessons become a series of 'one-offs'—work that can be completed in the course of one lesson. This obviously places considerable limitations on the type of work that is possible.

Apart from affecting the commitment of the children themselves and the type of work that can effectively be tackled, the final casualty of this system can be the teacher's own attitude to his work:

It is difficult to make eight or so lessons seem exciting and different all in one day and it is all too easy to fall into the trap of repeating the successful idea with several different groups. To conjure up twenty-four different ideas in a week in the knowledge that the quality of the work is going to be severely limited can be extremely frustrating for the teacher.

Different teachers will, of course, meet these challenges in different ways. But many teachers feel these frustrations. If the school is sufficiently convinced to introduce drama on to the timetable in the first place, as many undoubtedly are, then there is need to give serious thought to what will constitute adequate provision to ensure that its value is actually realized. Our own observations suggest that while there is something to be said in favour of having limited amounts of drama on the timetable rather than none at all, the complexity of the drama teacher's task raises serious questions about the continued value of short intermittent periods of drama as a general policy in the first three years of the secondary school. The answer to this problem is not necessarily to make unrealistic demands for more and more time for drama at the expense of other curriculum work, but rather to consider whether there are practical alternatives in organizing the time which can be made available. We shall return to the question of alternative patterns of organization below.

As we have seen the single drama teacher can be put under quite considerable pressure if he has sole responsibility for drama in the school, largely because of the large turnover of children and the subsequent difficulties of forming satisfactory working relationships. Any attempt to discuss the possible role of the specialist drama teacher in the school, therefore, must assume a reasonable staff/pupil ratio. Even where there is large non-specialist commitment to drama, the separate responsibilities of the specialist need to be taken into account here.

## Options: examinations in drama

One of the major problems facing the development of drama in schools is the option system leading up to examination entrance in the fourth and fifth years. Of course the problems of drama are by no means unique in this respect. Many curriculum areas, especially in the arts, find themselves low on the timetablers' list of priorities when faced with the demands of the examination system. The trouble here is that the children in most cases have too many options to choose between and too little time in the day to do everything they might want to. Faced with the necessity for quick and permanent decisions, their preferences necessarily turn towards those subjects which will give them a useful qualification for later employment or higher education. If arts teachers are to compete for their attention then, it seems reasonable that they should be prepared, along with other teachers, to offer examination courses themselves. In practice there has been an increase in the number of examination syllabuses in drama. There are a number of advantages in running such courses in the secondary school. Apart from attracting more children to drama in the upper years, the examination course makes drama more accountable in the eyes of both parents and other members of staff. It can also result in an increase in essential facilities. Yet many teachers are reluctant to introduce examinations in drama. What are the reasons for this?

It is important to distinguish here between assessment and examinations. Assessment, in the sense of making judgements about the progress and quality of classroom work, is an essential part of the teacher's everyday work. Examinations, on the other hand, are controlled and structured attempts to classify individual ability or achievement according to predetermined criteria. The results of this process are put to specific uses in grading pupils' work one against another. In practice examinations are associated with the idea of success and failure. But a major underlying ethic guiding the arts teacher's work is that there are no wrong answers and no entirely right ones either. Experiential work in the arts is to do with personal interpretations and subjective response. The teacher's judgements about the quality of work are largely value-laden, made in the context of each specific group. To introduce an element of competitive grading seems in many ways to be not only incompatible with what such teachers are trying to achieve, but also largely irrelevant to it. Even accepting a necessity to examine the work, the problem still remains of finding a form for the examination which takes account of the value judgements which the teacher includes in his assessments. To use these subjective judgements as the basis for objective gradings harbours an obvious paradox which many teachers would prefer to keep away from.

Quite apart from the ethical problems involved in examining drama, there is the problem of what to examine. In answering this, it is possible in fact to resolve some of the more philosophical problems. The drama teacher is concerned with the development of particular skills—in the use of dramatic media. Whether drama is being used as a creative process in its own right or as a way of understanding a range of themes or topics, its general content is tremendously wide-ranging. But taken in its total relationship with the arts, the area of content for which the drama teacher can claim a specific responsibility relates to the theatre as an art form. There seems to be no reason why these two aspects of the drama teacher's total work should not provide a reasonable basis for an examination course. Moreover such a course need not in itself involve the drama teacher in any contradictions in theory or in practice in the way he tackles the rest of his work in the school. As it happens, most of the existing examination courses are in the area of theatre arts.* For those children with a particular interest in the theatre these can provide a stimulating and at the same time challenging course of study. But there is a need for caution here. There are two further issues which must be taken into account when deciding whether or not to introduce such a course in the senior years of the school.

Firstly, an examination in theatre arts does not represent the total range of work for which the drama teacher is responsible. The drama teacher's general commitment is to the use of drama as a way of exploring and making sense of the child's own sub-jective experience. Although, as we have argued, this is related fundamentally to the functions and process of the theatre, it does not necessarily lead to a study of the theatre as such. The theatre is

---

* Schools Council English Committee, *Examinations in Drama*, Occasional Bulletins from the Subject Committees (Schools Council, Summer 1974).

merely one aspect of drama work. It is possible, and indeed likely in many schools, that there will be a group of children who will develop a specific interest in theatre work and these should be catered for. The danger is that in introducing an examination course, for whatever reason, the rest of the teacher's work, even in the lower school, might begin to be seen as a preparation for the examination option. The natural and logical planning of the drama work in the school should begin with the teacher's aims and objectives for drama as a whole, in the context of the school. Methods of assessment should grow out of this. This is a process which can easily be reversed through the introduction of an examination. Secondly, it must be accepted that examinations in theatre arts are likely to appeal to a minority of children. The teacher and the school therefore need to consider how to provide for older children who want to continue with the general work in drama but who do not have this specific interest in theatre work. If drama work in the first three years of the secondary school is seen mainly as a preparation for a subsequent examination in theatre arts, how is this to be justified in the case of the majority of children who, through lack of opportunity or lack of inclination, do not take up the option? It is essential that the majority of children are given a meaningful course of work and not a preparation for an examination they never take which leaves them frustrated by the work and wondering what it was all about.

Short of a school reviewing its upper-school curriculum altogether, it is likely that drama will continue as an option. The business of devising and operating a well-balanced option system can be extremely complicated, with many variables to be taken into consideration. The option schemes of most schools offer discrete package deals, but great care is normally taken to ensure that each course maintains some kind of balance between arts and sciences, and so on. The established core subjects, such as English and mathematics, are compulsory or tend to appear in most courses. A pupil whose strengths and interests lie in a minority subject, however, may well find that it only appears in one course of options. He then has to face up to the problem that in opting for one subject he is also opting out of a range of others. In one of the regional surveys, the working party considered this question of what the pupil who takes drama is likely to leave behind him. They found the answers (shown in table 3) disturbing.

In many cases the pupil opting for drama is unable to continue his work in any of the other creative arts.

The drama teacher needs to be clear about the specific reasons for introducing an examination into the school, the kind of children it is intended to cater for, and the functions the examination course will have. If it is intended to complement the child's overall work in drama rather than to pursue a specific interest in theatre studies, this should be reflected in the content and form of the examination itself. In other words, an examination not based on theatre arts should grow out of general course work in drama and reflect the kinds of learning the teacher has been anxious to encourage. This would suggest a scheme of examination where the bias is on practical work. Such examinations naturally present problems in moderating standards of achievement between individuals. Nevertheless a number of examination boards have begun to experiment along these lines. One board, for example, has developed an examination which does not have a written paper. Eighty per cent of the marks are awarded for practical work in acting-out (thirty-five per cent for improvised work on the day and forty-five per cent for work which has been prepared beforehand). The remaining twenty per cent are awarded for 'understanding texts'.* The criteria for assessment in any examination based largely on practical work should grow out of the teacher's general approach to assessment in the rest of his work and be related to the specific aims of the examination (see Chapters 4 and 5).

Table 3. *Subject options timetabled against drama in Cambridgeshire schools (educational year 1974-75)*

| Subject | Percentage of schools |
|---|---|
| Design (including art and craft) | 24 |
| Music | 20 |
| A foreign language | 12 |
| Any academic subject at O level | 12 |
| Social service | 8 |
| Environmental studies | 8 |
| Home economics | 4 |
| Office studies | 4 |
| Computer studies | 4 |
| Link courses with technical colleges | 4 |

The failure to provide adequate courses in drama, albeit as an option, for non-examination groups after the third year raises an

* For a discussion and comparison of existing syllabuses see Schools Council, *Examinations in Drama,* Occasional Bulletins from the Subject Committees (Schools Council, Summer 1974). Also see J. Compton, 'C.S.E. examinations in drama', *Young Drama 4,* (June 1976). Thimble Press in Association with Heinemann Educational Books.

interesting question. If the value of drama is sufficiently recognized to include it in the timetable in the first three years, why is it not provided for during the adolescent years when it is of equal importance?

It is equally disturbing, though the instances of this seem less, that in some schools drama can only be taken by pupils not involved in GCE O level examination courses. This may reflect a belief, which is however becoming less common, that drama is of most value with the academically less able child who finds difficulties in more formal work. While it is certainly true that drama has this value, there is no evidence to support the conclusion which is drawn from this that drama has no value for the intellectually-gifted child. While, in principle, most schools would agree that the value of drama is largely unrelated to such abilities, their belief is not always put into practice in the design of the option system.

There are then a number of problems for drama inherent in both the examination system itself and the option schemes which surround it. However the particular problems of dealing with the question of examinations are faced, we would suggest that the introduction of drama into more than one of the option courses offered would certainly allow the process of drama to make a more meaningful contribution to the curriculum of the upper school, as well as making more complete sense of including it in the timetable of the lower school.

## Existing attitudes to drama

Any consideration of the place of drama in the curriculum and the present provision for it on the timetable should take account of current attitudes to drama both of other members of staff and of those children with little previous experience in drama. The potential of drama as a way of teaching in many subject areas will only be realized, of course, if the staff concerned are convinced of its usefulness and have some direct experience of the process in action. Similarly any claims the drama specialist makes for more time, particularly in the upper school, will depend for their success on the general sympathy of the school for the kind of work he is trying to do. Because drama teaching is relatively new, many members of staff have not yet had the opportunity of forming a judgement of drama based on direct experience.

Drama involves the children and the teacher in a different kind of working relationship. One of the contributors to the project undertook a micro-study of attitudes to drama in a particular school.* He concluded from this study that other members of staff do not always interpret this new kind of relationship favourably. A lack of sympathy for drama, where it does exist, may be rooted in an overall concern for what is seen as a general decline in standards of behaviour in schools. Drama may be seen, mistakenly, as a contributor to this 'erosion of standards' since it does indeed demand a different kind of control and discipline from more formal methods of teaching. But it would be quite wrong to associate this in itself with a decline in teaching standards or levels of behaviour. This misconception perhaps arises from the fact that many teachers have not yet had the chance to see or take part in a drama session. This does raise the question of whether or not the drama teacher should feel under any more pressure than other teachers to show colleagues his work. The difficulty with drama is that usually the only work which the rest of the school sees is performance-based. This is not the kind of work with which the teacher is primarily concerned on a day-to-day basis in the classroom. In order to give a fuller impression of the nature of his work, the drama teacher should perhaps be prepared to give practical demonstrations to other colleagues.

Certainly there is a limited value in just describing what he does to interested teachers. In the study school mentioned above, the drama teacher was convinced of the need to involve other teachers. But he was sure that

talking to the staff in the staffroom was counter-productive. He had tried it but was now of the opinion that a demonstration in action was more likely to influence people than the staff-room commercial.

In trying to convince colleagues of the value of his own work, the drama teacher should be aware that

he could well find himself in the position of trying to convert other staff to his way of working while turning a deaf ear to other people's ideas. He must watch out that he's not rejecting while trying to attract.

Of course involving other colleagues in practical work is not always as straightforward as it might sound. A teacher in another school was asked to do just this.

Some time ago, after I had been on two or three drama courses, the headmaster asked me if I would pass on something of what I had learnt to the rest of the staff. This was the practice in the school at the time. People would come back from craft courses or music courses and take us in a short session passing on some of their new skills. The drama session was

*C.L. Winston, 'An enquiry into how teachers in one school perceive the nature, role and value of drama in education'. (Department of Education St Luke's College, Exeter.)

fixed for a Monday afternoon, so I went away and tried to think up a plan for a session in which they would feel safe. I tried really hard. I screwed up paper after paper as I rejected plans which I thought would make them feel uncomfortable. Finally, I had a plan which I felt they could do happily, without any embarrassment. When Monday afternoon came and I was due to take the staff, a message was sent along to me to say that 'the 20 children with whom you are going to take the drama demonstration lesson will be waiting for you outside the hall at 4 o'clock'! . . . I explained that I didn't want to take a drama session with the children but with the staff . . . Mutiny broke out. One said, 'I don't care what you are going to do or what you have planned, I am not going to do it.'

Q: What do you think they thought they were going to be asked to do?
A: I suppose they thought they were going to be asked to be trees. I had spent a quarter of an hour explaining to them that this wasn't the sort of work I wanted them to do. I had planned a gentle session where they didn't have to crawl around on the floor or anything, some simple exercises just so they could feel what it was like to be a member of a drama session. They had to experience it. They would not do it at all. In the end I was coerced into taking the session with the children as arranged. I wish I hadn't done this.
Q: And what did the staff think of the demonstration lesson they saw?
A: They thought it was super.

The tendency for teachers to judge the work of colleagues in terms of their ability to control their classes may well be counteracted by their experiencing the work at first hand, as participants. Having seen this class work, these teachers might then have been more prepared to become involved themselves. Nevertheless, the teacher's frustration is easily understood.

It must be said that the children themselves, in particular circumstances, are just as reluctant to become involved in drama. This is especially true of older children who are introduced to drama late in their school careers. The differences in criteria for success, the freedoms of response, can make the senior child critical of the value of drama, if it conflicts strongly with the forms of behaviour he has become accustomed to. This can lead in turn to quite real discipline problems for the teacher. The following account comes from the head of a creative arts department which makes extensive use of drama. The department is now meeting with increasing success in terms of pupils' responses and teacher co-operation. In the first year of the new department's work, however, they met with many problems particularly with those of the older children who were completely unused to such work.

Certainly with the fifth year we had probably arrived too late. The lower band were anti any kind of education and a subject that didn't even have an exam at the end of it *'must* be useless'. They were utterly unused to freedom of movement, thought and speech . . . their prejudices against any kind of friendly approach were immense and we were treated with distrust. The boys we certainly failed with. The girls we taught as a separate group were a little more responsive. Next to the first and second years, our work with them was the most exciting, rewarding and, we think, creative.

The fourth years also proved difficult. The upper band treated us with an air of condescending tolerance . . . The lower band had the impression that we were a filler-in for them. Although they hated their formal subjects, at least they could justify them—they had at least always been taught in schools. Often, whatever we tried was wrong:

Drama: 'Oh, this is silly.'

Writing: 'Oh, this is English.'

Painting: 'Oh, this is art!'

Discussions: 'Oh, this is boring, all we do is talk.'

Of course there were good moments and there were children who were openly responsive and understanding. More importantly, we had to be responsive and understanding, we had to realize their past history, make allowances and adapt.

The third years were rather unique. We worked with them in a building which was isolated from the main school and this presented many administrative and organizational problems. At first they were wary of us but were inclined to give us a chance. Unfortunately, after their initial acceptance their feelings changed. Due possibly to the influence of older children, staff impressions and possibly our own failings, they became less tolerant and old prejudices grew strong again. One of the worst body blows for us must have been their all-important Careers Talk: 'Decide now what exams you are going to take in the fourth year or your life will be ruined for ever.' What chance did Creative Arts have against a threat like that?

There is little doubt that streaming in the third, fourth and fifth years made our job a lot harder. Those that felt it most were the lower bands. By the fifth year they had more or less accepted themselves as second-class citizens, convinced everyone that they were unteachable and accepted failure long ago. To awaken a person to their own individuality, to their responsibility to themselves and to others . . . was something incomprehensible to the pupils.

This may be an extreme example. But these problems can be met in setting up courses in creative work late on in the school life of the pupils. Many of the issues raised in this situation are very wide-ranging. Of immediate importance to our own inquiry is the initial suspicion and reluctance which these teachers met in those children who had no previous background in expressive work. There is no doubt that these attitudes can be overcome with patience and experiment. But the development of them in the first place can be avoided through an early introduction to this kind of work lower in the school. If there is continuity in drama work from the lower school—and especially if there is a smooth carry-over from expressive work in the primary school—drama becomes a familiar experience with a known code of behaviour using skills which are gradually and permanently acquired.

Establishing drama in the school and exploiting its potential across the curriculum needs time and adequate facilities. It also depends on the specialist's abilities to build up co-operative relationships within the school, among both staff and children. This in turn relies on a favourable attitude to drama in the school, based on a clear understanding of the kind of process it is. If these elements are lacking drama can be caught up in a cycle of constraint in the timetable itself which will prevent it having any long-term impact.

*A cycle of constraint in the development of drama in the timetable*

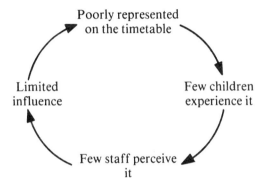

In many schools the problems of increasing the influence of drama, as a specialism and a non-specialism, are organizational. How can the work be blended into the timetable in such a way that its effect will be most strongly felt? Are there patterns of organization, beyond the ones we have described so far, which are better suited to the sort of experiences in which drama is based, and the kinds of developments the drama teacher is employed to bring about?

## *Some practical ways of organizing drama in the curriculum*

The timetable provision for drama is related to the overall planning, aims and objectives of the school itself. Where drama is simply being fitted into an existing timetable based on small periods, it is likely to be given only minimum time, possibly one period per week with each class. While it is still possible for valuable work to take place within such a framework, as we have seen, it can lead to a fragmentation of the work and have a negative effect, in the long term, on the attitudes of both staff and pupils. It often happens within this kind of planning of the timetable that 'priority' subjects are catered for first and then the gaps which remain are filled with the 'low status' subjects. Over time these subjects can come to be seen as ancillary to the 'main curriculum'. Moreover post third-year courses are often divisive between prestigious and non-prestigious subjects, defined within the terms of the examination system and the qualifications market. On the whole drama seems to have fared better, both in terms of opportunities and actual results, in the schools where its place is considered within a concept of the total curriculum—hence its strong presence in the comprehensive schools where the opportunities for a general reorganization of the day are so much greater. Although we would argue that more time should be made available for drama, there is the question of whether the best use is being made of the time which is available. There are a number of alternative ways of organizing drama which can give more opportunity for work to develop as well as increasing the variety and breadth of work which can be tackled.

## Block release

In a system of block release, large numbers of children, say a whole or a half year-group, are timetabled together with one department for an extended period of time. The teachers in the department then decide how best to divide the block of time according to the work which is planned. One way in which this can benefit the drama teacher is that instead of having a group of children for, say, six forty-minute periods of drama over half a term, the group are released from the normal timetable once during the half term to work with the drama teacher for a whole day, or longer. There are a number of advantages in this system. The most obvious of these is that the work which takes place within the block can develop at its own pace without the need to break off after a short amount of time and then having to wait for a week to elapse before the work can be resumed. Operating the system involves the co-operation of other departments who stand to miss their own periods with the group during the drama session, but this is largely counteracted by the fact of it happening only once in a period of six weeks or more. With only minimal interruption of the rest of the school timetable, the drama teacher can pursue his own work within a concentrated block of time. A disadvantage is that if the blocks are widely spaced, it is difficult if not impossible to ensure continuity of work from one session to the next.

A teacher who promoted and worked within a block-release system in his own school described its effects on the children's work as follows:

Under the new system, classes were receiving three and a half days of drama two or three times a year. An immediate advantage was that the children had a tendency to look forward to their drama lesson. Changing out of uniform for a day also made sense; but most of all, the bells, that so reduce the day to segments of time, became irrelevant. The day could be structured as we wanted it; the rhythm of the pupil's day could be controlled, could be more organic. The block period enabled a sense of overall achievement, for within the time we could have explored something and made a statement about it in some way. The pupils all had folders in which work that emerged could be kept and the room itself could take on the characteristic of the work being carried out.

Lessons were not a series of beginnings, the concerns and disciplines of the work being done predominated. The relationships were not built on knowing names and habits but on the relationship of both pupils and teacher to the work.

As a result of the success of the block system in the first and second forms of the school during its first year of operation in this school, it was subsequently extended to include the third year. Other subjects also began to be blocked. An unfortunate side-effect of this was that the drama block was increasingly being cut into. The growth of the school, and the consequent increase in the number of groups, meant that the number of times any one group could be blocked had to be reduced. For one year the system of block release operated in years one to four but encountered problems in the fourth year with the examination options. The system which eventually prevailed was a block release in years one to three, four single periods of drama with a fourth-year option group, four periods with a fifth-year option group and two periods each with a sixth-year option group and a fourth-year remedial class. Eventually a second drama specialist was appointed. Unfortunately the two teachers were not released to operate the block system. An alternative system was therefore devised which used both music and drama teachers as a team. The lessons were, in this case, called Combined Arts and revolved around half-day blocks with half year-groups. The teacher commented that this: 'was a logical step and enabled us to have drama throughout the school. At the same time it placed drama skills within a more sensible relationship and within an outward-looking context.'

There are a number of variations on the block-release system which allow it to be adapted to fit the particularities of different schools. Its essential advantage is that it allows the children and the teacher much more time to develop work through to satisfactory conclusions rather than continually starting projects or looking for less ambitious ideas which can be accommodated with much shorter periods. A disadvantage is that the children have less continuous experience of drama.

A variation within the block system which partially overcomes this is the 'circuit' or 'roundabout'. Here a group of teachers from different departments work within the same block of time, taking groups of children from the main block to work in their own discipline. This has the added advantage of encouraging opportunities for different subject specialists to co-operate in a shared course of work. In one secondary school, for example, which was using a circuit system, half year-groups were timetabled for half a day each week to a combination of the drama, music and religious education departments. In practice, the drama teacher would take a third of this group for the whole half-day each week over the course of half a term. Each of the other departments would also take a third of the group. After half a term the groups moved around on the circuit to one of the other subjects. This meant, in each case, that the specialist teachers worked with each group for an intensive period of about six weeks in every eighteen. Once again the opportunities for intensive work seemed to improve the children's commitment within each of the circuit subjects. At the beginning this system was set up only for the first two years. In year three, however, the drama teacher was still seeing five groups for an hour each week. Since he found this unsatisfactory he looked for ways of adapting the system within the existing timetable. As it happened, several of the third-year sessions were blocked with the English and music departments, but there was no co-operation between departments at that time.

Since we were basically a group of five or so teachers with the whole of the year-group it seemed as if a more rational use of the time could be made. I therefore approached these departments . . . and proposed a Combined Arts type of system which would put drama as a system at the service of music and English and give a meaningful context to their work. At the same time it would allow a flexible approach to the arrangement of groups and teachers, so that, for instance, in some weeks instead of seeing five separate groups I was only seeing one group for five sessions.

The benefits of seeing groups for longer periods of time also extended to both the music and the English teachers. There were some initial reservations in the other departments. The most strongly felt of these was that the children would feel confused by the apparent complications. They would not know where they were supposed to be and would be 'upset by change'. In practice, the system is less complicated in terms of the master timetable, and the actual changeovers within the blocks were easily arranged and · explained from week to week.

Using a block release system, whether or not it is associated with a circuit of specialist teaching, as in this case, can immediately benefit drama work through increasing the opportunities for in-depth work, and closer relationships between the teacher and his class. Although drama work becomes on the whole less frequent, there is reason to believe that this is compensated for by the intensity of the work when it does happen. This system obviously makes different demands on the teacher. Exploiting the potential of three hours' continuous work depends on the teacher's skill and resourcefulness in developing and challenging the children's ideas. In other words, he must be able to take the group beyond the initial, prerequisite stages of drama. If the value of the block system is to be realized, the staff involved need to recognize these new demands and be able to meet them. A danger is that if the circuit rotates too slowly—if there is too long a gap between drama sessions—there is little opportunity to encourage progression in the work from term to term. Arranging for block release involves relatively few complications in the master timetable. In many ways it makes timetabling simpler. There is no reason, of course, why less frequent work with the drama specialist for each class should reduce the amount of drama which can take place with non-specialists during other subject teaching. Indeed it is hoped that any such changes in organization would not be at the expense of non-specialist work.

In both the examples given, the drama teachers have tried to encourage integration with other departments. This can present tremendous opportunities for enriching the work of all the departments concerned.

## An illustration of drama and creative arts within a block timetable

In discussing the functions of drama at a theoretical level we suggested that drama is best understood within the general context of the arts. In practical terms we would also place drama within the general organization of the arts in the school. There are enormous possibilities here for practical integration of music, art and drama work. We want to qualify this, however, before discussing some of the ways in which this can be done. However much the arts are integrated, they each make quite distinctive demands on the child, as disciplines in their own right. Music, art and drama operate through different forms of expression, and draw and rely on the development of different skills in their own distinctive media. If integration is to be effective, each of these areas needs to be allowed sufficient time to itself at some point in the timetable for the children to become accustomed to different ways of working and to explore the potential of these different forms of expression.

While drama may flourish within a faculty of creative arts, such a faculty is probably best composed of separate departments made up of specialist teachers. Successful integration is not simply a matter of legislation within the timetable. Obviously it cannot happen in the first place unless adequate opportunities for co-operation are created. But where these opportunities exist there must also exist a willingness on the part of the staff involved to co-operate, and to work together in a compatible and complementary way.

By creating more amenable staff/pupil ratios, team-teaching can provide invaluable opportunities for attention to individual children and a high degree of concentrated involvement. The head of the creative arts department quoted earlier recognized the pressures of exposing one's work to other colleagues. But he emphasized that:

. . . one of the most valuable things to learn is sharing. In team-teaching the failures in front of others are embarrassing, the successes are exhilarating. But more important than all this, they are shared.

By becoming aware of your own teaching style, by self-criticism and by discussion with other members of staff, you learn to change, progress, consolidate, adapt, and adopt all that is good and eradicate all that is bad.

The success of integrated courses relies to an enormous extent on having adequate time for planning the work and reflecting on it afterwards. Without this essential planning the quality of the work can be severely affected. One of the dangers of working exclusively in an independent department is that the work of the specialist becomes isolated from the rest of the school. A comparable danger in integrated work is that with insufficient time to plan in advance, the work becomes diluted and dissipated. This means recognizing a need to allocate time for planning sessions between staff within the timetable itself.

Every Creative Arts session needs to be well and adequately planned. This in many cases, in our own school, has been impossible. The team-teaching sessions have suffered most. Even with break-time, lunch-time, after-school and holiday-time meetings, getting together for sufficient lengths of time has proved difficult. I know for a fact that many of the staff have accused us of being boring because we were always talking Creative Arts.

But the plain facts are that if we didn't use literally every available minute of our time for discussion, then Creative Arts would be worse off.

Without such planning it is extremely difficult for staff to explore different ways of working with each other except in action in the classroom, where the immediate pressures and demands from the children, for whom the work is after all designed, may leave them little time to develop their thinking about general principles and organization. More than one attempt at integration has failed precisely through the frustration and sense of imminent failure which this situation can breed. The long-term effect may be that the initial enthusiasm wanes and the individual specialists go back to working exclusively in their own departments where they feel more sure of their ground.

Once the organizational mechanisms for integration have been established, it is for the staff themselves to experiment with and evaluate different patterns of co-operation, in the light of the children's responses. Finding a satisfactory formula will only happen through trial and error. The following account of the evolution of a creative arts project describes some of the alternatives which were explored in a large middle school.

In the first year the whole year-group was timetabled together for two double periods. After a short time this was changed to a whole morning for it was found that the team could work more effectively in continuous block of time. They used hall/gym, the Drama room, four ordinary classrooms, the Woodwork room and the Arts room. Staff engaged in this: teachers of (i) Woodwork, (ii) Housecraft, (iii) Art, (iv) English, (v) Dance. It was difficult at first because only two teachers had any real leanings towards Creative Arts or to team-teaching, but they were all prepared to have a go. They began by choosing a theme and dividing the year-group into four groups and the teachers did their own specialism with each group.

They would be horrified to work in this way now because children were only exploring the theme in one medium. There was no actual integration at all.

Very soon they began to rotate the children from medium to medium while still working on the same theme, within each of them. But this still did not seem to them to be true team-teaching or Creative Arts.

The next stage therefore was to choose a theme, and some sort of starter activity, and then let the children choose which medium they wanted to work in—the teachers still working within their own specialisms. Certain aspects of this worried them:

(i)   Children were choosing teachers and/or a medium rather than asking, 'How do I most want to express this theme?'

(ii)  It became too heavily weighted in the arts and dance/drama areas and other aspects of the course, e.g. writing, had few customers.

To combat this the team of teachers designed pamphlets about the theme containing some starter ideas in all arts areas. One pamphlet was given to each small group of five children and as a group they had to cover all the arts areas.

Teachers were still worried that they were being over-directive. Yet there was a danger that the children would be spoilt for choice if there was no direction. Moreover they might not develop their skills sufficiently in particular arts to express their ideas to any degree of satisfaction.

A small group of children who did not want to do anything were picked up by a fifth, floating teacher and allowed to do anything that interested them. While coping with this problem, the floating teacher also had to assist with large groups of children in other activities as a general member of the team.

All of these developments within the team's original conception of Creative Arts, took place during its first year of operation. In the second year this year-group carried on with a whole morning as did the new third year. Because the school had increased its numbers, the year-groups now had to work in only four spaces: hall/gym, Drama room, Art room, Music room. This meant that some groups were now too big. The pressures and problems caused the Art teacher to lose interest in the block. There was a new Music teacher who worked well on his own but did not like team-teaching. The Art teacher eventually attended a course and came back into the scheme more committed than ever to this way of working. He took over the leadership of the team and moved the work away from exploring themes to that of making statements in individual or mixed media, on topics of direct interest to the children.

By this time a full-time drama teacher had been appointed to the school and became the fifth member of the team (Music, English, Dance, Drama.) Generally work on any topic could last one week or as much as half a term. Later they felt that spending half a term on a topic did not put the children under enough pressure. It also tended to make them over-elaborate their statements and lose their immediacy.

Eventually they worked on the theme of 'Black and White' (it is a multiracial school). Children working in each area completed their work in half a morning and in the second half of the morning they all came together in the hall/gym to create a joint statement. There was large-scale art work creating an overall environment with dance, music, drama and some writing taking place within it.

It was at this point that the team felt they had come much nearer to discovering what team-teaching within the Creative Arts was all about. There was a flow of staff and children from room to room and from medium to medium during the exploration period. This led to the final coming together in the shared expressive statement. Staff had become advisers and consultants, helping and encouraging the children to take the work in the direction they wanted it to go in.

As they began to plan the work for the third year this became the basis for their thinking. There are still difficulties. There are more children and they are down to four staff again. But they have developed a much more flexible approach with a variety of ways of working and a number of organizational structures being tested within the general block of time. They have also realized that working with the Creative Arts should leave pupils opportunities to make individual statements or to stay in smaller groups on occasions. There should not be a constant emphasis on bringing everything together as one large piece of work.

The task for teachers co-operating in a team is to experiment and try out different patterns of work to find those ways which best meet the challenges of their particular situation. Some thought has to be given by the school as a whole, however, to the best ways of allocating time both for the work to happen and for it to be well planned. Given these conditions and, of course, adequate space and materials, the possibilities are limitless, and the effects on the involvement of the children far-reaching.

## The modular timetable

The keynote of success in the expressive arts is flexibility of organization. Apart from the brevity of the forty-minute period as a general foundation for the timetable, it is also fairly inflexible. It can be doubled to eighty minutes or trebled. But in practice something between these extremes is often more suitable. Not all groups need the same time-frame in drama, and some subjects need different time-frames from others. Also, where the whole school is working in the same time-frame, it means that the available facilities are not always being fully exploited. For long periods of the day teachers are competing for facilities. For short periods throughout the day—breaks and lunchtimes—some facilities are probably not being used at all. Balancing all of these factors and trying to fit them into a rigid time structure can require great ingenuity and does not always meet with success.

This has led some schools to experiment with the so-called 'modular timetable'. This is essentially a different way of managing the time available to the whole school during the week. It does not apply solely to drama. It provides a new conception of the timetable within which drama and other subjects can be given much more appropriate and flexible time allocations. The principle on which this system is based is that the week is divided into a number of small units or modules of time: for example one hundred modules of fifteen minutes. This provides a much more flexible unit for time management. There are a number of ways of using these modules in the organization of the master timetable. In every case the first step is to consider the aims of the school's curriculum and the subjects which make it up. In consultation with the various departments it is decided how many modules of each subject the children in each class need from year to year. The timetable is then composed accordingly. At this level the organization of the timetable is done very much along the lines of the period system. The principal advantage is that subjects are not fixed to the same time-frames. The French teacher, for example, may feel that fifteen or thirty minutes of French every day is a better arrangement for first-year children than three single or two double periods per week. The modular system would lend itself more easily to this. If the school is divided into faculties, however, the management of the master timetable is considerably simplified. The school decides how many modules of time each child should spend with each faculty. These modules are then allocated to the faculty in a block and the faculty members themselves plan how to deploy the time for each group within the separate departments. If the block system is associated with faculties and block timetabling, the only remaining problem for the master timetable is the allocation of space. The use of blocks of time makes this simpler. But there is another advantage. The timetable can actually be staggered during the day, because of the different time-frames. So, for example, while the language faculty is working a block of, say, eight modules (a total of perhaps two hours) with the first year in the morning—the arts faculty may be working with a year-group for six or seven modules. This means that the morning break would come at different times for them. In principle this then means that all available facilities can be put to constant use, thereby avoiding periods of overcrowding followed by periods of empty spaces.

In the particular case of drama, the limited facilities which are usually available can be the scene of continuous activity with different groups—providing of course that there are sufficient staff in proportion to the numbers of children in the school. This system does not mean that integration has to occur. But it does mean that the opportunities for integration are much easier to provide.

A thirteen to eighteen high school associated with the drama project was organized around a faculty structure using the modular system. Faculties were allocated modules and then used the time as they felt most appropriate to the achievement of the school's aims and their own objectives within this. Whole year-groups were taken together with teams of teachers. Lead lessons were followed by group work with individual teachers. Options existed within some modules for children to make choices from the second year onwards. In all cases, except in one second-year module, children could choose drama at some point in the week without prejudicing their selection of examination options. At fourth- and fifth-year level there were both examination and non-examination courses and the modular system was so devised within the option blocks to permit any child who wanted to, to take either course. Also in the fourth year modules were devoted to 'taster' courses each of which extended over six weeks. If a pupil liked the 'taste' of any of these courses he could follow them through as an evening activity in the school's integrated youth centre.

When they appointed a drama teacher, the school wanted to extend the range of drama in the curriculum and this led to the establishment of a creative arts faculty incorporating art, dance, drama and music. The drama teacher led this faculty which taught as a team for most of the time, but also taught within other subject areas.

The level of collaboration and positive achievement which resulted from this confirmed the school's belief in the value of team-teaching and the faculty structure as a whole. When this first drama teacher left for promotion, his successor and other members of the faculty felt that a new approach might be tried. Drama is now within the general studies faculty often linking with other areas of study but also being used separately in the drama studio as a specialism in its own right.

# Conclusions

What general conclusions can be drawn then about the place of drama in the curriculum? There is a clear place for the teaching of drama both by specialists and non-specialists. In the primary and middle schools the possibilities for integrated teaching are enormous. By developing more structured work from the child's natural activities in play, the primary teacher can both enhance his own work in the classroom while laying the foundations in expressive work for the secondary teacher to build on in later years. In the present situation, the lack of continuity from primary to secondary education can lead to real problems as children meet what seem to them to be unusual demands in drama and the creative arts. This in turn can lead to a lack of commitment which helps to establish a cycle of constraint in drama teaching in the timetable. The specialist and non-specialist have related but distinctive roles in the secondary school. However much drama is developed as a non-specialism, we would argue that the provision of trained specialists, in a reasonable proportion to the numbers of children, is essential and that sufficient time should be given for the development of drama in its own right.

The extent to which the value of drama is actually realized in the school depends on two conditions: the quality of the teaching; and adequate provision on the timetable. If drama is to have a significant effect, serious thought needs to be given by the school to the most appropriate ways of organizing it into the curriculum, taking into account the time which is available overall. The greatest opportunities for development to occur are in situations where the drama sessions are not too short or too widely spaced.

Given the opportunities, drama can have an all-embracing relationship in the life of the school. It should be seen as an integral part of the system rather than as a luxurious appendage to the timetable when other curriculum demands have been satisfied. At the same time drama is not an educational panacea. It is one component in the broad process of education. But in the end its introduction into the school will be most rewarding where it is seen in the light of overall aims and objectives of the school's curriculum. If the aims of the drama teacher and the school are compatible and if the teacher is thorough in his approach to his work, he ought reasonably to expect that timetable provision, resources and space will be made available. If drama teachers do not feel these things are happening, they should look at their own work to consider if their methods are appropriate; initiate fuller discussions and involvement with other members of staff and the head; and draw on the help of the Drama Advisory Service.

If a school has clear aims and objectives in introducing

drama—or any new area—into the curriculum in the first place, it is possible, fairly simply, to devise timetable structures which will facilitate the achievement of those objectives and repay their investment. A broader view of the place of drama in the curriculum might help it to break out of the cycle of constraint which currently limits its growth.

# Chapter 8
# Resources for Drama
## Provision in the school

So far we have discussed time allocation, staffing and possible patterns of organization for drama in schools. We now need to consider the kind of facilities necessary for drama. Where is drama currently being taught in the school? In a classroom, an adapted space (hall, gym) or a purpose-built studio/workshop? Does the size of the working space relate to the size of the group? Where is the drama space in relation to other teaching areas and what constraints/freedoms does this offer? What is the effect of working in different kinds of spaces? What provision in terms of facilities can best serve the needs of pupils and teachers engaged in drama? Does drama need or benefit from specialist equipment?

## Space for drama

There is some truth in the view that drama can take place almost anywhere, with no special facilities. Unfortunately this has led some administrators to place drama at the bottom of their list when allocating rooms and resources each year. It partly explains why drama has been observed in places as unlikely as dining-rooms, cloakrooms and even corridors. In general, spaces allocated for drama can be divided into three categories: purpose-built studios/workshops; rooms converted for drama; unconverted classrooms, gyms, halls. In a sample of 259 schools it was found that drama was taught in 587 different spaces during the week; 22 per cent of these spaces used were purpose-built, 28 per cent were converted and 50 per cent were unconverted.* Converted areas refer to any space that has been adapted specifically for drama work. This usually involves providing blackout facilities, a clear, smooth floor space, possibly additional lighting equipment and a simple sound system. Often two classrooms are knocked together to provide a larger space; conversely, partitions may be put up in over-large spaces to give a more intimate working area. Half of the

*K. Robinson, *Find a Space*, a report on the teaching of drama based on a survey of 259 secondary schools, prepared for the University of London School Examinations Department, 1975 (mimeo).

spaces used for teaching drama were unconverted areas, usually classrooms or assembly/dining halls. it is not surprising, therefore, that nearly half the teachers in the survey (42 per cent) felt that the areas available for drama work were inadequate. Yet, if drama can take place almost anywhere, why do so many teachers insist that facilities are inadequate? What is wrong with a classroom or an assembly hall? What is so special about a purpose-built studio? Will good drama automatically occur if the space is right? What are the advantages and disadvantages of working in different spaces?

Successful drama can and does take place in classrooms which sometimes provide the right kind of intimate atmosphere. For the general class teacher or non-specialist it also means that as the opportunity for drama work arises naturally, the teacher can seize it without changing rooms. This is not always easy though. The nature of the work will probably require some clear floor space which means moving desks, tables, chairs, to the side of the room or by stacking them. This may result in a lack of enthusiasm which can affect the pupils' attitude towards drama. Equally, having to prepare a classroom for drama and clear up afterwards can mean that ten minutes of the lesson is lost. This loss is considerable if the teacher only has the class for thirty or forty minutes. Classrooms are almost always built adjacent to one another. What is a tolerable level of noise for drama work may not be tolerable for French or Mathematics, taking place next door. Therefore the teacher is placed in the unenviable position of either curbing the natural and often necessary noise level of the drama by nagging reminders or else having to deliberately structure 'quiet' drama work out of consideration for the needs of colleagues working nearby. The noise level and the necessity for freedom of movement that drama requires are two of the key factors in making it unpopular with other staff. If the space for drama were reasonably separate from teaching areas in subjects requiring long periods of quiet, this hostility need not arise.

If drama takes place in the main hall there are also a number of constraints. The advantage that a hall has over a classroom is the amount of space and fewer physical obstacles. But the disadvantages of a public space can be enormous. First, the hall may be used for a number of different purposes—assembly, outside speakers, dining, PE/Dance, public examinations, and school occasions. It may even be a thoroughfare for the rest of the school. Teaching drama in such a space means the class and teacher are never certain that the lesson will not be cancelled or interrupted for a number of reasons: perhaps the school orchestra needs to practise for open day; desks have to be set out for public exams, the PTA are having a 'function' and need to get the hall ready, etc. As well as the uncertainty there are the distractions. Often the kitchens are adjacent to the hall and as well as rattling their pots and pans, always at inappropriate moments in the acting-out, the kitchen staff have to lay and clear tables which makes the periods before and after lunch virtually unworkable. Linked with this is the question of atmosphere.

Children associate work with the kind of environment that it takes place in. An art room, science laboratory, or housecraft room sets the atmosphere for that activity and in most cases is reserved exclusively for that purpose. It is difficult for some children to commit themselves seriously to drama knowing that in forty-five minutes they will be eating their lunch on the same spot. The greatest distraction and inhibiting factor to any drama work is probably having the space used as a corridor by the rest of the school. Projecting into symbolic roles and 'as if' situations can be a vulnerable activity requiring privacy and trust. It is impossible to create such an atmosphere when pupils and other staff amble through the hall, causing embarrassment to many pupils. These 'intruders' are reminders of the 'real' roles at work alongside their 'symbolic' acting-out and often prevent a sustained commitment on the symbolic level.

So drama *of sorts* can take place almost anywhere. But drama work of quality requires certain practical consideration. Drama work, of whatever kind, is essentially practical. It requires space to move, and space for individual and group work to be done without the interference which results from overcrowding. The basic requirements are: a skilful teacher and a space *in which anything can happen*. This last point is important. In real terms it is not so important whether the space is an adapted room or a purpose-built one, providing it fulfils these basic requirements and offers space, privacy, and possibilities. But possibilities for what? For movement; for sound/music; for constructing environments—physically/atmospherically; for painting; craft; reading; writing; discussion . . . all of which may be legitimate.

An ideally equipped workshop does not necessarily produce the best drama, just as beautiful equipment is no substitute for bad teaching. But the more facilities a good teacher has, the more opportunities he has to heighten and refine the quality of the drama experience. Some teachers only use technical facilities in performances yet their reasons for doing so apply equally to curriculum work. There is no one ideal type of space to suit everyone. But a space 'in which anything can happen' will automatically demand certain practical considerations. If the children are to move freely, perhaps barefoot, the texture of the floor is important. If they are to paint or build environments, it must be durable. If lighting is to be used, the floor must have a non-reflective surface. Equally the walls must be considered. If lighting is to be used to maximum effect, the walls should be very darkly painted in a matt finish. If there are windows, they should have heavy blackouts. If there are no windows, it is important that the ventilation system is quiet. Films or slides may need to be shown, so that one of the four walls might remain matt white for this purpose. In a space 'in which anything can happen' children should be allowed to use the equipment and resources available; therefore safety is an essential consideration. All equipment must be safe, durable and easily accessible. This implies towers or catwalks, patching units, a variety of stations for plugging in controls, controls in the same room, good storage space. Such considerations have led to the design of purpose-built drama studios or workshops. These are most commonly found in recently built schools; in particular the larger comprehensives. Designs for these vary tremendously. Some double as theatres for school productions and concerts, while a few exceptional schools have both a theatre and a studio.

Some authorities have clear specifications for the facilities they feel schools require.

In Leeds it is now established policy that a new secondary or high school will have one purpose-built drama studio per 750 children. This studio is intended primarily as a teaching space for curriculum drama, but each one is individually designed to give maximum flexibility, and also suitability for small audience performance work.

Some of our schools are specifically designed as a community complex, in which case a purpose-built theatre is included in the schedule in addition to the drama studio. A new studio costs, at present, in the region of £10,000 to equip with lighting, sound, rostra, drapes, percussion instruments etc.

It is more difficult to find funds to provide facilities for existing schools. If drama work is being purposefully developed in the school one looks for suitable spaces to be converted into a drama studio that has the same essential facilities as those provided in a new school.

When teachers in Devon were asked by questionnaire to list the two or three facilities or resources they had available and found most useful in their work, the items of equipment most frequently mentioned were: record-player, tape-recorder, lighting and blackout. Music or other recorded sounds may be a stimulus for drama work or a means of underpinning a statement. They may be previously arranged or arise spontaneously. Children may select music/sound or record their own. Therefore a simple yet effective sound system (including a tape-recorder and/or record-player) is a high priority. Lighting equipment has much the same function in creative drama as in theatre. It is used primarily to build environments, create atmosphere, suggest locations, to isolate areas so as to focus attention and increase concentration, for work in groups or with the whole class.

While drama teachers place special importance on good sound and lighting systems, other items of equipment can also be immensely valuable. Portable drama rostra that stack easily and are relatively lightweight allow new dimensions to be created through the construction of a variety of levels and the arrangements of these shapes. Percussion instruments are an immediate source of improvised sound and allow children to experiment with the effects of sound in their representations during acting-out. A slide projector is useful, though it may not need to be permanently housed in the drama space. Slides projected on to walls can quickly create atmospheres, in the same way as sound and general lighting. Videotape recorders are being used increasingly in drama. One advantage is that they provide immediate playback for comment and evaluation. They can also be used as a creative medium. Somewhere in the drama space there needs to be a large cupboard or library containing a range of literature, play texts, tapes, records, slides, visual and documentary material, art and craft materials, and the tools (brushes, scissors, glue, string, cardboard, etc.) for creating. Somewhere there might also be room for an assortment of hats and accessories, bits and pieces of costuming rather than elaborate costumes. A collection of paraphernalia is useful as well—walking sticks, spectacles, bags, buckets, balloons—anything that can be stored easily and might lend significance to the symbolic exploration. While none of the above equipment is essential for acting-out to take place, it can enrich the experience considerably as well as involve the use of a whole range of skills.

# Provision outside the school

Where can the practising teacher look for help, advice and resources outside the school?

## *Advisory service*

At present the provision of a drama advisory service for an area is the decision of a local education authority. Consequently some areas of the country have well-established advisory services, based on a clearly defined policy and receiving financial support; other areas unfortunately have no advisory service and, either as a cause or an effect of this, there is usually little drama work in the schools in such areas.

There is no established national drama policy as such in the advisory service. However, the National Association of Drama Advisers may indirectly influence this through its meetings and encouragement of 'shared work experiences'. As well as working within their authority, advisers meet regularly on a regional basis to share ideas and discuss areas of mutual interest. It is not possible here to explain the full range of an advisory team's work. In most authorities the service is not confined to the teaching which takes place between 9.00 am and 4.00 pm during the school term. It provides a service for the whole community. Consequently, it is not surprising to discover that the work of an adviser and his team involves:

In-service training in schools
Courses for children and teachers at drama centres
TIE work
Youth theatre work
Integrated work in school departments
Teachers' workshops
Work with local arts associations
School and youth drama festivals
Workshop courses for children after school and during holidays
A hire service of lighting and equipment
Technical advice and courses in lighting, etc
Public relations and liaison with headteachers, adult evening colleges
Administration and planning.

Although this is a very general list it may give an idea of the wide area of responsibility of the service. Some of these responsibilities are more directly related to work in schools than others.

## The drama adviser

In some areas there is just one adviser who has to co-ordinate all of these responsibilities. In other areas the adviser works with a team of advisory teachers. The size of the team varies according to the size of the county, its needs and the adviser's influence, but generally he will have several advisory teachers working under him. These advisory teachers may have specific responsibilities related to their skills and interests, or have overall responsibility for a geographical area within the authority. This is how one drama adviser sees his role:

'It is my responsibility to advise the Authority, Heads and teachers in schools and colleges on all aspects of education through drama. This involves direct contact with all types of school to advise teachers and to assess the quality and range of work undertaken, and to help, guide and assess teachers in their probationary year; advise on the design and provision of specialist accommodation and equipment for the teaching of speech and drama; promote curriculum development through the integration of drama with other subjects.'

The principal function of his team of advisory teachers is to 'aid in the development of drama both as an activity in its own right and as a general teaching method'. In addition they have area responsibilities for the development of in-service education in drama. Each advisory teacher is responsible for advising a group of schools, in this case about fourteen schools each. These 'Area Advisory Drama teachers are available to work with all teachers, interested in beginning or extending their drama work. The nature of the work consists of planning, discussing, implementing, and developing ideas and work structures. Specific needs of teachers are catered for and any other teacher who becomes interested in drama work through these visits also receives assistance'.*

## In-service training

Advisory teachers vary in their individual methods and strategies. Generally they will go into a school and work with a class and teacher on a team-teaching basis for a half or whole term.

To begin with the Advisory Teacher 'takes the leading role and the class teacher observes; soon the teacher is involved in the lessons and gradually begins to share the teaching until the roles are reversed and the class teacher is taking the responsibility for the lesson'.†

Some advisory teachers also run teachers' workshops so that the teacher can meet with others to discuss problems, share ideas and experiences, as well as experiment and work at their own level.

In Devon, one of the advisory team visits all the teachers who attend her weekly workshop. By this means she becomes very much a partner alongside the teacher, rather than the visitor whom the teacher might thank at the end of the day for giving the children an enjoyable hour or two. Another of the Devon advisory staff's concerns is to 'help the teacher in the area of procedural changes in the session: how does this situation lead to another, how are the changes (from all class to group, from static to moving, etc) engineered?' The advisory teacher achieves this by demonstrating teaching over a period of several weeks, encouraging the teacher to question both what he sets up and how he advances an improvisation.

Teachers have commented on the usefulness of this 'in-the-classroom' approach:

It was very important for me. Having seen someone else making it work, making it relevant, and working in some depth with the class, I wanted to be able to do this with my future class.

*Structures of Advisory Drama Work in Great Britain*, compiled and edited by Christopher Day for the National Association of Drama Advisers, 1975 (mimeo).

† From a paper by John Coultas, Drama Adviser for Somerset in C. Day, op. cit.

Similarly, working with and observing other teachers on the same staff can be a rewarding experience and a valuable resource. A teacher describes his thoughts at the end of the year of team-teaching:

Through this experience we have gained in knowledge of our own teaching methods and techniques and of those of others. I can think of no better way of being made to see yourself for what you truly are. . . . What we learned in exchanging ideas, experimenting with each other's approaches and adopted through observation is incalculable.

Teachers need opportunities to work at their own level as well as with children. A workshop session, because of its flexible nature, can meet all these needs. Most advisory services run weekly workshops in the evening, although this is more difficult in rural areas. Where organized workshops do not exist it is useful for groups of schools to organize their own; each teacher taking it in turn to lead or define a session. In some areas as well as the teachers' workshops, combined workshops for teachers and children are organized to allow teachers to experiment prior to taking work into their own classroom.

In addition to the individual help given by the adviser and his team, a number of courses and conferences are run centrally throughout the year. Most authorities offer a variety of courses varying in content, length and venue. A London Borough provides an example of the kind of comprehensive programme of courses. The aim is to:

'(a) extend teachers' knowledge and skills in the teaching and practice of speech and drama activities;
(b) provide opportunities for discussion of problems and the free exchange of ideas as well as provide for particular needs requested by teachers;
(c) give opportunities for teachers to extend their own personal skills and interest in speech and drama and teach new skills and demonstrate new material resources.'

'There is an average of two Borough courses each week.' They are staffed by the Adviser or by guest tutors and they run from 5 pm to 7.30 pm. Two residential and two non-residential weekend courses are held each year as well as three one-day courses. The content ranges from 'ADB (Ed) teachers' workshop, which meets throughout the year, to Community Theatre' and methodology courses for particular age ranges.*

---

*C. Day, op. cit.

## The ADB (Ed)

Of all the courses offered throughout the country the ADB (Ed) is the only part-time course that offers an examination and qualification and is nationally moderated. The Advanced Drama Board (Education) Examination is 'a criterion-referenced examination indicating that its holder has mastered the basic principles of drama in education and is capable of applying those principles to classroom practice'.*

The examination consists of four sections, although not all people who take the course elect to take the examination. There is written work; a personal project, 'which is a study of any aspect of drama or theatre selected by the candidate'; practical work where 'the candidate works with a class of children of his choosing, for the normal lesson length. The lesson is then discussed in the viva-voce over forty-five minutes'. All this is supported by continuous assessment submitted by the course tutors.

The qualities expected in a holder of the ADB (Education) Certificate are set out by the Board as follows:

As this is a further qualification, not an initial one, the candidate should be more than usually proficient as a teacher. At a theoretical level, he should have an overall view whereby he can relate his work to education in general. He should have a broad knowledge of the changing nature of the child's mental, social and emotional development and of his individual needs, and of the corresponding changes in the types of dramatic activity which can be utilised (by the drama teacher). The teacher should be aware of the importance of group and inter-personal relationships and, without hindering the flow of the group's ideas or imposing his own upon them, be at hand to solve any problems that arise. He should be sensitive to the group's needs as they work and help them achieve the best of which they are capable, with—ideally—a sense of achievement at the end of the session. In order to do this, he must be alert and perceptive to changing situations and must gain the confidence of the group and its co-operation. He should be able to relate his own beliefs to what he sees drama in education to be; e.g. it is useless believing in the value of individual work when the lessons are solely concerned with conformity.

The minimum number of hours recommended for the course is 120 although decisions are left to individual tutors. The course not only offers a total approach to the understanding of drama in education, combining the practical and theoretical, it also puts teachers in touch with the advisory service, since advisers are often the tutors. In this way the teacher has back-up support in his school while the course functions as a workshop. Although the

*'The ADB (Education) Examination—the First Three Years, 1970-1973', a paper from the Drama Board, September 1973.

examination is a further qualification, not an initial one, a number of proficient teachers of other subjects have been introduced to drama in this way. At a conference on teacher training, held by the Project in December 1975, it was stated that 75 per cent of students on the ADB (Education) courses had had no initial drama training.

In interviews with some Devon primary teachers who had taken the ADB (Ed) Course, they revealed how it had introduced them to drama and been of positive value.

*Q:* Before you came on any drama courses were you doing any drama work?

*A:* Yes, I was but I didn't know I was doing drama.

*Q:* Could you be more clear?

*A:* Well, I remember doing some work on shops, and one shop that went down particularly well was a travel agency, and so the whole class tried out different ways of travelling. We turned the classroom into an aeroplane or into a train or into a coach and I realize now that it was drama. Also I remember doing some work on *The Lion, the Witch and the Wardrobe*, the story which I had been reading with the class. I noticed while on playground duty that they were acting-out parts of this story at playtime and also beginning to alter it and extend it. I wondered whether this was something I could do with them in the classroom and so eventually we would try out ideas from the story in the classroom and I used to like to try to change stories—try out different endings and so on.

*Q:* Why did you confine this work to your classroom? Why didn't you try out ideas in the hall at this stage?

*A:* Well, I was a bit scared of trying out drama anywhere else in case people wondered what on earth I was doing with the children, and also I found that a big space inhibited the kids. We used to go in there for music and movement and always they would get into a little huddle in the middle. Once I started the ADB (Ed) Course, I started to notice more and more things about my kids. I think this is because drama definitely does develop your own awareness.

*Q:* What to you was the most important aspect of the ADB (Ed) Course?

*A:* How to work with other people of your own ability and learning to criticize constructively your own work and other people's.

*Q:* What happened at the end of the course?

*A:* Well, I must admit I didn't do any drama for a bit—for about a term I suppose. But now I have gone back to it again. The difference is that whereas then I was trying it out, now I am really using it.

*Q:* Let's think back to your ADB (Ed). How did you find this affected you?

*A:* It made me much more adventurous—willing to put myself more at risk with the children. I was not so afraid of failure. It made me a lot more flexible. I felt, especially with the older children, that I could just walk in and make a statement and take it from there.

*Q:* Can you give me an example of what you mean?

*A:* Well, even something as ordinary as saying, 'what a lousy day it is today, I'm fed up' and sitting in the corner and seeing what the children would come and say to me. Then building something up from there. With the older ones this would help them to start talking about something that happened to them and we would go on to develop a situation out of this.

As an extension to the ADB (Ed), the Drama Board also run a diploma course. The ADB (Ed) counts as the first third of the diploma. It can be taken as a one-year course, or over two years as a mixture of part-time and a full term; or just part-time over three years.*

Finally, teachers in Devon were asked by questionnaire to state their preferences for different kinds of in-service training. Six types were listed and teachers ticked three in order of priority. (In arriving at 'scores', a number 1 vote counted three points, number 2 counted two, and number 3 counted one.)

| | |
|---|---|
| Long residential courses, e.g. 5 to 7 days | 88 |
| Short residential courses, e.g. weekends | 47 |
| Local teachers' centre short courses, e.g. 5 'tea-time' sessions | 38 |
| Regular evening teachers' workshops | 96 |
| Lectures on specific topics | 35 |
| School-based help by county drama staff | 107 |

## Drama centres

Drama centres have already been mentioned as places where courses or workshops may be held for teachers. But they have a much wider brief than this and can be an added resource to the work of the school. Not all authorities are fortunate enough to have them, and where they do exist they are often the result of imaginative conversions.

The buildings that the staff use range from a Theatre Arts Complex in a 6th form College to two houses knocked into one; from an old police station . . . to a Nissen hut in the middle of a football field; from a converted domestic science centre to a disused civil defence centre to, finally, a purpose-converted arts centre based around a Water Tower. All the buildings have a tremendous working atmosphere and can quickly be converted from a drama studio into a theatre or into whatever working environment is required. All buildings are fully equipped with lighting and sound hardware and most have a variety of tools/machines for building as well as materials and equipment for a variety of areas of art work. †

---

* For further information, contact the Drama Board, De Montfort House, De Montfort Street, Leicester LE1 7GH.

† From a paper by Julian Sluggett, Director, Crookham Arts Centre, in C. Day, op. cit.

Where Drama Centres exist their function is to serve the whole community, although much of the day is devoted to schools. One London centre is 'used regularly by over 200 primary-school children each week during the daytime; five Youth and Adult Drama Groups on four evenings each week; and one Saturday morning children's Drama Club. The Centre is also used for the evening performances of the Schools, Youth and Community Festivals.'* In some schools, particularly the smaller rural ones, there is no hall or space for drama so it is severely limited. One county is experimenting by 'bringing children from local rural schools' to a centre 'for a whole day's drama. The same children have come back for three or four weeks and then another group have their turn.'†

Not all the centres are specifically used for drama. Some have been set up as regional arts centres/workshops to foster interest in all the arts. In Inner London, 'The Cockpit' fulfils such a function.

The Cockpit is the only purpose-built youth arts workshop in London, as distinct from a theatre centre, and one of only a handful of such centres built by an education authority in Great Britain.

It is in part a specialist activity youth centre and a resource centre of complementary education in the arts for senior secondary-school pupils. It is also in part a public theatre for new and experimental presentations in many art forms and a springboard into all kinds of community situations in the City of Westminster.

But its central function is the opportunity it offers through its resources and its 'animateurs' to act as a Teachers' Centre and to run courses and workshops for youth leaders and teachers of many subject areas. Here its twin priorities are to promote the idea of music, art and drama forming the core disciplines of a Faculty of Arts Department in every Secondary School and to advocate that the arts must be central to any educative process where new pupil-teacher relationships are to enrich the concern for learning and where the inner worlds of the pupils are valued as highly as their outer worlds.

Northumberland and North Tyneside also have similar arts centres, though not purpose-built, fulfilling the same function in a rural community. From documents submitted by the Northumberland Working Party it is possible to give an impression of the staffing, finance and timetable of such a centre. Alnwick is the smallest of the complex of three centres. The other two have larger staffs and more working space. One of them offers residential accommodation.

*C. Day, op. cit.

† From a paper by John Coultas, Drama Adviser for Somerset in C. Day, op. cit.

Alnwick Drama Centre employs a full-time teacher in charge (A) financed by the Northumberland Education Committee, and several occasional staff: a Youth Theatre Adviser (1 session) (B) paid by FE and Youth Service; Alnwick County Secondary School staff (C) paid by the Northumberland Education Committee; as well as volunteer helpers (D) and a drama tutor (1 session) (E) paid by FE. The working spaces are one studio and one meeting/canteen room.

| | Morning | Afternoon | Evening |
|---|---|---|---|
| | | TIMETABLE | |
| Monday | C. Curriculum drama | C. Curriculum drama | C. School drama club |
| | A. Administration | A. Administration | E. Alnwick Theatre Club |
| | | | A. Seahouses CS School Rehearsal with Bamburgh Drama Group |
| Tuesday | A. Visiting school day course | A. Visiting school day course | D. Top Class Club (8-10 years) |
| | | A. Meeting with local teachers | D. Adult group rehearsal |
| | | | A. Rothbury Village Hall Young Farmers' Club rehearsal |
| Wednesday | A. Visiting school day course | A. Visiting school day course | D. Junior Youth Theatre (11-13 years) |
| | | | D. Alnwick Young Farmers' Club rehearsal |
| | | | A. Holy Island Village Hall rehearsal with drama group |
| Thursday | A. Visiting school day course | A. Visiting school day course | B. Alnwick Youth Theatre |
| | | | E. Alnwick Theatre Club |
| | | | A. (in own club room) |

| | | | |
|---|---|---|---|
| *Friday* | C. Curriculum drama<br>A. School visits | C. Curriculum drama<br>A. Preparing for evening performance | A. Visiting theatre group, public performance |
| *Saturday* | A. ADB (Ed) day course on stage lighting | A. ADB (Ed) day course on stage lighting | A. Ponteland College adjudicating Young Farmers' Club competition |
| *Sunday* | E. Alnwick Theatre Club setting up for production | E. Alnwick Theatre Club setting up for production | E. Alnwick Theatre Club setting up for production |

Where 'curriculum drama' appears on the timetable, classes are invited to the centre for sessions taken by the tutor, sometimes in conjunction with the class teacher. Follow-up visits to the schools are then arranged. Sometimes when a class is taken to a drama or arts centre, they participate in a programme devised by members of the resident staff.

## Theatre-In-Education teams

Not all TIE teams are members of, or attached to centres. Some are attached to the local theatre and some are independent companies. The drama adviser or one of his staff usually acts as liaison where these teams are not part of the advisory team itself. The resource that they provide cannot be provided by the teacher in the school.

Unlike a general theatre production, TIE programmes are carefully researched and devised for particular age-groups, often in conjunction with teachers and advisers. The experience of the TIE visit is not intended to be an end in itself; it is intended rather as a stimulus for further work around the subject by the class and teacher. To make sure that teachers understand this, teams are increasingly employing Schools Liaison Officers whose specific responsibility it is to contact schools, find out about the children who are intending to see the programmes, invite the teacher to workshops, both before and after the performance, to give help and guidance with follow-up material. Unlike Children's Theatre which sets out to provide an early experience of theatre for its own sake, TIE programmes are devised with special teaching/

educational needs in mind. In Wales, a junior-school drama project was devised along the following lines for several local schools:

(a) A panel of teachers decided on the theme for the project and a research team was appointed to compile a dossier on the background and data necessary. The dossier was printed and issued to schools.
(b) Class teachers used the folder as a basis for academic and creative work.
(c) Members of the (actor/teacher) team would visit the school for two separate sessions and work with the children through movement, language and improvisation.
(d) They would then visit the school with a Theatre in Education Programme based on the topic under investigation.
(e) They would individually visit the schools for a follow-up session. This visit also provided the opportunity for discussion with interested class teachers on ways of continuing education through drama until the next visit by the team, usually about a year later.*

In urban areas the pattern of TIE might be based in one place inviting schools to visit them. Most are adaptable enough to offer this or a visit to the school. The content of programmes varies enormously since they are devised with particular groups of children in mind (see pages 47-51). The Cockpit Theatre-in-Education policy is broad:

to research, devise and present projects relevant to secondary-school pupils within the ILEA. Projects aim to relate to the ongoing work in the schools and explore themes across the curriculum. These projects may range from a creative exploration of a text to an investigation of social issues. A wide range of techniques are used to encourage the pupils to explore and analyse issues—these techniques include strong theatre stimuli, practical workshop activity, discussion and a range of role-play situations. In conjunction with the projects, the team provide teachers' workshops and supportive, preparatory and follow-up material where relevant.

The Bowsprit Company is a TIE team which operates from the theatre at Greenwich. Their performances take place in the theatre, in the local drama centre or in schools.

A Schools Liaison Officer deals with the publicity, mailing, bookings and arrangements necessary for visiting a school, or a school visiting the theatre or centre. A drama advisory teacher working for the Authority acts as a link between the Company and schools. He provides help for teachers, holds courses and arranges meetings with the local Drama Teachers Association. He also helps the Company research and plan programmes, compiles teachers' notes and handouts, organizes pre-visits and follow-up work in schools. He is the educational adviser for all these things and feels that 'TIE is essentially a further means of educating, and should bring to schools a resource they have not already got'.

*From a paper by Derek Hollins, Drama Adviser, Clwyd, Wales in C. Day, op. cit.

Most TIE teams offer a variety of programmes. They also cater for pupils studying play texts, particularly those for examination. The Bowsprit team offered a study of the text of *Twelfth Night* to fifth- and sixth-year students. The programme examined the various comic elements as well as trying to recreate the atmosphere and environment of London at the time of the first performance of *Twelfth Night*. They also devised a programme about D. H. Lawrence based on his novel, *Sons and Lovers*, for A-level students of English.

Some authorities subsidize the cost of visiting TIE companies as well as visits to theatres to see productions of plays. Seats at West End productions are subsidized by some outer London boroughs and the ILEA so that special matinees for school children are arranged. In ILEA seats are offered to teachers free of charge. But they have to apply in writing for tickets and allocation is on a rotation basis.

In one London Borough a voucher scheme operates, whereby children receive vouchers, through the Advisory Service, entitling them to greatly reduced seat prices at the local theatre. The theatre is now working closely with the Drama Adviser and there is 'a Children's Theatre performance every alternate Saturday morning'. Children are also 'introduced to all technical aspects of theatre work' when they visit the theatre for a full day. In the afternoon this is followed by a complete performance. 'Plays are often chosen from "O" level or CSE syllabuses'.*

A questionnaire sent to Cambridgeshire schools to discover the extent to which theatre and TIE visits are used by schools showed that the number of visits to the theatre increases with the age of pupils and that 92 per cent of visits were thought to be valuable. Twenty-six per cent of schools questioned did not organize theatre visits at all.

# Conclusions

The resourcefulness of any teacher is limited, not infinite. He should avoid thinking of himself as the only resource. First, there are the children brim-full of ideas; then other members of staff, both drama and other subjects teachers, often prepared to exchange ideas, attempt team-teaching or look for areas where work might be combined. This is the most difficult resource to tap, but it is also one of the most rewarding. Teachers in other schools, feeling equally frustrated or isolated, may welcome the chance to meet on a regular or occasional basis. This can be arranged through

---

* From a paper by Maureen Garth, Drama Adviser, London Borough of Havering, in C. Day, op. cit.

local teachers' associations or by organizing workshops.

In his day-to-day work the teacher should know the possibilities of, and how to operate, the equipment he has available to him. Often teachers have expensive lighting systems or video equipment that they do not know how to exploit. They should seek the advice of the drama adviser in these and other matters and ask for courses to be run or individual help to be given. The advisory service in turn should ensure that all teachers are aware of the full range of services they can offer.

In conclusion, it is important for the teacher to be sure about the kind of resources which best suit his educational aims. He needs to be able to make use of available resources inside his school and argue his case for adequate provision. The standards of his teaching and his ability to link drama in the school with the community are affected by what he knows about outside agencies provided by the advisory service and how he uses them. The school itself must recognize the very real demands which drama makes, both in terms of space and facilities, if it is to be given practical opportunity to realize its potential.

# Chapter 9
# Summary and Conclusion: the Future of Drama in Education

In this book a number of questions have been asked:

1.  How can drama be defined?
2.  What is the distinctive nature of drama? What are its distinctive contributions to the development of children?
3.  What kinds of learning can be achieved through drama? What are the practical implications of placing different emphases on the drama process?
4.  What decisions can teachers take into account before and during sessions so that they can achieve best results?
5.  Can drama be assessed? If so, how?
6.  What kinds of long-term development should be expected of children who have had continuous experience of drama over a number of years?
7.  What should be the place of drama in the curriculum? How can drama be organized in schools?
8.  What facilities are necessary for good drama work? What resources are available outside school?

In this chapter two further questions will be asked:

1.  What are the implications of the views given in this book for teacher training?
2.  In the light of the project's findings, what recommendations could be made for the future of drama in education?

We have argued that drama should be seen as an arts process; that experience in the arts should be considered a basic part of every child's education. Its value lies in that it gives children opportunities to explore, interpret, express and communicate feelings and ideas by representing them in a variety of symbolic forms. Through active exploration, it allows a deeper understanding and experiencing of a vast range of human feelings and perceptions which otherwise may not be dealt with in the rest of the curriculum. This is done by using various media as vehicles for representation, and involves learning how to control them. Differences between the arts are mainly related to the different media used which, in turn, affect the ways in which meaning can be explored.

In drama, people are themselves the main medium of

expression. The whole person—voice and body (speech and movement)—is used symbolically to represent meaning. Patterns of meaning are explored through the interrelationships of imagined roles. This is usually done by and through social interaction. The process can include finding areas of exploration, selecting, rejecting, modifying, elaborating ideas and feelings, organizing them into patterns or forms and communicating them to others.

Differences in drama occur because children are encouraged to focus on different aspects of the process at a given time. They may be asked purely to develop skills as part of learning to control dramatic media. They may be asked mainly to be responsible for choosing their own content and symbolic forms or they may be expected to work within someone else's imagined situation. Certain kinds of learning are stressed more than others. For instance, if children are being encouraged to learn to use the process, it is more likely that they will be allowed to take most decisions during acting-out. On the other hand, if pupils are using drama to focus on deepening their understanding of particular themes, topics or issues, it is more likely that the teacher will ask them to act-out within an already defined situation, sometimes with given roles. If teachers wish pupils to present their ideas to others, they are likely to focus on activities which improve skills of communication.

Decisions teachers make concerning what they are going to teach in any session will be affected by the kinds of learning they want to achieve. They will also be influenced by other factors such as the environmental context in which drama is taught—how much space and time they are given; the kinds of pupils they are teaching (age, ability, attitude to drama, states of readiness); their ability in acting-out and relating to each other. These will influence what decisions the teacher makes. These include how he structures the overall activities of the lesson; how the class is grouped; and the kinds of roles he might adopt during acting-out. At any time the teacher may become aware that children need particular help with certain aspects of the process and might intervene to help. He might find he needs to change his intentions because pupils throw up a more profitable line of exploration. Because of this, teachers need to be alert and flexible enough to recognize and seize opportunities as they occur.

All teachers, regardless of the kinds of learning they wish to emphasize, should be concerned with improving the quality of children's acting-out. Questions could be asked about achievements in the following ways: whether children have found adequate forms of representation; whether they are able to crystallize their ideas into some kind of form; and whether they have been able to use and control dramatic media in expressing and communicating meaning. There may be excellence in any one of these features but this does not necessarily mean that the work as a whole is of quality. For this, there needs to be a simultaneous combination of all these elements where exploration occurs mainly at a symbolic level, patterns of meaning unfolding through exploration and effective use of the media. It is necessary for children to be able to identify with the chosen content and be committed enough to want to explore it. A right combination of thinking and feeling needs to develop if work of real significance is to occur.

The quality of acting-out is one of the factors that teachers should take into account when assessing drama sessions. Because each drama session is the result of the unique interaction between the teacher and his pupils, there is no one way of assessing every drama lesson. It is necessary to ask a number of questions concerning drama sessions with regard to both pupil's and teacher's performances:

1. What significant factors affected learning during the lesson?
2. What were the teacher's aims and intentions? Were they realized? If not, why not?
3. Were adequate methods/strategies used for achieving aims and intentions, and for improving the quality of the work?
4. What kinds of decisions can be made about future work based on assessment of the current lesson?

In asking questions such as these it is important to recognize the effect that structuring certain activities can have and whether the strategies used are appropriate for what teachers are trying to achieve. It is important to be aware of the stages of development that pupils have reached in order to give appropriate help.

Assessment is seen as part of a continuous attempt to improve children's achievements in acting-out over a period of time. Just as teachers should be aware of what has been achieved during a single session, they should also consider work in the context of the child's total drama experience during his school career. Children who have had drama for a number of years should have had some experience of all its aspects. Development should therefore occur along the following lines:

1. Improvement in learning to use the process: the capacity to project into 'as if' situations in exploring and representing meaning; to be able to organize ideas and appreciate form; to use and control the media (in particular, verbal and physical means of expression); increased ability to work with others on both real and symbolic terms (improvement in corporate decision-making, giving, accepting, modifying and developing ideas together); greater sensitivity to how others react and awareness on the part of the individual of how he functions in groups.

2.  In being able to deepen understanding of particular themes, topics and issues, either by translating their understanding of certain concepts, etc, into dramatic terms, or by using their experience of drama to understand the general nature of specific issues, concepts, etc. Children should also improve their ability in discussion.

3.  Presentation involves improving communication skills; learning to sustain work for longer periods of time; to work with a large number of other people towards a production, and to become aware of the effect that they as individual people have on the overall success of a performance. Successful presentations can give children a degree of satisfaction that can improve their general self-confidence.

4.  By appreciating other people's dramatic presentations and statements, children should understand how other people use dramatic symbols to convey and present ideas/ perceptions/feelings.

5.  Finally, through long-term experience in drama, children should be able to discriminate between different aspects of the process, gain mastery in each of them and be able to ask questions about the quality of their own and others' work.

This book has shown with numerous examples that drama can enable children to achieve certain kinds of learning, many of which cannot be brought about in other ways. Experience in acting-out, because of its distinctive media, can help children express themselves better in everyday life. Drama can enable the child to think hypothetically about other people. He is therefore able to react to and cope with a variety of imagined and real social situations, some of which are of relevance to his present or future life, or might extend and widen his general knowledge of people and the ways they think and feel. Acting-out is a useful way of enabling the child to gain self-confidence in learning to express himself both physically and verbally. Because drama can help the development of the child in a number of specific ways, it should be seen as an essential part of the school curriculum.

## *The place of drama in the school curriculum*

It is argued that drama should be seen as a core subject rather than as an appendage to the curriculum. Acting-out can be used in a number of ways. It is of value both in terms of a process in its own right and as a technique for exploring certain kinds of content. These can include the use of drama in various subjects: language development, including the teaching of second languages, and the use of drama for children with special problems.* Drama should occur in the curriculum because it is one of the main art forms in our culture. If the general contributions that drama can make to development are recognized as valid, then the number of trained drama teachers ought to be in proportion to the number of children in the school. Also some thought should be given to alternative ways of timetabling drama, particularly more flexible systems such as block release and modular timetabling. Adequate time and facilities, especially space with privacy, should be given to allow maximum opportunities for development to take place.

In primary schools drama is mainly used by class teachers and is often only taken when the hall is available. However, many opportunities arise during normal classroom work when drama work would greatly benefit children's learning. Headteachers should encourage teachers to try using drama and enable them to go on courses and to invite advisers to visit the school and work alongside teachers in the classroom.

In secondary schools, in addition to drama specialists being responsible for developing drama in its own right, they can also play an important part in encouraging and helping non-specialists use drama for their own purposes. If drama is to be given fullest opportunity to develop, it must be given the same status as other subjects/disciplines and drama teachers must be graded accordingly. Because drama is not fully accepted, many drama teachers with ability leave to be promoted in other areas, often to pastoral posts.

How drama is actually organized in terms of departments depends mainly on how the school as a whole functions, and what the practical possibilities are in terms of staffing, time and facilities. We believe that drama should fundamentally be seen within the context of the arts rather than having an exclusive relationship with English. However, drama does have a special role to play within the teaching of English, both in language and literature.

# Implications for teacher training

So far some assertions and recommendations have been made concerning the teaching of drama and its role in the curriculum. If these are accepted, a number of points must be raised concerning the effective training of drama teachers, and the basic elements that should be included in any professional course.

* Lynn McGregor. 'The use of drama for children with difficulties', Drama Therapy Centre, Pitman's Conference, December 1973.

A competent drama teacher should have a knowledge of the drama process and how it can be used. He should also have at his disposal a wide variety of methods and activities. He should be aware of the effects of making certain decisions about the practical nature of the work. He should be able to emphasize aspects of it so that certain kinds of learning can be achieved. He should be sensitive to learning opportunities as they arise; be aware of what pupils are struggling with at a given time, and have a clear idea of how to improve work from minute to minute. This means that not only does he have to have a knowledge of how drama works, but also needs to be able to participate at his own creative level. He should be able to devise a range of situations through which children can work and, where necessary, to adopt roles himself. He ought to know how to structure his work in such a way that he can best achieve the kinds of learning he wants to develop. He ought to be able to recognize the children's general states of development and adapt to their particular needs.

Many of these qualities can only develop with time and experience. Training should lay the foundations for this approach to the practical teaching of drama. Practical training for drama teachers should contain two interrelating elements: they should be able to learn to use the process themselves at their own levels; and they should have direct experience of practical classroom work and what it entails.

Because drama can be used for various purposes, it is important for teachers to have a knowledge of the different functions of drama within the school curriculum and the implications for time and facilities. Specialists should be aware of the relationship of drama to other subjects. Because of the scarcity of drama teachers and the low priority which schools often give drama, there is great need to set aims in the context of the school. They ought to be aware of the organization of different school systems and how these might affect their teaching—by what freedoms and constraints, especially those of time and facilities, they might be affected.

## Initial training

The elements mentioned above should be included in all courses aimed at training drama specialists. There are, however, a wide variety of different kinds of course in which they could be included, ranging from an emphasis on the performing arts to drama as part of a broader training in education. If a teacher is to be given overall responsibility for the development of drama in a school, he should at least be aware of and have practised the variety of ways in which drama can be used.

The question is: do existing courses contain the basic elements of training suggested here? Although many courses contain some 'method work' there is evidence that in a number of courses practical training for the classroom is not considered to be of paramount importance.* Many courses have in the past concentrated on the personal development of the student with particular regard to theatre arts. It has been argued that 'academic courses in drama which relied heavily upon the teaching of literary and traditional theatre skills were not necessarily appropriate for the preparation of those who were to teach drama in schools'. Although all members of a working party considering teacher training felt that 'in their experience there was a considerable need for more highly competent teachers of drama', they also felt that 'few teachers in initial training received adequate preparation for teaching drama in schools',† This often resulted from the fact that not enough time was allocated for practical work. One of the dangers of the now popular unit system is that there is a tendency for academic units to be adopted at the expense of the professional units. One of the reasons for this may be because of the difficulty of validating practical work as part of degree qualifications. Many people are reluctant to submit courses which contain a large practical element because they feel that their submissions will not be accepted. However, a representative from the Council for National Academic Awards has said that validating panels welcomed the application of courses which contained elements of practical training.‡ We recommend that 'every initial course for the training of drama teachers should include a unit of drama in education. This course should be compulsory for main-course drama students and could be used by non-specialists who wish to learn about drama methods and strategies for their own purposes.'§

In structuring courses for the training of drama teachers 'two problems immediately come to mind. One is the ever present pressure of time and the other is the choice of subject matter. . . Clearly a way must be found to use the practical skills of drama within both the subject teaching area and the method work, as well as providing the students with the ability to use these in the school experience. This must be done through integration of subject

---

* Sheila M. Sharpless, 'The training of drama teachers', A dissertation for the Master's Degree in Education, University of Sussex, 1975.

† Schools Council Drama Teaching Project (10-16), 'Report of the Teacher Training Conference', 5 December, 1975. (mimeo).

‡ Ibid.

§ Ibid.

matter with method . . . rather than the imposition on to an existing pattern.'*

The problem of organizing initial courses is, therefore, how much importance and time is to be given to both practical and academic aspects of training. Some courses have managed to combine these effectively and offer their students a sound basis for their work in schools. But however good an initial course may be, the quality of teaching is usually developed through experience in the classroom. This means that education for the teacher should not stop after his initial training.

## In-service training

In arguing the case for further training the point has been made that

the newly qualified teacher has seldom absorbed and balanced these experiences to the extent that they enable him to commence teaching in an organized and competent manner. . . . . By virtue of the nature of initial training . . . the experience of continuous teaching, sustained contact with children, adaptation to particular school conditions, relating work to the total learning pattern (cannot) be given.†

While working in the classroom, the drama teacher needs constantly to devise new ways of working, to try out new methods of teaching so that the quality of his work can be improved. For this he often needs help and advice. For drama teachers, in-service training should constitute a vital element in the development of their own teaching.

The questions are not general or theoretical. They relate to that syllabus, these children, this school. There is a precision about the discussion. The teachers also get lengthy opportunity to catch up on development they have missed, or acquire expertise in aspects of teaching drama that they were unable to gain in their initial training.‡

In-service training in terms of follow-up work from colleges can be of great benefit to the inexperienced teacher. Many new teachers lose confidence and often give up trying to teach drama because they lack the important transitional help which outside advice might offer to them.

A number of possible opportunities exist for the further training of drama teachers. They range from teachers working with advisers

---

* Sheila M. Sharpless, op. cit., p.68.

† David Male, 'Some thoughts on in-service training', Homerton College, Cambridge, 1975.

‡ Ibid.

and advisory teachers in schools; to attending short courses in drama centres and colleges; to taking lengthy ADB (Ed.) courses which are both practically and academically demanding; to doing full-time advanced courses, including diplomas and master's degrees, for qualified and experienced teachers (for example, at the University of Newcastle upon Tyne, and the Advanced Diploma Course of the Central School of Speech and Drama, and diploma and MA courses at the University of Durham).

## *Training for the non-specialist*

Because drama can play a valuable part in deepening the understanding of content in certain ways, it is suggested that many teachers would benefit from some training in drama techniques. Indeed one working party felt that 'all of those intending to teach in primary and middle schools should have some basic teaching competence in this area.' Learning basic drama techniques need not involve a lengthy process of training. This could easily be part of a modular system or provided during in-service training. Once teachers have had a basic training, the only way to develop is through experience. It should be remembered that many non-specialists take time to lose their own inhibitions and to take the kinds of risks demanded of effective drama teaching. Courses in methods alone will not equip teachers to teach drama in its own right; a more balanced course would be necessary for this.

It is all very well to discuss teacher training and the value of drama in education in terms of what ought to happen. The picture that is emerging for the future training of drama teachers, either specialist or non-specialist, is at best hazy and at worst gloomy. If drama is to develop as a valid educational process and is to survive, then it is essential to take realistic measures. The fact is that in the current reorganization and financial stringency drama has been one of the main casualties. It is quite likely that the number of drama teachers will diminish in the future. Unless this tendency is corrected, the future of drama teaching is bleak.

Given present circumstances what can be done to improve the prospects? Firstly, the standards of drama teaching must improve so that other colleagues become convinced of the value of drama. Practising teachers should ask themselves what they think the needs of their particular pupils are with regard to development in drama. They should ask themselves whether they are aware of the variety of methods and strategies available to them and what aspects of the process they feel they can best work with depending on their own strengths and weaknesses. They should question the quality of their own and their pupils' work. They should be able to discuss in concrete terms the kinds of short-and long-term development they are trying to achieve through drama. In other words, teachers should ask themselves how much they know about drama, how well they can use it for their purposes. They should also ask themselves how they as participants can operate within the process as well as the children. Teachers should also question their overall role within the school itself: whether demands are being made upon them which they are unable to meet; whether the time and facilities they are given allow for development to occur. Teachers should also consider ways of encouraging the use of drama in other areas of the curriculum and perhaps make suggestions about how this could be done.

Secondly, heads of drama departments should consider whether drama and its values are understood by the rest of the school; how specialists in the school can be organized to help other subject teachers; whether responsibility for school performances should be placed on the drama department or whether other members of the school staff could also be involved. It is suggested that people with responsibility for drama should have a long-term perspective about the kinds of development they would like children to achieve over a five-year period. To do this it is necessary for them to find out how other drama teachers are teaching and attempt to see that a balanced programme is achieved. It is necessary for the head of the drama department to be clear about what he and his department's long-term aims and objectives are and to put forward a case as clearly as possible so that those planning timetables and facilities are aware of what is needed if drama is to be taught effectively in that school.

Thirdly, people with administrative responsibilities for developing drama in schools should ask how drama can best be structured within the existing timetable to make use of present resources; whether the way drama is organized in school is the most effective; if it is best to work towards an integrated or a separate department; whether drama should be part of an arts faculty or an English department, for example; whether, if there is only one specialist, to begin with he should be allowed to 'float'. The way in which these questions are resolved will depend on the staff available at the time and what the relationships are between them. If headteachers wish to develop drama in its own right they should ask whether the time they have given is sufficient for worth-while development to occur. They should ask how many teachers have had actual drama training and how many teachers, either within an existing drama department, or in other departments, can help other subject teachers who wish to use drama. They should be aware of the exhausting demands made on teachers, not only because drama demands the teachers' emotional and intellectual involvement all the time, but also because some are required to teach six to eight periods a day without a break. They should also consider the pressures put upon teachers who not only teach a full timetable but are also often expected to organize school performances involving large numbers of people and run out-of-school clubs as well.

Fourthly, for people involved in the organization of drama on a regional basis, we recommend that if the value of drama is recognized, drama should have at least the same status and resources in terms of budgeting and staff allocation as other arts. The development of drama in a region will depend on how many specialists are employed, and the kind of facilities available in schools. If there are very few specialists in any one region, how can they best be employed? Is it better to concentrate them in one school? Would it be more useful to extract them from one school and have them servicing a number of schools, as part of a team? Perhaps they could be used to run courses for teachers who wish to start drama in their own schools.

There is no doubt that drama is best developed in those areas with a drama adviser or an advisory team. If it is felt that there is a need for the development of drama in certain regions profitable links could be made between local training colleges in drama and other agencies for in-service training in schools.

In this book we hope to have shown that drama in education has valuable and distinctive contributions to make to the development of the child. It is not an easy option, but makes definite cognitive, affective and social demands on the child. If drama is recognized as an essential element in children's education, every attempt must be made at all levels of education to ensure that its development continues in spite of the increasing financial and political pressures which are threatening its future.

# Bibliography

Artaud, A. *The Theatre and Its Double.* Calder & Boyars, 1970.

Bolton, G. *Some Notes Prepared for London Teachers of Drama.* University of Durham, October 1973 (mimento).

Britton, J. *language and Learning.* Allen Lane, Penguin Press, 1971.

Bruner, J.S. *Studies in Cognitive Growth.* John Wiley, New York, 1966.

Cassirer, E. 'Selected writing of Edward Sapir', in *Culture, Language and Personality,* ed. David G. Mandlebaum. University of California Press, Berkeley and Los Angeles, 1949.

Clegg. D. 'The dilemma of drama in education', *Theatre Quarterly,* **3,** Jan.-Mar. 1973, 31-42.

Courtney, R. *Play, Drama and Thought.* Cassell, 1974.

Creber, P.J.W. *Sense and Sensitivity.* University of London Press, 1968.

Crystal, D. *The English Tone of Voice.* Edward Arnold, 1975.

Day, C., ed. *Structures of Advisory Drama work in Great Britain.* National Association of Drama Advisers, 1975 (mimeo).

Department of Education and Science. *A Language for Life.* Report of Committee of Inquiry appointed by Secretary of State for Education and Science, under Chairmanship of Sir Alan Bullock. [Bullock Report.] HMSO, 1975.

Education Survey 2: *Drama.* HMSO, 1968.

Education Survey 22: *Actors in Schools.* HMSO, 1977.

Dewey, J. *Art as Experience.* Putnam, New York, 1958.

Dodd, N.A. and Hickson, W. *Drama and Theatre in Education.* Heinemann Educational Books, 1971.

Eisner, E.W. 'Do behavioural objectives and accountabilities have a place in art education?', *Art Education,* **26,** May 1973.
*Instructional and Expressive Objectives. The Formulation and Use of Curriculum. Instructional Objectives.* AREA Monograph Series on Curriculum Evaluation, ed. W. James Popham. Rand, McNally, Chicago, 1969.

Fines, J. and Verrier, R. *The Drama of History: Experiment in Co-operative Teaching.* New University Education, 1974.

Hodgson, J. and Banham, M. *Drama in Education, The Annual Survey,* Vols 1, 2, 3. Pitman, 1972, 1973, 1975.

Kelly, G. *A Theory of Personality.* Norton, New York, 1963.

Langer, S.K. *Feeling and Form.* Routledge & Kegan Paul, 1953. *Philosophy in a New Key.* Harvard University Press, Cambridge, Mass., 1957.

Luria, A.R. and Yudovich, R.I. *Speech and the Development of the Mental Processes in the Child,* trans. O. Korasc and J. Simon. Penguin Books, 1971.

McCaslin, N. *Children and Drama.* David McKay, New York, 1975.

McGregor, L. *A Sociological Investigation of Drama Teaching in Three Schools,* M. Ph. thesis, Institute of Education, University of London, 1975 (mimeo).

*Developments in Drama Teaching,* The Changing Classroom Series, ed. J. Eggleston. Open Books, 1975.

Millar, S. *The Psychology of Play.* Penguin Books, 1969.

Piaget, J. *Play, Dreams and Imitations in Childhood.* Trans. C. Gattegno and F.M. Hodgson. Routledge & Kegan Paul, 1951.

Read, H. *Education Through Art.* Faber, 1943.

Robinson, K. *Find a Space,* a report on the teaching of drama based on a survey of 259 secondary schools, prepared for the University of London School Examinations Department, 1975 (mimeo).

Rogers, C.R. 'Towards a theory of creativity', *ETC; A Review of General Semantics,* Vol ii, 1954, 249-60. Reprinted in *Creativity,* ed. P.E. Vernon, Penguin Books, 1970.

Ross, M. *Arts and the Adolescent,* Schools Council Working Paper 54. Evans/Methuen Educational, 1975.

Schools council. *Examinations in Drama.* Occasional Bulletins from the Subject Committees. Schools Council, Summer, 1974.

Seely, J. *In context—Language and Drama in the Secondary School.* Oxford University Press, 1976.

Slade, p. *Child Drama.* University of London Press, 1954.

Stanilavski, C. *An Actor Prepares.* Trans. E.R. Hapgood, Bles, 1937.

Taylor, J. and Walford, R. *Simulation in the Classroom.* Penguin Papers in Education, Penguin Books, 1972.

*Theatre News,* **vii.** May 1976, Washington DC, USA.

Vygotsky, L.S. *Thought and Language,* MIT Press, 1962.

Walton, J., ed. *The Integrated Day in Theory and Practice.* Ward Lock Educational, 1971.

Way, B. *Development Through Drama.* Longman, 1967.

Witkin, R.W. *The Intelligence of Feeling.* heinemann Educational Books, 1974.

# Acknowledgements

We said at the beginning of this book that it was not intended as a survey of the views of all of those who were involved with the project. The work of the project developed through the contributions of a great many people throughout the country. It would be impossible to acknowledge our specific thanks to everyone who took part. However, we would like to thank the following for their special and, in many cases, sustained commitment of energy and ideas.

## The six local education authority areas
### Cambridgeshire

*Co-ordinator:* John Boylan, Senior Adviser for Drama.
*Cambridgeshire Working Party:* J. Boylan, (Chairman); N. Blyth, Head of English Department, Sawston Village College; A. Brown, Head of English Department, Comberton Village College; A.M. McMurray, Headmaster, Ernulf School; Miss S. Macklin, Lecturer in Drama, Homerton College; R.E. Martin, Warden, Burwell Village College; R.E. Smith, Senior Advisory Teacher for Drama; Mrs G. Truckle, Teacher, Paston Ridings County Junior School.
*Schools:* Ernulf School; Kings Hedges Junior School; Jack Hunt School.
*Heads:* A.M. McMurray; M. Taylor; L.N. White.
*Teachers:* Cliff Knight; Miss Dorothy Loftus; Tim O'Grady.

### Devon

*Co-ordinator:* Terry Jones, County Drama Adviser.
*Devon Working Party:* T. Jones, (Chairman); A. Bacon, Headmaster, Priory High School; J. Butt, County Adviser for Curriculum Development; S. Cockett, Head of Drama, St Luke's College of Education; P. Creber, Senior Lecturer in Education, University of Exeter School of Education; G. Fox, Lecturer in Education, University of Exeter School of Education; D. Price, Head of Drama, Plymstock Comprehensive School; A. Roberts, Deputy Headmaster, Lifton Primary School; Mrs P. Sneddon, Teacher, Haywards County Primary School; L. Winston, Lecturer in Drama, South Devon College. The working party also received papers from A. Delzenne; J. Percival; K. Rattray; and Miss M. Sanders (Devon Drama Area Advisory Teachers).

*Schools:* Exmouth School; Newton Abbott Grammar School; South Molton School and Community College.
*Heads:* R. Hawkes; J.I. Sturt; P.E. Thorne.
*Teachers:* Mrs Yvonne Harkin, Mrs Wendy Mason, Mrs Sue Pike.

## ILEA

*Co-ordinator:* Mrs Cecily O'Neill, Drama Warden.
*ILEA Working Party:* G. Hodson, Senior Inspector for Drama (Chairman); C. Brantingham, Headmaster, Southfields School; A. Davison, Director, Cockpit Theatre and Arts Workshop; R. Jerome, Lecturer in Drama, Battersea College of Education; Miss D. McKone, Deputy Head, Ellerslie Infant Schools; Mrs C. O'Neil; Miss M. Price, Inspector for Drama; R. Read, Deputy Head, Henry Thornton School; P. Skinner, Head of Drama, William Penn School.
*Schools:* Acland Burghley School; Addison Primary School; William Ellis School.
*Heads:* R.S. Fisher; D. Kent, R.L. Perry.
*Teachers:* Peter Gray, Miss Celia Greenwood, Mrs Margaret Sawday.

## Leeds

*Co-ordinator:* David Morton, General Adviser (Drama).
*Leeds Working Party:* D. Morton (Chairman); J. Auty, Head of Drama, Intake High School; R. Duckworth, Senior Adviser (Secondary); A. Lynskey, Headmaster, Greenbank County Primary School; Mrs R. Mallins, General Adviser (Drama); J. Mee, Lecturer in Drama, Leeds Polytechnic; S. Rowley, Head of Community Drama, Ralph Thoresby High School; Mrs N. Senior, Senior Mistress and Head of Dance and Drama, Harehills Middle School; B. Strong, Head Teacher, Priesthorpe School. Visitors to the working party; R. Chapman, Director, Theatre-in-Education, Leeds; C. Gardiner, Head Teacher, Intake High School.
*Schools:* Foxwood Secondary School; Holt Park Middle School; Primrose Hill School; Wetherby High School.
*Heads:* H. Fitton; L.A.G. Lowton; R. Smith; R.T. Spooner.
*Teachers:* Miss Pauline Majerus; Eric Prince; Colin Rimmington; Mrs Kathy Webster; Tony Webster.

## Northumberland and North Tyneside

*Co-ordinator:* Keith Williams, Drama Adviser.
*Northumberland and North Tyneside Working Party:* K. Williams (Chairman); Miss J. Bailey, Teacher Adviser in Drama; P.

Chamberlain, Principal Lecturer in Drama, Northern Counties College of Education; I. Finch, Head of Drama, Cramlington High School; A.J. Hales, Drama Teacher, Summerville Middle School; S. Harvey, Drama Adviser; Miss M. Osborne, HMI; Miss E. Robinson, Drama Warden, Alnwick Drama Centre; G. Whitehouse, Headmaster, Queen Elizabeth Grammar School. Contributions were also received from the teams at the Backworth and Gosforth Drama Centres.
*Schools:* Queen Elizabeth Grammar School; Ridley High School
*Heads:* L. Brown; G. Whitehouse.
*Teachers:* David Garrett; Chris Kelly; Harry Pearson.

### *Redbridge*

*Co-ordinator:* Hugh Lovegrove, Drama Adviser.
*Redbridge Working Party:* H. Lovegrove, (Chairman); R. Gibson, Senior Education Officer; A. Goode, Head of Creative Studies, Gearies Secondary School for Boys; M. Griffin, Head, William Torbitt Junior School; Mrs M. Horne, Headmistress, Fairlot Secondary School for Girls; D. Mackay, Head, Wanstead High School; L. Scott, Head of Lower School, Seven Kings High School; Miss J. Tennant, Redbridge Drama Centre.
*Schools:* Dane Junior High School; Wanstead High School; William Torbitt Junior School.
*Heads:* M. Griffin; D. Mackay, J.I. Westbury.
*Teachers:* Miss Jo Butterfield; Don Hendy; Alan Wright.

# Schools Council Consultative Committee

| P. Creber (Chairman 1975-1977) | Senior Lecturer in Education, University of Exeter School of Education; representing Schools Council English Committee and English Drama Sub-committee |
| Professor J.N. Britton (Chairman 1974-1975) | Goldsmiths' Professor of Education in the University of London; representing the grant-holder, 1974-1975 |
| J. Allen | Principal, Central School of Speech and Drama, London |
| Mrs B. Anderson | Deputy Head, Overmede First School, Oxfordshire |
| D. Cobley | Advisory Teacher, West Glamorgan |
| N. Dodsworth | Representing Schools Council Steering Committee B |
| C. Godden | Representing English Committee of the Associated Examining Board |

Miss V. Gottlieb — Drama Department, Goldsmiths' College, University of London

P. Haeffner — HM Inspectorate

Dr R. Hoggart — Warden, Goldsmiths' College, University of London; representing the grant-holder, 1975-1977

D. Mackay — Headmaster, Wanstead High School, London

J.B. Parnaby — HM Inspectorate; representing Schools Council English Drama Sub-committee

G. Scotney — Representing Schools Council Steering Committee A

T. Stabler — Headmaster, Kingsley County Primary School, West Hartlepool; Director, Schools Council Drama 5-11 Project; representing Schools Council English Committee, and English Drama and Sub-committee

R. Staunton — Teacher/Adviser, Loughborough Drama Centre; representing Schools Council English Drama Sub-committee

Miss A. Williams — Teacher, Ursuline High School, Ilford

Mrs M. Wootton — Lecturer in Drama, University of London Institute of Education

## Project Evaluators

Gavin Bolton, Lecturer in Drama in Education, University of Durham Institute of Education
Brian Davies, Senior Lecturer, Department of Sociology, University of London Institute of Education

## Project's Film: 'Take Three'

Our thanks to all of those involved in the production of the project's film, *Take Three,* especially Roger Crittenden (Editor), John Slater (Producer/Director), Roger Deakins and Dick Pope (Camera), and Bob Alcock (Sound). We are also grateful for the co-operation of the schools, teachers and children who took part in the film: Don Hendy at Wanstead High School; Yvonne Harkin at South Molton School and Community College; and Eric Prince at Primrose Hill School.

# Other Contributors

Among the many other people who contributed to the project, we would like to thank the following:

David Clegg, Lecturer, Ulster College

Christopher Day, Drama Adviser, London Borough of Barking

Mrs Kay Dudeney, Assistant Inspector (Drama), Surrey

Greenwich Young People's Theatre

Peter Husbands, Secretary, The Drama Board, Leicester

Mrs Olga Ironside-Wood, Senior County Drama Adviser, Suffolk

Miss Kathy Joyce, Curriculum Development Leader for Drama, Manchester

David Male, Senior Lecturer in Drama, Homerton College, Cambridge

Ray Moss, Drama Adviser, London Borough of Ealing

John Norman, Director, Outreach (Cockpit Theatre and Arts Workshop)

The Redbridge Drama Centre

Robin Rook, Lecturer, Balls Park College of Education, Hertford

John Seely, author of *In Context—Language and Drama in the Secondary School* (Oxford University Press, 1976)

Mrs Sheila Sharpless, Lecturer in Drama, Garnett College of Education, London

Lawrence Surridge, Lecturer in Drama, Coventry College of Education

Leslie Williams, County Adviser for Education through Drama, Dorset.

## *Teacher Training Conference*

*Speakers:*

Miss Joan Lestor, Parliamentary Under-Secretary to the Department of Education and Science

Dr Alan Davies, Principal, Bretton Hall College of Education, Wakefield

Mrs Dorothy Heathcote, Course Tutor in Drama in Education, University of Newcastle upon Tyne

Geoffrey Hodson, Senior Inspector of Drama, ILEA

David Morton, General Adviser (Drama), Leeds

Dr Ronald Mulryne, Chairman of the Drama Panel, Council for National Academic Awards.

## Theatre-in-Education Conference

*Speakers:*
Jem Barnes, Director, Basingstoke Regional Drama Centre
Don Hendy, Director of Drama, Wanstead High School, London
Terry Jones, County Drama Adviser, Devon
Bert Parnaby, HM Inspectorate
John Samson, Bolton Octagon Theatre
Miss Pam Schweitzer, Drama Advisory Teacher, London Borough
of Barking.

## Seminar on the Relationship of Drama to English Teaching

Eric Bolton, HM Inspectorate
Brian Coxall, Head of English Department, Abbey Wood School,
London
Professor David Crystal, Head of Linguistics Department,
University of Reading
Harold Gardiner, Staff Inspector for English
Gerard Gould, English and Drama Adviser, Oxford
Paul Haeffner, HM Inspectorate (Drama)
David Herbert, Central School of Speech and Drama, London
Derek Hollins, County Drama Adviser, Clwyd
Bert Parnaby, HM Inspectorate

Finally our special thanks to Maurice Plaskow, Curriculum Officer at the Schools Council, for his continuous advice and support throughout the project's work. And to Mrs Mavis Benford, our secretary, for her help, encouragement and especially her organizational panache. We are indebted to her for all her time and hard work.